RITUAL MUSIC

Studies in Liturgical Musicology

Edward Foley, Capuchin

The Pastoral Press
Beltsville, Maryland

Acknowledgments

"A Mighty Fortress." Music and English text from *Martin Luther, Liturgy and Hymns*, ed. Ulrich Leupold (Philadelphia: Fortress Press, 1968); original German from *D. Martin Luthers Werke* (Weimar: Herman Bohlaus Nachfolger, 1923).

"Psalm 91" by Christopher Willcock, © 1982, International Commission on the Liturgy, Inc. All rights reserved. Used with permission.

Ubi Caritas by Jacques Berthier, © 1979, Les Presses de Taizé. Used by permission of GIA Publications, Exclusive Agent.

ISBN: 1-56929-057-1

Copyright © The Pastoral Press, 1995

The Pastoral Press
5640-D Sunnyside Avenue
Beltsville, MD 20705
(301) 474-2226

Printed in the United States of America

Contents

Abbreviations iv
Preface v

1. Judaeo-Christian Ritual Music:
   A Bibliographic Introduction to the Field 1

2. The Auditory Environment of
   Emerging Christian Worship 37

3. The Cantor in Historical Perspective 65

4. Martin Luther: A Model Pastoral Musician 89

5. Toward a Sound Theology 107

6. From *Music in Catholic Worship*
   to the "Milwaukee Document" 127

7. Musical Forms, Referential Meaning, and Belief 145

8. The Evaluation of Roman Catholic Ritual Music:
   From Displacement to Convergence 173

Index 191

Abbreviations

All scripture translations, unless otherwise noted, are taken from the *New American Bible*.

CCL	*Corpus Christianorum, Series Latina.* Turnhout and Paris.
CSEL	*Corpus Scriptorum Ecclesiasticorum Latinorum.* Vienna.
CSL	Constitution on the Sacred Liturgy, 1963.
DOL	*Documents on the Liturgy 1963-1979.* Collegeville: The Liturgical Press, 1982.
EJ	*Encyclopaedia Judaica,* ed. Cecil Roth and Geoffrey Wigoder. 16 vols. Jerusalem: Keter Publishing, 1972.
GCS	*Die griechischen christlichen Schriftsteller.* Leipzig.
H-MM	Andrew Hughes. *Medieval Music: The Sixth Liberal Art.* rev. ed. Toronto: University of Toronto Press, 1980.
IDB	*The Interpreter's Dictionary of the Bible,* ed. George Buttrick, et al. 4 vols. Nashville-New York: Abingdon, 1962.
LMT	Bishops' Committee on the Liturgy. *Liturgical Music Today.* Washington, DC, 1982.
Mansi	J.D. Mansi. *Sacrorum Conciliorum Nova et Amplissima Collectio.* Florence, 1759-1798. Reprint and continuation: Paris and Leipzig, 1901-1927.
MCW	Bishops' Committee on the Liturgy. *Music in Catholic Worship.* 2nd ed. Washington, DC, 1982 [1972].
MGG	*Die Musik in Geschichte und Gegenwart.* 17 vols. Kassel: Bärenreiter, 1949-1986.
MSCC	*The Milwaukee Symposia for Church Composers: A Ten-Year Report.* Washington, DC: National Association of Pastoral Musicians, and Chicago: Liturgy Training Publications, 1992.
NGDMM	*The New Grove Dictionary of Music and Musicians.* 20 vols. New York: Norton, 1980.
NJBC	*New Jerome Biblical Commentary,* ed. Raymond Brown, Joseph Fitzmyer, and Roland Murphy. Englewood Cliffs, NJ: Prentice-Hall, 1988.
PG	Migne, *Patrologia, Series Graeca.*
PL	Migne, *Patrologia, Series Latina.*
SC	*Sources chrétiennes,* ed. H. de Lubac and J. Daniélou. Paris.
TDNT	*Theological Dictionary of the New Testament,* ed. Gerhard Kittel and Gerhard Friedrich, trans. Geoffrey W. Bromiley. 10 vols. Grand Rapids: Wm. Eerdmans, 1964.
TLS	*Tra le sollicitudini,* 1903.

Preface

One of the myths of publishing is the aura of finality that surrounds any article or monograph that makes it into print. Often for reader and author alike, the publishing of a work announces its completion and bestows an almost irrevocable quality upon the piece.

My experience of writing about music and worship over the past fifteen years is somewhat different. Because of mentors like Robert Taft and colleagues like Herbert Anderson and Robert Schreiter, I have learned that publishing an article or monograph is the beginning of a dialogue and not the end of one. Writing has often been the opportunity to test a hypothesis, present preliminary findings, or float an idea in print. Sometimes the conversation that ensues is mostly with myself. Thus, for example, the article "The Cantor in Historical Perspective" in this volume has been revised in view of further historical information that I have gathered since first writing the piece. Other articles, such as "From *Music in Catholic Worship* to the "Milwaukee Document," were the fruit of years of dialogue with other participants in the Milwaukee Symposia for Church Composers, or members of the Music Study Group of the North American Academy of Liturgy. Finally, some relatively new explorations, like "The Evaluation of Roman Catholic Ritual Music: From Displacement to Convergence," were the result of conversations with students in my seminars on ritual music at Catholic Theological Union over the past decade.

These revised and sometimes wholly rewritten essays are not presented even here as the final word but rather as one more phase of an ongoing conversation about ritual music in North America today. My hope is that they will stimulate the conversation, and move us further toward the goal of effective musical liturgy.

I am grateful to Virgil Funk and Larry Johnson of the Pastoral Press for inviting me to publish this collection of studies. I am particularly grateful to four dialogue partners and friends who have sustained me through many conversations about worship and the arts: Mary Lynch, Marchita Mauck, Mary McGann, and Mary Prete. It is to this quartet of gifted women that I dedicate this volume.

22 November 1994
Feast of St. Cecilia

1
Judaeo-Christian Ritual Music: A Bibliographic Introduction to the Field

Introduction

THE FIELD OF RITUAL MUSIC IS A VAST AND FAR-RANGING ONE, DIVERSELY partitioned, studied, and presented. Unlike some other subdisciplines of liturgics, there is little standardization in the study of ritual music, and syllabi for courses of study in the area often cover very different terrain employing a variety of methods.[1] There is barely agreement on the appropriate language for accessing the field,[2] as symbolized by the many dictionaries on the topic which are diversely titled and arranged.[3]

Although there is little standardization in the field, there are a few reoccurring methods and areas of interest in the field—some more prevalent than others—which dictate something of the content of an introductory survey such as this. The three most important of these, from my perspective, are (1) historical studies; (2) theological reflections upon the relationship between music and worship or faith; and (3) the recent turn to non-traditional methods—often borrowed from the social sciences—to examine worship music ritually and culturally.

Whereas there are innumerable other areas of interest that could occupy us, we will focus on these three. And although my perspective is Roman Catholic and my own cultural lens that of the dominant culture, I will attempt to map these areas ecumenically and cross-culturally, with special attention to their influence on

Judaism and western Christianity in the U.S. Since this essay is intended to be an introduction to the field, it is designed as a bibliographic essay, with selective references to works that are important because of the quality of their scholarship, the relevance of the topic, or the uniqueness of their perspective.[4] It is hoped that such referencing will help to balance my own presuppositions which will inevitably permeate the essay.

Historical Studies

Just as initial studies in liturgics showed a preference for the historical method, so does this approach dominate most earlier as well as many contemporary studies of ritual music.

General Histories

Books and Articles: Apart from the many general histories of music, in particular of western art music,[5] which contain much information on ritual music, there is an abundance of general works on the history of worship music. Three well-known examples available in English are Friedrich Blume's *Protestant Music: A History* (New York: Norton, 1974 [1965]); Abraham Z. Idelsohn's *Jewish Music in Its Historical Development* (New York: Schocken Books, 1967 [1929]); and Karl Fellerer's *The History of Catholic Church Music* (Baltimore: Helicon Press, 1961 [1949]; reprint ed., Westport, CT: Greenwood Press, 1979).[6]

There are a few significant difficulties with these and similar works.[7] The first is that the sheer amount of current scholarship on a given topic makes it very difficult for any single author to provide a competent overview of such a vast field. Consequently, the various entries in a great dictionary such as *Die Musik in Geschichte und Gegenwart,* 17 vols. (Kassel: Bärenreiter, 1949-1986), *The New Grove Dictionary of Music and Musicians,* 20 vols. (New York: Norton, 1980), or even in one of the more accessible, smaller dictionaries[8] are sometimes a better source of historical information than single-volume, general histories of worship music. There are also some very good survey articles on the history of liturgical music which are a good place for the uninitiated to begin their study.[9]

A second difficulty with books on the history of worship music is that—given the reality of the sociology of knowledge today—

our information about a given field such as liturgical music doubles almost every ten years. Consequently, much of the historical nuancing in many of the standard works on liturgical music is eclipsed or significantly challenged even before such are widely distributed. The ground breaking work in the history of liturgical music—as is true in other disciplines—often appears in various scholarly journals. These need to be consulted by the serious student of liturgical music.[10]

A final difficulty with many general histories of liturgical music—and this is also true of many of the dictionary and survey articles—is that they are often more histories of the music than of the musical-liturgical event. Thus a book will often enumerate which musical works were employed in worship, or offer extended analysis of that music, but seldom analyze how the music interacted with the rite, how it was experienced by those who heard it or those who performed it, or how it was considered theologically or in terms of its spirituality. For example, there are many histories that discuss Mozart's (+ 1791) Masses, *Requiem*, and other "sacred" compositions: seldom, however, do these works examine how or even if such works were employed in worship. Consequently, many histories are not histories of "liturgical music" properly speaking but of the music that was, in some way, connected to the church or synagogue. One notable exception is Solange Corbin's *L'Eglise à la conquête de sa musique* (Paris: Gallimard, 1960).[11]

Manuscripts, Editions, and Recordings. Besides writings about the history of liturgical music, there are three other important genres of sources for this history. Prior to the invention of printing by movable type in the 1450s, all written music appeared in manuscript form.[12] Although there have been some claims to have deciphered exactly the notation in manuscripts previous to the tenth century,[13] it is only Daseian notation—appearing around 900 CE—which is the first nonalphabetic western European notation that can be so deciphered. The basic resource for identifying music manuscripts before 1600 is *Répertoire international des sources musicales* (RISM).[14]

Besides manuscripts, there are many printed editions of individual liturgical musical manuscripts as well as historical (critical)[15] editions of the works of individual composers compiled from multiple manuscripts available today. A basic tool for accessing these editions is Anna Heyer's *Historical Sets, Collected Editions, and*

Monuments of Music, 3rd ed. (Chicago: American Library Association, 1980).[16] The most important collection for Jewish music in general, and Jewish liturgical music in particular, continues to be Abraham Z. Idelsohn's *Hebräische-orientalischer Melodienschatz*, 10 vols. (Leipzig: Breitkopf & Härtel, 1914-1932). There is no collection of such singular importance for Christian liturgical music. Notable monuments for the latter include various editions of the collected works of important composers like Johann Sebastian Bach's (+ 1750) *Werke* (Leipzig: Breitkopf & Härtel, 1851-1926),[17] collections of liturgical music from specific eras or geographic areas such as Hanna Stäblein-Harder's *Fourteenth-Century Mass Music in France* ([Rome]: American Institute of Musicology, 1962),[18] and more broadly defined collections of liturgical import like *Monumenta Musicae Sacrae* (Macon: Protat Frères, 1952-).[19]

Finally, those interested in music of any type, including liturgical music, require resources demonstrating that music is not notation on a page, but a sonic event. Recordings are invaluable in studying or teaching the history of liturgy music. Discographies describe and catalogue recordings. Recordings of most liturgical, sacred, or religious music composed before the twentieth century are categorized as "classical." One useful guide to discographies about this music is Michael H. Gray and Gerald D. Gibson's *Classical Music, 1925-1975* (New York: Bowker, 1977), which is a bibliography of discographies.[20] Another important resource for medieval, Renaissance, and baroque music—much of which would be considered liturgical—is Trevor Croucher's *Early Music Discography: From Plainsong to the Sons of Bach* (Phoenix: Oryx Press, 1981). Resource Publications in San Jose CA annually publishes a series of *Christian Music Directories*, one of which is subtitled *Recorded Music*, listing recordings of contemporary Christian liturgical, sacred, and religious music. *Schwann Opus* is a widely used quarterly journal, which lists "classical" recordings currently on the market.[21] The elasticity of the recording industries and markets has spawned the development of new electronic resources for accessing recorded music. One of the better of these is a quarterly cd-rom service entitled Music Library,[22] whose contents are copied from the OCLC[23] online Union Catalogue and consists of all types of musical sound recordings from all time periods, including lp's, 45's, cassettes, tape reels, cd's and piano roles. Another such resource—available in book format, on cd-rom, or through internet—is the *All Music Guide*.[24]

Focused Histories

Even more numerous than general historical works are the many studies that focus on particular times, places, or people in the history of liturgical music. The history of western music is commonly divided into six or seven discreet segments.[25] Sometimes the general divisions of western music are followed when studying liturgical music. Often, however, these prove problematic for chronicling worship music, and various authors construct different schemes for the periodization of liturgical music.

Judaism. In Judaism, for example, the music of the Bible is an important historical subdivision of the field. In addition to various monographs on the topic, such as Bathya Bayer's *The Material Relics of Music in Ancient Palestine and Its Environs* (Tel Aviv: Israel Music Institute, 1963),[26] there are important articles on the subject in many biblical dictionaries and commentaries,[27] the standard musical dictionaries noted above, and Jewish dictionaries and encyclopedias. Especially valuable are the many articles in *Encyclopaedia Judaica*, ed. Cecil Roth and Geoffrey Wigoder, 16 vols. (Jerusalem: Keter Publishing, 1972).[28] Another fruitful source of information about biblical music are key publications on the worship of Ancient Israel, such as H.H. Rowley, *Worship in Ancient Israel: Its Forms and Meaning* (London: SPCK, 1967) 176-212.

The rise of the synagogue[29] usually serves as the delineating factor for setting a second major period of Jewish music.[30] Notable monographs include two publications by Hanoch Avenary: *The Ashkenazi Tradition of Biblical Chant between 1500 and 1900* (Tel Aviv: Tel Aviv University, 1978), and *Hebrew Hymn Tunes: The Rise and Development of a Musical Tradition* (Tel Aviv: Israel Music Institute, 1971).[31] Dictionary and encyclopedia entries provide information on key developments such as the metrical prayer-poems known as *piyyutim* and the rise of the *hazzan*. Two major liturgical studies that shed some light on the music of the synagogue are Joseph Heinemann, *Prayer in the Talmud* (Berlin and New York: Walter De Gruyter, 1977) and Lawrence Hoffman, *The Canonization of the Synagogue Service* (Notre Dame: University of Notre Dame Press, 1979).[32] Much scholarly literature on synagogue music has appeared across the spectrum of periodic literature.[33] There are also a number of theoretical works from this period, and a body of accompanying literature, some of which will be discussed below.

The nineteenth-century reforms in Judaism provide the focus for delineating a third major period in Jewish liturgical music.

There are fewer monographs or individual articles on this period than the previous two. Two articles in *Sacred Sound and Social Change* (Geoffrey Goldberg's "Jewish Liturgical Music in the Wake of Nineteenth-Century Reform," 59-83; and Benjie-Ellen Schiller's "The Hymnal as an Index of Musical Change in Reform Synagogues," 187-212) provide a helpful overview of some of the developments and literature for this era.

Christianity. The New Testament period (1st century) is one of the Christian eras least considered by musical scholars—partly because there is little that could properly be isolated as "music" in the New Testament.[34] The studies by scriptural and other scholars on the general topic of "music" in the New Testament include J.A. Smith's recent "First Century Christian Singing and Its Relationship to Contemporary Jewish Religious Song," *Music and Letters* 75 (1994) 1-15.[35] Such scholars have also given us numerous studies on particular texts,[36] or of "musical" genres—especially hymnody—suggested by the New Testament, for example, Jack Sanders, *The New Testament Christological Hymns* (Cambridge: Cambridge University Press, 1971).[37]

General histories of western music usually say very little about Christian worship music before Ambrose (+ 397). One of the better general treatments of the era of the early church (c. 100-600) is Giulio Cattin's *Music of the Middle Ages,* vol. 1 (Cambridge: Cambridge University Press, 1984).[38] One of the better collections of patristic texts on music is James McKinnon's *Music in Early Christian Literature* (Cambridge: Cambridge University Press, 1987).[39] There are significant studies on various musical forms from this period, especially hymnody[40] and psalmody. Helmut Leeb's *Die Psalmodie bei Ambrosius* (Vienna: Herder, 1967) is a classic when it comes to the latter.[41]

Some monographs examine the contributions of important individuals in this era.[42] More numerous are articles examining a wide variety of topics such as the role of instruments in early Christian music and the role of the cantor.[43] Since this era also witnesses the rise of the Byzantine liturgy and its distinctive music, there is significant study of this repertoire[44] as well as the distinctive repertoires of Rome,[45] Jerusalem[46] and other centers of worship.[47]

Histories of western music often date the Middle Ages from 500 to 1430, followed by the Renaissance (1430 to 1600). From the viewpoint of liturgical music, it may be preferable to consider the liturgical-musical continuity between these two periods by speaking of the early Middle Ages (seventh to twelfth centuries) and the late Middle Ages (thirteenth to the mid-sixteenth centuries). A good overview, especially of the early Middle Ages, is provided in Richard Crocker and David Hiley, *Early Middle Ages to 1300*, vol. 2 of *New Oxford History of Music*, 2nd ed. (New York: Oxford University Press, 1994).[48] There are numerous theorists who write about music during this era.[49] As important for the history of liturgical music are the various ecclesiastical instructions on how music is to be employed in worship. The best source for this material is André Pons, *Droit ecclésiastique et musique sacrée*, 4 vols. (St. Maurice: Editions de l'Oeuvre St. Augustin, 1959-1961).[50] The major topic in the early Middle Ages vis-à-vis liturgical music is plainchant. David Hiley's *Western Plainchant: A Handbook* (Oxford: Clarendon Press, 1993) is the best single-volume introduction to the topic.[51] A key issue in this area is the origin of Gregorian chant and especially its relationship to Old Roman chant. Peter Jeffery rehearses most of the relevant material on this issue in *Reenvisioning Past Musical Cultures: Ethnomusicology in the Study of Gregorian Chant* (Chicago and London: The University of Chicago Press, 1992).[52] A major area of study in the late Middle Ages is polyphony and its effects upon the liturgical text. A good introductory article is Marion Gushee, "The Polyphonic Music of the Medieval Monastery, Cathedral and University," *Antiquity and the Middle Ages: From Ancient Greece to the 15th Century* 143-169.[53] From a liturgical music perspective this would include Palestrina (+ 1594) and the Council of Trent (1545-1563) for, although they chronologically overlap into the next period, musically and liturgically they are more backward than forward looking, and could be considered the culmination of the late medieval period.[54] Another key topic is the development of Latin hymnody: a splendid introduction in an important series (Typologie des sources du moyen âge occidental) is Josef Szövérffy, *Latin Hymns* (Turnhout: Brepols, 1989).[55] Not to be overlooked are the popular religious songs, especially of the laity, such as the *cantiga, cantio, cantique,* carol, *Geisslerlieder, lauda, Leise,* and *Ruf*,[56] as well as the expansion of musical-liturgical forms at this time.[57]

The Reform and Counterreform (sixteenth to nineteenth centuries) was a period of unusual musical-liturgical ferment. No single volume adequately summarizes the period. Most general histories give more attention to "sacred" non-liturgical music of this period—especially for Roman Catholicism—than to music actually employed in the rites. In multi-volume works on the history of western music, information on this period is often scattered across numerous volumes. For Protestant liturgical music, Blume's *Protestant Music: A History* (1974 [1965]) remains a useful guide;[58] Fellerer's second volume of *Geschichte der katholischen Kirchenmusik* is similarly useful for the music of the Roman Catholic Counterreform. Among the many valuable monographs on this period is Anthony Lewis and Nigel Fortune's *Opera and Church Music 1630-1750* (New York and Oxford: Oxford University Press, 1986).[59] There are numerous parallels between the broad categories of Protestant[60] and Roman Catholic worship music during this period. These include the introduction of concerto style composition for worship, the growth of instrumental music in the liturgy,[61]—in particular, the organ[62]—and the development of new vocal forms such as the cantata, oratorio, and passion music.[63] Vernacular psalmody and hymnody are especially important for emerging Protestantism. There are fewer general works on the former; Erik Routley's *The Music of Christian Hymns* (Chicago: GIA, 1981) offers a good overview of Reformation psalmody (28-58), including many musical examples.[64] The general works on hymnody are more plentiful, including various bibliographies (Keith C. Clark, *A Selective Bibliography for the Study of Hymns 1980* [Springfield, OH: Hymn Society of America, 1980])[65] and dictionaries (a standard is John Julian's *Dictionary of Hymnody*, 2 vols. [Grand Rapids: Eerdmans, 1985 {1907}]).[66] The hymns of many reformers are available in various editions,[67] and there are numerous specific studies on various aspects of Reformation hymnody.[68] Although many of the above cited sources also document the hymnic developments in Roman Catholicism, more particular to its musical-liturgical history in this era was the revival of Gregorian chant, especially symbolized in the Cecilian movement.[69] There are a host of important liturgical composers during these centuries and many other luminaries who also write some liturgical or sacred music.[70] The musical-liturgical giant of this era is Johann Sebastian Bach. The literature about him and his music is daunting. An outstanding introduction to the liturgical Bach is Günther Stiller's *Johann Sebastian Bach and Liturgical Life in Leipzig*, ed. Robin Leaver (St. Louis: Concordia, 1984).[71] Finally, it was during this period that liturgical music developed in various churches in the United States. A good introduction to this study is Victor Gebauer's

"'Look Again!' Writing about America Church Music," *Currents in Theology and Mission* 16:3 (1989) 180-186.[72]

The twentieth century has been a period with few parallels in regard to the amount of scholarship, legislation, composition, and change in Christian liturgical music. Although there has been much historical writing in this century, there are few general works on the history of liturgical music in this era. The writings of Erik Routley provide something of an introduction to this period, for example, *Twentieth Century Church Music* (New York: Oxford University Press, 1964).[73] There has been a great deal of writing, especially among Roman Catholics, about the liturgical-musical developments that have occurred since the Second Vatican Council (1963-65).[74] Some of the key issues of this era—the role of culture, the nature of ritual music, and the theology of liturgical music—will be addressed below. Other central developments for Roman Catholics include the spate of legislation and other documents on liturgical music in this century,[75] while key for many Protestant communities has been the publication of new hymnals.[76]

Theological Studies

Besides historical studies of liturgical music there is a growing body of literature about liturgical music which is of a more overtly theological nature.[77] Though there are few conventions for organizing this material, one useful way to divide this material is to distinguish between theological reflections (1) on the nature of music and sound itself, (2) on the role of music in worship, and (3) on the relationship between music and texts.

On the Nature of Music/Sound

In some respects, much of our earliest material about music in the Judaeo-Christian tradition could be considered under this category. There is no generic word in biblical Hebrew for "music," and music *per se* was not the point of theological speculation. There was an awareness in ancient Judaism and emerging Christianity, however, that public worship required a heightened auditory environment—especially in the proclamation of sacred texts.[78] Music was valued by the rabbis because of its capacity for enabling the praise of angels and of people.[79] Under the influence of Neo-Platonism, later Jewish writers, such as the tenth-century philosopher Sa`adya in *Emunot vedeot* and Joseph Aknin (+ 1220) in his *Tibb al-Nufus*, acknowledged the power of music to move the spirit, and the innate ethical implications of music and its rhythms.[80] The great philosopher Maimonides (+ 1204)—not unlike some Christian counterparts of the same era—was severely distressed by the power of music and poetry to distract the worshiper.[81] The positive power of music was emphasized by the Kabbahlistic mystics who stressed music's vital role in contemplation.[82]

In Christianity, as well, many of the musical allusions or writings about music in the early church are implicit reflections on music or sound as vehicles or obstacles to the self-communication of God and to the assent of the soul to that gracious self-communication.[83] Although *De Utilitate Hymnorum* by Niceta of Remesiana (+ after 414) contains some instruction on musical performance in worship, it is essentially a pastoral-theological reflection on the value of singing hymns and psalms.[84] Although ordinarily classified as one of the "philosophical" works of his youth, Augustine's (+ 430) *De Musica*—especially book six—also needs to be considered for its theological reflections on rhythm, and the manner of ascent from mutable numbers to the immutable number, who is God.[85] Also notable is the philosophical work of Boethius (+ 525), *De Institutione Musica*, in which he asserts—as did the Greeks before him—that music is intimately related to morality.[86] Finally, many ecclesiastical instructions, from John XXII's (+ 1334) *Docta Sanctorum Patrum* to Pius X's (+ 1914) *Tra le sollicitudini*—although usually providing pastoral instruction—also include theological reflections on the nature of music itself, as well as thoughts about the relationship of music to the rites.

There have been a number of contemporary attempts to articulate a general theology of music or liturgical music—such as my own "Toward a Sound Theology," *Studia Liturgica* 23:2 (1993) 121-139.[87] Jon Michael Spencer has even advocated the recognition of a specific discipline for addressing music and theology which he calls "theomusicology," as in his *Theological Music: Introduction to Theo-Musicology* (New York and Westport, CT: Greenwood Press, 1991).[88] The search for appropriate language in which to speak about music theologically or its role in worship is further symbolized in the literature which raises questions about the very concept of liturgical, religious, or sacred music. A recent article that raises such questions is Claude Duchesneau's "Musique sacrée, musique d'église, musique liturgique: changement de mentalité" in *Notitiae*,

n. 256, 23:11 (1987) 1189-1199.[89] Whereas most of the writing on the interplay between music and theology has an implicit religious or denominational perspective, some works are explicit in their attempt to articulate a theology of music for a specific denomination. Besides Roman Catholics,[90] this trend is especially apparent among some Lutherans as exemplified in Joyce Irwin's "Shifting Alliances: The Struggle for a Lutheran Theology of Music," *Sacred Sound*, ed. Joyce Irwin (Chico, CA: Scholars Press, 1983) 55-69.[91]

Music and the Rites

For the liturgical theologian, systematic reflection on sound or music presumes that one take seriously the rites themselves. This means, for example, considering the liturgical-theological dynamics between worship and its music. One such classic work in Roman Catholicism, written on the brink of the Second Vatican Council, is Joseph Gelineau, *Voices and Instruments in Christian Worship*, trans. Clifford Howell (Collegeville: The Liturgical Press, 1964).[92] An important post-conciliar work in this genre is Bernard Huijbers, *The Performing Audience*, 2nd ed. (Phoenix: North American Liturgy Resources, 1974).[93]

Some studies in this category have focused on particular liturgical units and considered the implications of music in these specific subdivisions of the rite. Mary McGann and I attempted such a study in our *Music and the Eucharistic Prayer* (Washington, DC: The Pastoral Press, 1988).[94] Also, there has been some inquiry about the theological implications of various genres of liturgical-musical forms,[95] in particular the hymn.[96]

The Interplay of Music and Texts

Another area of inquiry, related to the previous concern about the relationship between music and the rite, focuses on the intersection of text and music in worship. Apart from historical studies analyzing the treatment of texts by one composer or another, there are a limited number of more theological works that explore the faith dimensions of the text, and the influence of the music on the same. Noteworthy is Eugene Brand's unpublished dissertation from the University of Heidelberg (1959), "The Liturgical Function of Music: Music in Its Relationship to the Texts of the Liturgy."[97] More recently, as part of the larger discussion about the translation of texts and issues of inclusivity, there has been significant writing about the appropriate language for worship and worship song, both in terms of inclusivity as well as poetics. Reflections from well-respected text writers, such as Thomas Troeger ("Theological Considerations for Poetic Texts Used by the Assembly," *Worship* 59:5 [1985] 404-412) and Brian Wren (*What Language Shall I Borrow: God Talk in Worship—A Male Response to Feminist Theology* [New York: Crossroads, 1990]) have enriched this discussion.[98] Such discussions raise sometime larger questions about the pastoral-theological responsibilities of composers and/or text writers in the shaping of worship music.[99]

Pastoral and Cultural Studies

Apart from historical studies, or systematic reflections on the relationship between faith and music in general—or liturgical music, in particular—there have also emerged a variety of new approaches for considering worship music, largely borrowed from the social sciences. This evolution is reliant upon precedents both in musicology over the past century, as well as later, parallel developments in the field of liturgy.

Musicologically, the late nineteenth and early twentieth centuries were a time of diverse developments in the methods for the study of music. Some pioneered musical research from the perspectives of psychology, including Karl Stumpf (see his *Tonpsychologie* [Leipzig: S. Hirzel, 1883-1890]), and Carl Seashore (e.g., his *Psychology of Music* [New York: McGraw-Hill, 1938]).[100] Others approached music from the viewpoint of sociology[101] or anthropology.[102] Musical studies, employing methods from these varying disciplines, spawned many of new fields of inquiry. Of special import for liturgical music is the field of ethnomusicology (originally "comparative musicology").[103] Although initially focused on music of non-western cultures, there have been recent efforts within ethnomusicological circles to study the music of any culture. Of particular interest to some has been the study of music in ritual, which has become a rubric frequently employed for organizing presentations at the annual meeting of the Society for Ethnomusicology.[104]

Within the study of liturgy over the past few decades there has been a noticeable influence of psychology, anthropology, ethnology, and other social sciences. Gilbert Ostdiek provides a splendid overview of these developments in his recent article "Ritual and

Transformation: Reflections on Liturgy and the Social Sciences," *Liturgical Ministry* 2 (1993) 38-48. A memorable articulation of the need for such methodological shifts was Mark Searle's 1983 vice-presidential address to the North American Academy of Liturgy, in which he outlined a new branch of liturgical scholarship, which he called "pastoral liturgical studies."[105] Since that time, the recently defined field of ritual studies has emerged which, in large measure, has taken up the concerns outlined by Searle. A key figure in this discipline is Ronald Grimes (e.g., *Reading, Writing and Ritualizing: Ritual in Fictive, Liturgical, and Public Places* (Washington, DC: The Pastoral Press, 1993).[106]

The influence of the social sciences on the study of music, and their parallel ascendancy in liturgical studies—as well as the new work in ritual studies—has begun to affect the study[107] and even the composition and publication of liturgical music.[108] Of particular importance is the concern about varied cultural expressions of liturgical music and the development of appropriate frameworks for understanding and evaluating this music. A related concern is creating an experience-based method for ascertaining how music actually functions in worship and faith through the techniques of field observation.

The Culture of Worship Music

The worship music of Jews and Christians, like that of other world religions, is culturally conditioned—a fact not always readily recognized. One common presupposition about worship music is the alleged superiority of certain works or a body of works that originated from a particularly prized era, geographic location, or composer.[109] Such music has often been exported outside its culture of origin, and sometimes imposed regardless of the cultural tastes or standards of the receiving culture. Pius X's claim about the superiority of Gregorian chant in the previously cited *Tra le sollicitudini* is a classic example of this in Roman Catholicism. It is especially through the influence of cultural anthropology and ethnomusicology that such practices are being studied and challenged.[110]

The number of studies—as compared with "reports"—of non-traditional music in Christianity and Judaism is small but growing. Some of these studies are of a more reflective or theological nature, such as James Cone's "Black Spirituals: A Theological

Interpretation," in *Music and the Experience of God*, ed. Mary Collins et al. (Edinburgh: T. and T. Clark Ltd., 1989) 41-51.[111] Other works—many of them the product of University study—are based on field observation, such as Stephen Frederick Duncan, "Christian Bhajans: A Study of the Uses of Indigenous Music in the Rites of the Catholic Church on the Subcontinent of India since the Second Vatican Council with Particular Attention to *Bhajan* and *Kirtan*" (unpublished Ph.D. dissertation from Memphis State University, 1991).

African-American music has received the bulk of such attention in the U.S.[112] One important scholar in this area is Mellonee Burnim (for example, her "Culture Bearer and Tradition Bearer: An Ethnomusicologist's Research on Gospel Music," *Ethnomusicology* 29 [1985] 432-447).[113] There is less scholarly work on the current ritual music of Hispanics in this country,[114] although there are some studies of music of the Spanish missions in North America.[115] A growing awareness of the value of these non-dominant cultural expressions has lead to the inclusion of a sampling of "non-traditional" worship music in some recent major hymnals,[116] as well as the publication of particular hymnals—especially for African-Americans and Hispanics—in this country.[117]

Field Work and Liturgical Music

There are—and always have been—a variety of opinions about worship music and how it should function in worship.[118] The development of field methods in anthropology and ethnomusicology, as well as the use of such methods in ritual and liturgical studies,[119] have spurred some investigators to explore new ways for understanding how music does function in worship. Most of these studies to date—and there are few of them—have been conducted by ethnomusicologists or anthropologists, who often do not ask explicitly the theological question in their work, such as Jacqueline DjeDje's "Change and Differentiation: The Adoption of Black American Gospel Music in the Catholic Church."[120] A few studies have been conducted by liturgists or musicians with little experience or training in field work in consultation with experts from the social sciences.[121] An unusual collaboration between liturgists and social scientists was the *Notre Dame Study of Catholic Parish Life*, which gave some attention to worship and its music.[122] Unfortunately, the specifically musical data was very difficult to retrieve from this study.[123]

Whereas there is certainly further need for historical and theological studies of worship music, this author believes that further field work in liturgical music—and the employment of disciplines such as semiotics[124] for the interpretation of the data collected from such field work—are critical for the advancement of the field today. As this introduction itself demonstrates, historical studies dominate the field. It is necessary to balance those efforts, so that we not only acquire adequate knowledge of the liturgical music in our past, but develop an understanding for how it can serve our worship in the future.

Notes

1. See, for example, *Teaching Seminarians Music: Course Descriptions from Nine Seminaries*, ed. Anthony DiCello (Washington, DC: NPM Publications, 1991).

2. The most common of these are: church or synagogue music, liturgical music, worship music, religious music, ritual music, and sacred music. For a further discussion of this terminology, see my "Liturgical Music" in *The New Dictionary of Sacramental Worship*, ed. Peter Fink (Collegeville: The Liturgical Press, 1990) 854-870; also n. 89 below.

3. Examples include Joseph Robert Carroll, *Compendium of Liturgical Musical Terms* (Toledo: Gregorian Institute of America, 1964); James Robert Davidson, *A Dictionary of Protestant Church Music* (Metuchen, NJ: Scarecrow Press, 1975); Utto Kornmüller, *Lexikon der kirchlichen Tonkunst* (Regensburg: Coppenrath, 1870 [corrected and expanded 1891-1895]; reprint ed., Hildesheim: G. Olms, 1975); Salomon Kümmerle, *Enzyklopädie der evangelischen Kirchenmusik*, 4 vols. (Gütersloh: Bertelsmann, 1888-1895; reprint ed., Hildesheim: G. Olms, 1974); Hans Musch, *Musik im Gottesdienst* (Regensburg: Gustav Bosse, 1975); Joseph Ortique, *Dictionnaire liturgique, historique et théorique de plainchant et de musique d'église* (Paris: Migne, 1853; reprint ed., New York: Da Capo Press, 1971); Jacques Porte, *Encyclopédie des musiques sacrées*, 4 vols. (Paris: Editions Lagergerie, 1968-); David Poultney, *Dictionary of Western Church Music* (Chicago: American Library Association, 1991); Carl Schalk, *Key Words in Church Music* (St. Louis: Concordia, 1978); G.-W. Stubbins, *A Dictionary of Church Music* (London: Epworth Press, 1949); E. Valentin, and F. Hofmann, *Die Evangelische Kirchenmusik. Handbuch für Studium und Praxis* (Regensburg: Bosse, 1967); Andreas Weissenbäck, *Sacra Musica: Lexikon der katholischen Kirchenmusik* (Klosterneuburg: Augustinus Druck, 1937). A new ecumenical dictionary which I am editing with Mark Bangert, Carol Doran, and Lawrence Hoffman is tentatively entitled *Worship Music: A Concise Dictionary*.

4. General bibliographies on the topic include: Bard Thompson, *A Bibliography of Christian Worship* (Metuchen, NJ: Scarecrow Press, 1989) 656-739; Walter Buszin, Theodore Finney, and Donald McCorkle, *A Bibliography on Music and the Church* (New York: National Council of the Churches of Christ, 1958); Irene Heskes, *The Resource Book of Jewish Music: A Bibliographical and Topical Guide* (Westport, CT: Greenwood Press, 1985); Martin Rossler, *Bibliographie der deutschen Liedpredigt* (Nieuwkoop: de Graaf, 1976); Alfred Sendery, *Bibliography of Jewish Music* (New York: Columbia University Press, 1951); Gino Stefani, "Bibliographie fondamentale de musicologie liturgique," *La Maison-Dieu* 108 (1971) 175-189; Richard von Ende, *Church Music: An International Bibliography* (Metuchen, NJ: Scarecrow Press, 1980); Albert Weisser, *Bibliography of Publications and Other Resources on Jewish Music* (New York: National Jewish Music Council, 1969); Paul Yeats-Edwards, *English Church Music: A Bibliography* (London: White Lion, 1975). More specific bibliographies will be noted throughout this chapter.

5. A standard single-volume work in English is Donald J. Grout and Claude V. Palisca, *A History of Western Music*, 4th ed. (New York and London: Norton, 1988); of the multi-volume works on the history of western music, two of the best in English are the *New Oxford History of Music*, 10 vols. (London: Oxford University Press, 1954-); and, *Prentice Hall History of Music Series*, 10 vols., ed. H. Wiley Hitchcock (Englewood Cliffs, NJ: Prentice-Hall, 1965-).

6. Better is the collection Fellerer edited, *Geschichte der katholischen Kirchenmusik*, 2 vols. (Kassel: Bärenreiter, 1972).

7. For example, Ch. L. Etherington, *Protestant Worship Music: Its History and Practice* (New York: Holt-Rinehart-Winston, 1962); Paul Huot-Pleuroux, *Histoire de la musique religieuse des origines à nos jours* (Paris: Presses Universitaires, 1957); Paul Hume, *Catholic Church Music* (New York: Dodd, Mead, 1956); Frits Mehrtens, *Kerk & Muziek*, 2 vols. ('s-Gravenhage: Boekencentrum, 1961); William Carroll Rice, *A Concise History of Church Music* (New York: Abingdon Press, 1964); Alec Robertson, *Christian Music* (New York: Hawthorn Books, 1961); Hans Sabel, *Die liturgischen Gesänge der katholischen Kirche* (Wolfenbüttel: Möseler Verlag, 1965); Alfred Sendry, *Music in Ancient Israel* (New York: Philosophical Library, 1969); Oskar Söhngen, *Musica sacra zwischen gestern und Morgan*, 2 Aufl. (Göttingen: Vandenhoeck & Ruprecht, 1981); Otto Ursprung, *Die katholische Kirchenmusik* (Potsdam: Athenaion, 1931); Eric Werner, *The Sacred Bridge*, 2 vols. (New York: Columbia University Press, 1959; New York: Ktav Publishing House, 1984).

8. Two of the best in English are *The New Harvard Dictionary of Music*, ed. Don Michael Randel (Cambridge, MA: Belknap Press, 1986), and *The New Oxford Companion to Music*, ed. Denis Arnold, 2 vols. (Oxford and New York: Oxford University Press, 1983).

9. For example, Margot Fassler and Peter Jeffery, "Christian Liturgical Music from the Bible to the Renaissance," *Sacred Sound and Social Change: Liturgical Music in Jewish and Christian Experience,* ed. Lawrence A. Hoffman and Janet Walton, vol. 3 of *Two Liturgical Traditions* (Notre Dame: University of Notre Dame Press, 1992) 84-123; also the older but still useful article by Joseph Gelineau, "Music and Singing in the Liturgy," *The Study of Liturgy,* ed. Cheslyn Jones et al., rev. ed. (New York: Oxford University Press, 1992) 493-507.

10. A sampling of current journals includes *Bulletin of the Hymn Society of Great Britain and Ireland* (Edinburgh); *Il Canto dell' Assemblea* (Torino); *Church Music* (River Forest, IL); *Eglise qui chante* (Paris); *Etudes grégoriennes* (Solesmes); *Jahrbuch für Liturgik und Hymnologie* (Kassel); *Black Sacred Music* (Durham); *Journal of Jewish Music and Liturgy* (New York); *Kirchenmusikalisches Jahrbuch* (Regensburg); *Musica Judaica* (New York); *Musik und Altar* (Freiburg im Br.); *Musik und Gottesdienst* (Zurich); *Musik und Kirche* (Kassel); *Plainsong and Medieval Music* (Cambridge); *Reformed Liturgy and Music* (Philadelphia); *Revue grégorienne* (Paris); and *Zeitschrift für evangelische Kirchenmusik.*

There is no single, comprehensive list of music journals or journals on liturgical, sacred, or church music. Three basic resources on music periodicals are *The Music Index* (Detroit: Information Service, 1949-); *RILM* [Répertoire international de litérature musicale] *Abstracts of Music Literature* (Flushing, NY: New York RILM, 1967-); and *Bibliographie des Musikschrifttums* (Leipzig: Staatliches Institut für deutsche Musikforschung, 1936-1939; Frankfurt a.M.: Institut für Musikforschung, 1950-).

11. A translation and revision of this work is currently underway.

12. Even after Gutenberg's invention, it took some time for music to be printed. In 1457 a *Psalterium* was printed by Johanna Fust and Peter Schöffer—associates of Gutenberg—but in this work only the staves were printed, whereas the notes were written by hand. The earliest known book of printed music appears to be a German gradual, possibly from 1473. On the history of music printing, see A. Hyatt King, *Four Hundred Years of Music Printing,* 2nd ed. (London: British Museum, 1968). A useful resource for identifying printed liturgical music before 1500 (incunabula), is Kathi Meyer-Baer's *Liturgical Music Incunabula* (London: The Bibliographical Society, 1962).

13. For example, Suzanne Haïk-Vantoura, who claims to have deciphered one of the Masoretic systems (the Tiberian) of accents (te'amin) dating from the ninth century CE. She claims that this system of accents reflects a musical system that developed before the emergence of Christianity and that it can be reconstructed today. See her *The Music of the Bible Revealed,* trans. Dennis Weber, ed. John Wheeler (Berkeley, CA: Bibal Press, 1991); a recording of her transcription, under the title *La Musique de la bible revélée* is available on disk (HMA 190989).

14. This is a joint project of the International Association of Music Libraries and the International Musicological Society begun in 1952. The two publishers of RISM are Bärenreiter in Kassel and Henle in Munich.

15. Critical editions in music are a late 19th century development: one of the first being Friedrich Chrysander's *Denkmäler der Tonkunst* (Bergedorf, 1869-1871).

16. Also see Sydney R. Charles, *A Handbook of Music and Music Literature in Sets and Series* (New York: Free Press, 1972).

17. A sampling of others includes William Billings (+ 1800), *Complete Works* (Charlottesville: University Press of Virginia, 1978-); Guillaume Dufay (+ 1474), *Opera Omnia,* Corpus Mensurabilis Musicae 1 ([Rome]: American Institute of Musicology, 1951-1966); Giovanni Gabrieli (+ 1612), *Opera Omnia,* Corpus Mensurabilis Musicae 12 ([Rome]: American Institute of Musicology, 1956-); Josquin Desprez (+ 1521), *Werken* (Amsterdam: G. Alsbach and Leipzig: Kistner & Siegel, 1922-1969); Guillaume de Machaut (+ 1377), *Oeuvres complètes* (Paris: Le Droit Chemin de Musique, 1977); Giovanni Pierluigi da Palestrina (+ 1594), *Le opere complete* (Rome: Edizione Fratelli Scalera, 1939-1965, 1973-); and Heinrich Schütz (+ 1672), *Stuttgarter Schütz-Ausgabe* (Neuhausen and Stuttgart: Hänssler-Verlag, 1971-).

18. Also see Laurence Feininger, ed., *Monumenta Polyphonae Liturgicae Sanctae Ecclesiae Romanae,* ser. I-II (Rome: Societas Universalis Sanctae Ceciliae, 1947-); Knud Jeppesen, *Italia sacra musica* (Copenhagen: W. Hansen, 1962); Fernando Liuzzi, *La Lauda e i primordi della melodia italiana,* 2 vols. (Rome: La libreria dello stato, 1935); *Monumenta Liturgiae Polychoralis Sanctae Ecclesiae Romanae,* ser. I-IV (Rome: Societas Universalis Sanctae Ceciliae, 1950-); Felipe Pedrell, *Hispaniae Schola Musica Sacra* (Barcelona: Juan Baptista Pujol, 1894-1898); and *Tudor Church Music* (London: Oxford University Press, 1922-1929).

19. Also see Wilhelm Bäumker, *Das katholische Kirchenlied* (Freiburg, 1883-1911); Charles van den Borren, *Polyphonia Sacra,* rev. ed. (University Park, PA: Pennsylvania State University Press, 1963); François Delsarte, *Archives du chant* (Paris: F. Delsarte, 1860-1870); *Paléographie musicale,* 21 vols. in 2 series (Solesmes: Imprimerie St. Pierre and Tournai: Desclée, 1989-; reprint ed., Bern: H. Lang, 1969-); Karl Proske, *Musica Divina* (Regensburg: F. Pustet, 1853-1876); and Yvonne Rokseth, *Motets du XIIIe siècle* (Paris: L'Oiseau-Lyre, 1936).

20. Also see the more general work by Brian Rust, *Brian Rust's Guide to Discography* (Westport, CT: Greenwood, 1980).

21. *Schwann Spectrum* is the quarterly which lists "popular" recordings currently available. Both are published by Stereophile, 208 Delgado St., Santa Fe, NM 87501.

22. Available from SilverPlatter, 10 River Ridge Dr., Norwood, MA 02062 (telephone: 617-769-2599).

23. Acronym for the Online Computer Library Center (originally, the Ohio College Library Center).

24. Available from Miller Freeman Inc., 600 Harrison St., San Francisco, CA 94107 (telephone: 415-905-2470).

25. For example, Ancient (Greek antiquity to 500 CE), medieval (500-1430), Renaissance (1430-1600), baroque (1600-1750), classical (1750-1825), romantic (1825 to early 20th century) and modern (20th century).

26. Also Abraham Wolf Binder, *Biblical Chant* (New York: Philosophical Library, 1959); Wolfgang Blissenbach, *Musik in Bibel und Gemeinde* (Erzhausen: Leuchter-Verlag, 1975); Sigmund Mowinckel, *The Psalms in Israel's Worship*, trans. D.R. Ap-Thomas (Oxford: Basil Blackwell, 1962); and the previously cited *Music in Ancient Israel* by Alfred Sendrey.

27. For example, Edith Gerson-Kiwi, "Musique dans la bible," *Dictionnaire de la Bible,* supp. 5 (Paris: Letouzey & Ané, 1957); and Eric Werner, "Music" in the *Interpreter's Dictionary of the Bible,* ed. George A. Buttrick, 4 vols. (New York-Nashville: Abingdon, 1962) 3:457-469.

28. Also the various entires in NGDMM, such as "Jewish Music, I. Liturgical" by Eric Werner et al. (9:614-634); various entires in Macy Nulman, *Concise Encyclopedia of Jewish Music* (New York: McGraw-Hill, 1975); one would also anticipate two forthcoming volumes to be valuable here: the *Dictionary of Biblical Judaism,* edited by Jacob Neusner from Macmillan, and the *Dictionary of the Jewish Religion,* edited by R. J. Zwi Werblowsky and Geoffrey Wigoder from Oxford. I am grateful to Prof. Lawrence Hoffman for these references.

29. As to the origin of the Jewish synagogue, see the articles by Joseph Gutmann ("Synagogue Origins: Theories and Facts") and Marilyn Chiat ("First Century Synagoguges: Methodological Problems") in *Ancient Synagogues: The State of Research,* ed. Jacob Neusner et al. (Chico, CA: Scholars Press, 1981).

30. Sometimes this period is divided around the year 1000 CE; the later period is often subdivided by consideration of two emerging traditions in Judaism: Ashkenazic and Sephardic.

31. Also Alfred Sendrey, *Music of the Jews in the Diaspora* (up to 1800) (New York: T. Yoseloff, 1970); the previously cited two volume work by Eric Werner, *The Sacred Bridge* (appropriate cautions about Werner's work are outlined in Peter Jeffery, "Werner's Sacred Bridge, Volume 2: A Review Essay," *Jewish Quarterly Review* 77 [1987] 283-298); id., *A Voice Still Heard: The Sacred Song of the Ashkenazi Jews* (University Park, PA: Pennsylvania State University Press, 1976).

32. Though it needs to be read with caution, Ismar Elbogen's *Der judische Gottesdienst in seiner geschichtlichen Entwicklung* (Leipzig: G. Fock, 1913), recently edited by Joseph Heinemann et al. as *Jewish Liturgy,* trans. Raymond P. Scheindlin (Philadelphia: The Jewish Publication Society, 1993) is also of value.

33. A sampling includes Higini Anglès, "La musique juive dans l'Espagne médiévale," *Yuval* 1 (1968) 48-64; Hanoch Avenary, "Contacts between Church and Synagogue Music," *Proceedings of the World Jewish Congress on Jewish Music* (Jerusalem 1978) Tel Aviv, 1982, 89-107; Joseph A. Levine, "Toward Defining the Jewish Prayer Modes with Particular Emphasis on the Adonay Malakh Mode," *Musica Judaica* 3 (1980-1981) 13-41; James W. McKinnon, "On the Question of Psalmody in the Ancient Synagogue," *Early Music History* 6 (1986) 159-191; Baruch David Schreiber, "The Woman's Voice in the Synagogue," *Journal of Jewish Music and Liturgy* 7 (1984-1985) 27-32; Avigdor Shinan, "Sermons, Targums and the Reading from Scripture in the Ancient Synagogue," *The Synagogue in Late Antiquity*, ed. Lee I. Levin (Philadelphia, 1987) 97-100; Johanna Spector, "Chant and Cantillation," *Musica Judaica* 9 (1986-1987) 1-21; and Max Wohlberg, "The History of the Musical Modes of the Ashkenazic Synagogue and Their Usage," *Journal of Synagogue Music* 4:1-2 (April 1972) 46-61.

34. See my *Foundations of Christian Music: The Music of Pre-Constantinian Christianity* (Bramcote Nottingham: Grove Books, 1992), especially chapter 1.

35. There are many good articles in various biblical dictionaries and commentaries, including the 10 vol. *Theological Dictionary of the New Testament*, ed. Gerhard Kittel and Gerhard Friedrich, trans. Geoffrey W. Bromiley (Grand Rapids: Wm. Eerdmans, 1964). Also see Gerhard Delling, *Worship in the New Testament*, trans. Percy Scott (Philadelphia: Westminster Press, 1962) chapters 5 and 6; Franz Josef Dölger, *Sol Salutis: Beget und Gesang in christlichen Altertum, mit besonderer Rücksicht auf die Ostung in Gebet und Liturgie*, 3. Aufl. (Münster: Aschendorff, 1972); J.A. Smith, "The Ancient Synagogue, the Early Church and Singing," *Music and Letters* 65 (1984) 1-16; William Sheppard Smith, *Musical Aspects of the New Testament* (Amsterdam: Uitgeverij w. Ten Have N.V., 1962); and Samuel Terrien, *The Magnificat: Musicians as Biblical Interpreters* (Mahwah, NJ: Paulist Press, 1994).

36. For example, Klaus Berger, "Das Canticum Simeonis (Lk 2:29-32)," *Novum Testamentum* (1985) 27-39; Pierre Grelot, "Le Cantique de Siméon Luc 2.29-32," *Revue biblique* 93 (1986) 481-509; F. Manns, "Un hymne judéo-chrétien: Philippiens 2, 6-11," *Euntes Docete* 29 (1976) 259-290; R.P. Martin, *Carmen Christi* (Cambridge: Cambridge University Press, 1967); R. Schnackenburg, "Logos-Hymnus und johannischer Prolog," *Biblische Zeitschrit ns* 1 (1957) 69-109; and G. Wilhelmi, "Der Versöhnen-Hymnus in Eph. 2:14ff," *Zeitschrift für neutestamentliche Wissenschaft* 78 (1987) 145-152.

37. Also Máximo Brioso Sanchez, *Aspectos y problemas del himno cristiano primitivo* (Salamanca: Consejo Superior de Investigaciones Científicas, 1972); Reinhard Deichgräber, *Gotteshymnus und Christushymnus in der frühen Christenheit* (Göttingen: Vandenhoeck & Ruprecht, 1967); Michael Lattke, *Hymnus: Materialien zu einer Geschichte der antiken Hymnologie*,

Novum Testamentum et Orbis Antiquus 19 (Fribourg: Editions Universitaires, 1991); W. Richardson, "Liturgical Order and Glossolalia in 1 Cor. 14:26c-33a," *New Testament Studies* 32 (1986) 144-153; and Klaus Wengst, *Christologische Formeln und Lieder des Urchristentums* (Gütersloh: Mohn, 1972).

38. Besides previously mentioned works, see C. Hannick, "Christian Church, Music of the Early," *NGDMM* 4:363-371; A.W.J. Holleman, "Early Christian Liturgical Music," *Studia Liturgica* 8 (1972) 185-192; James McKinnon, "Christian Antiquity," *Antiquity and the Middle Ages: From Ancient Greece to the 15th Century*, ed. James McKinnon (Englewood Cliffs, NJ: Prentice Hall, 1991) 68-87; Johannes Quasten, *Music and Worship in Pagan and Christian Antiquity*, trans. Boniface Ramsey (Washington, DC: NPM Publications, 1983 [1929, rev. 1973]); Bruno Stäblein, "Frühchristliche Musik," *MGG* 4:1036-1064; Gino Stefani, "L'expressione vocale nella liturgia primitiva," *Ephemerides Liturgicae* 84 (1970) 97-112.

39. Also Théodore Gérold, *Les Pères de l'église et la musique* (Paris: Alcan, 1931; reprint ed., Geneva: Minkoff Reprint, 1973); and Robert Skeris, *Chroma Theoi*, Catholic Church Music Associates 1 (Altötting: Alfred Coppenrath, 1976).

40. For example, James H. Charlesworth, *The First Christian Hymnbook: The Odes of Solomon* (New York: Crossroad, 1993); Jacques Fontaine, "Les origines de l'hymnodie chrétienne latine," *La Maison-Dieu* 161 (1985) 33-74; Josef Kroll, *Die christliche Hymondik bis zu Klemens von Alexandreia* (Darmstadt: Wissenschaftliche Buchgesellschaft, 1968 [1921]); Gottfried Gottfried, *Frühchristliche Hymnen* (Berlin: Evangelische Verlagsanstalt, 1965); and E.R. Smothers, "Phos Hilaron," *Recherches de science religieuse* 19 (1929) 266-284.

41. Also J. Dyer, "Monastic Psalmody of the Middle Ages," *Revue bénédictine* 99 (1989) 41-74; Everett Ferguson, "Psalm-Singing at the Eucharist: A Liturgical Controversy in the Fourth Century," *Austin Seminary Bulletin* 98 (1983) 52-77; Balthasar Fischer, "Der liturgische Gebrauch der Psalmen im altchristlichen Gottesdienst, darfgestellet am ältesten bezeugten Beispiel: Jerusalem, 5. Jahrhundert," *Liturgie und Dichtung: ein interdisziplinäres Kompendium*, ed. Hansjakolo Becker and Reiner Kaczynski, 2 vols. (St. Ottilien: EOS Verlag Erzabtei, 1983) 1:303-313; Joseph Gelineau, "Les psaumes à l'époque patristique," *La Maison-Dieu* 135 (1978) 99-116; and Peter Jeffery, "The Introduction of Psalmody into the Roman Mass by Pope Celestine," *Archiv für Liturgiewissenschaft* 26 (1984) 147-165.

42. For example, *Ephrem the Syrian: Hymns*, trans. and intro. Kathleen McVey, pref. John Meyendorff, The Classics of Western Spirituality (New York: Paulist Press, 1989); Richard L. LaCroix, *Augustine on Music* (Lewiston, NY: Mellen Press, 1988).

43. For example, J. Dyer, "Augustine and the 'Hymni ante Oblatium,' the Earliest Offertory Chants?" *Revue des études augustiniennes* 27 (1981)

85-99; Margot E. Fassler, "The Office of the Cantor in Early Western Monastic Rules and Customaries: A Preliminary Investigation," *Early Music History* 5 (1985) 29-51; my "The Cantor in Historical Perspective," below pp. 65-87; A.W.J. Holleman, "The Oxyrhynchus Papyrus 1786 and the Relationship between Ancient Greek and Early Christian Music," *Vigiliae Christianae* 26 (1972) 1-17; James McKinnon, "The Church Fathers and Musical Instruments," unpublished Ph.D. dissertation (New York: Columbia University, 1965); id., "The Meaning of the Patristic Polemic against Musical Instruments," *Current Musicology* 1 (1985) 69-82.

44. Besides the various entries in the *Oxford History of Byzantium*, ed. Alexander Kazhdan, 3 vols. (New York: Oxford University Press, 1991), see Dimitri Conomos, *Byzantine Hymnography and Byzantine Chant* (Brookline, MA: Classical Folia Editions, 1984); Oliver Strunk, ed., *Essays on Music in the Byzantine World* (New York: Norton, 1977); Josef Szövérffy, *A Guide to Byzantine Hymnography: A Classified Bibliography of Texts and Studies*, 2 vols. (Brookline, MA: Classical Folia Editions, 1978-1979); Egon Wellesz, *Eastern Elements in Western Chant* (Copenhagen: Munksgaard, 1947); id., *A History of Byzantine Music and Hymnography*, 2nd ed. (Oxford: Clarendon Press, 1961). Further bibliography is in Andrew Hughes, *Medieval Music: The Sixth Liberal Art*, rev. ed. (Toronto: University of Toronto Press, 1980) nn. 390-475. Also see key works on the history of the Byzantine Liturgy, such as Hans-Joachim Schulz, *The Byzantine Liturgy*, trans. Matthew J. O'Connell (New York: Pueblo, 1986), and the important works by Robert Taft, e.g., *The Great Entrance* (Rome: Pont. Institutum Studiorum Orientalium, 1978).

45. For example, Paul F. Cutter, *Musical Sources of the Old-Roman Mass*, Musicological Studies and Documents 36 (Stuttgart: American Institute of Musicology, 1979); id., "The Question of the 'Old Roman' Chant: A Reappraisal," *Acta Musicologica* 39 (1967) 2-20; id., "Oral Transmission of the Old-Roman Responsories?" *Musical Quarterly* 62 (1976) 182-194; Helmut Hucke, "Gregorian and Old Roman Chant," *NGDMM* 7:693-7; also the references in H-MM nn. 605-631.

46. Peter Jeffery, "The Sunday Office of Seventh-Century Jerusalem in the Georgian Chantbook (ladgari): A Preliminary Report," *Studia Liturgica* 21 (1991) 52-75; Helmut Leeb, *Die Gesänge im Gemeinegottesdienst von Jerusalem vom 5. bis 8. Jahrhundert* (Vienna: Herder, 1970); we look forward to the publication of Peter Jeffery's *Liturgy and Chant in Early Christian Jerusalem: The Sources and Influence of a Seminal Tradition*.

47. See the introductory bibliography on the Ambrosian, Aquileain, Beneventan, Mozarabic, and Gallican chant in Cattin, *Music of the Middle Ages*, vol. 1, 217-219; also the relevant articles in NGDMM, and the further bibliography in H-MM.

48. Other general introductions include John Caldwell, *Medieval Music* (Bloomington, IN: Indiana University Press, 1978); Cattin, *Music of the*

Middle Ages, vol. 1; F.A. Gallo, *Music of the Middle Ages,* vol. 2 (New York: Cambridge University Press, 1985); Richard Hoppin, *Medieval Music* (New York: Norton, 1978); Gustav Reese, *Music in the Middle Ages* (New York: Norton, 1940); Albert Seay, *Music in the Medieval World,* 2nd ed. (Englewood Cliffs, NJ: Prentice Hall, 1975); and Jeremy Yudkin, *Music in Medieval Europe* (Englewood Cliffs, NJ: Prentice Hall, 1989). A helpful reference work, especially for the later medieval period, is Jerome and Elizabeth Roche, *A Dictionary of Early Music: From the Troubadours to Monteverdi* (New York: Oxford University Press, 1981). The best annotated bibliography for the medieval period is H-MM.

Parts of the Late Middle Ages are often treated in histories of western music as the Renaissance. General introductions include Heinrich Besseler, *Die Musik des Mittelalters und der Renaissance* (Potsdam: Athenaion, 1931); Howard Mayer Brown, *Music in the Renaissance* (Englewood Cliffs, NJ: Prentice Hall, 1976); Friedrich Blume, *Renaissance and Baroque Music: A Comprehensive Survey,* trans. M.D. Herter Norton (New York: Norton, 1967); Anselm Hughes and Gerald Abraham, eds., *Ars Nova and Renaissance 1300-1540, New Oxford History of Music,* vol. 3 (London: Oxford University Press, 1960); André Pirro, *Histoire de la musique de la fin XIVe siècle à la fin du XVIe* (Paris: H. Laurens, 1940); Gustav Reese, *Music in the Renaissance,* rev. ed. (New York: Norton, 1959).

Particular studies with relevance to liturgical music of this era include: Hugh Benham, *Latin Church Music in England, c. 1460-1575* (London: Barrie & Jenkins, 1977); Douglas Bush, "The Liturgical Use of the Organ in German Regions Prior to the Protestant Reformation," Unpublished Ph.D. dissertation (Austin: University of Texas, 1982); Susan Rankin and David Hiley, eds., *Music in the Medieval English Liturgy* (New York: Oxford University Press, 1993).

49. The principle theorists in the west, with accompanying bibliography are listed in H MM nn. 900-1016.

50. Also Robert Hayburn, *Papal Legislation on Sacred Music* (Collegeville: The Liturgical Press, 1979); Fiorenzo Romita, *Codex Iuris Musicae Sacrae* (Rome: Desclée, 1952); id., *Ius Musicae Liturgicae: Dissertatio Historico-Iuridica,* 2nd ed. (Rome: Ephemerides Liturgicae, 1947).

51. See the substantial bibliography (pp. xxxii-xcvii); also H-MM especially nn. 476-714.

52. Unfortunately Jeffery's inability to be self-critical about his own presuppositions sometimes results in a skewed representation of the facts, especially regarding thoughts on Gregorian chant amongst those he calls "pastoral musicians" (present author included, pp. 77 and 83). Suffice it to say that, from my perspective, the decline in congregational singing within the liturgy during the Middle Ages was not a "result" of the emergence of Gregorian chant (thus, no simple cause-effect relationship as Jeffery seems to posit as the "pastoral" version of history); rather,

the ascendancy of the Gregorian repertoire as well as the decline in congregational singing were both symptoms of much larger ecclesiological and theological developments in the medieval west, especially the monasticization of the church and the theological assertion of the superiority of the monk (and eventually the priest) over the baptized.

53. Consult the general histories on the Middle Ages [or Renaissance] and the various dictionary articles on *conductus,* organum, motet, polyphony, and polytextuality; also Richard Hoppin's *Medieval Music* is unusually good regarding medieval liturgical polyphony (chapters 8-10, 14, 16-17). An important edition is the previously cited *Fourteenth-Century Mass Music* in France (n. 18); also various volumes in *Polyphonic Music of the Fourteenth Century* (Monaco: L'Oiseau Lyre, 1956-). Specific places and individuals of note in this vast topic include: St. Martial, Notre Dame (Leonin [+ 1201] and Perotin [fl. c. 1200]), Machaut, Dunstable (+ 1453?), Binchois (+ 1460), Dufay, and Deprez. Consult H-MM (nn. 1335-1748) for further bibliography.

54. The classic work on Palestrina is Knud Jeppesen, *The Style of Palestrina and the Dissonance,* 2nd ed., trans Margaret W. Hamerick (Copenhagen: E. Munksgaard, 1946; reprint ed., New York: Dover, 1970); also Herbert Andrews, *An Introduction to the Technique of Palestrina* (London: Novello, 1959); Malcolm Boyd, *Palestrina's Style: A Practical Introduction* (London: Oxford University Press, 1973); Jerome Roche, *Palestrina* (New York: Oxford University Press, 1971).

Specific works on music and the Council of Trent include Karl Gustav Fellerer, "Church Music and the Council of Trent," *Musical Quarterly* 39 (1953) 576-594; also Hugo Leichentritt, "The Reform of Trent and Its Effect on Music," *The Musical Quarterly* 30 (1944) 319-28; Raphael Molitor, *Die nachtridentinische Choralreform zu Rom,* 2 vols. (Hildesheim: G. Olms, 1967 [1901-1902]).

55. A key collection is *Analecta Hymnica Medii Aevi,* 55 vols. (Leipzig: Reisland, 1886-1922; reprint ed., New York: Johnson Reprint, 1961); also see Helmut Gneuss, *Hymnar und Hymnen in englischen Mittelalter* (Tübingen: M. Niemeyer, 1968); James Mearns, *Early Latin Hymnaries: An Index of Hymns in Hymnaries before 1100* (Cambridge: Cambridge University Press, 1913); Alain Michel, *In Hymnis et canticis: culture et beauté dans l'hymnique chrétienne latine* (Louvain: Publications Universitaires, 1976); Bruno Stäblein, ed., *Monumenta Monodica Medii Aevi,* vol. 1: Hymnen (Kassel: Bärenreiter, 1956); Josef Szövérffy, *Die Annalen der lateinischen Hymnendichtung: Ein Handbuch,* 2 vols. (Berlin: Erich Schmidt, 1964-1965).

56. Besides the various dictionaries and encyclopedia, see Higini Anglès, "The Various Forms of Chant Sung by the Faithful in the Ancient Roman Liturgy," *Scripta Musicologica,* 3 vols., ed. José López-Calo (Rome: Edizioni Storia e Letteratura, 1975) 1:57-75; Cyrilla Barr, *The Monophonic Lauda and the Lay Religious Confraternities of Tuscany and Umbria in the Late Middle Ages* (Kalamazoo: Medieval Institute, 1988); Blake Wilson, *Music*

and Merchants: The Laudesi Companies of Republican Florence (Oxford: Oxford University Press, forthcoming); José Romeu Figeras, "La canción popular navidena, fuente de un misterio dramático de técnica medieval," *Anuario Musical* 19 (1964) 167-184; Johannes Janota, *Studien zu Funktion und Typus des deutschen geistlichen Liedes im Mittelalters* (Munich: Beck, 1968); Walther Lipphardt, "'Laus tibi Christe'—'Ach du armer Judas,' Untersuchungen zum ältesten deutschen Passionslied," *Jahrbuch für Liturgik und Hymnologie* 6 (1961) 71-100; Johannes Riedel, *Leise Settings of the Renaissance and Reformation Era* (Madison, WI: A-R Editions, 1980); W. Wiora, "The Origins of German Spiritual Folk Song: Comparative Methods in a Historical Study," *Ethnomusicology* 8 (1964). Also H-MM nn. 1313a-1334, and 1816-1848.

57. Most notably *clausulae*, motets, *prosulas*, sequences, and tropes. Besides the many studies on these forms, important editions of these works are to be found in *Analecta Hymnica Medii Aevi*, especially vols. 47 and 49 (tropes), and 53-55 (sequences); and *Corpus Troporum*, ed. Ritva Jonsson et al. (Stockholm: Almqvist & Miksell, 1975-). Numerous other collections and individual publications are detailed in *The New Harvard Dictionary of Music*, s.v. "sources (pre-1500)"; also H-MM e.g., tropes (nn. 715-783) and "Notre Dame and the thirteenth-century motet" (nn. 1390-1494).

58. A handy introduction to the music of the Protestant Reformation is Robin Leaver's "Christian Liturgical Music in the Wake of the Protestant Reformation," *Sacred Sound and Social Change* 124-144; and Robert Stevenson, *Patterns of Protestant Church Music* (Durham: Duke University Press, 1953). Also see Konrad Ameln et al., eds. *Handbuch der deutschen evangelischen Kirchenmusik*, 3 vols. (Göttingen: Vandenhoeck & Ruprecht, 1930-1976).

59. Others include Conrad Donakowski, *A Muse for the Masses: Ritual and Music in an Age of Democratic Revolution* (Chicago: University of Chicago Press, 1977); Arthur Hutchings, *Church Music in the Nineteenth Century* (London: Jenkins, 1967; reprint ed., Westport, CT: Greenwood Press, 1977); Paul Nettl, *Luther and Music*, trans. F. Best and R. Wood (Philadelphia: Muhlenberg Press, 1948); Johannes Riedel, ed., *Cantors at the Crossroads* (St. Louis: Concordia, 1963); Carl Schalk, *Luther on Music: Paradigms of Praise* (St. Louis: Concordia, 1988); Gino Stefani, *Musica e religione nell'Italia barocca* (Palermo: S.F. Flaccovio, 1975); Elwyn Wienandt, *Choral Music of the Church* (New York: Free Press, 1965).

60. James White subdivides "Protestant worship" into nine traditions: Lutheran, Reformed, Anabaptism, Anglican, Separatist and Puritan, Quaker, Methodist, Frontier and Pentecostal, in *Protestant Worship: Traditions in Transition* (Louisville: Westminster/John Knox Press, 1989).

61. Both in combination with voices, as well as independent instrumental compositions such as the *canzona* and *sonata da chiesa*. Besides the various entries in the NGDMM, as well as the expansion of some of these

articles in *New Grove Dictionary of Musical Instruments,* ed. Stanley Sadie, 3 vols. (London: Macmillan, 1984), see the fine overview article "Performing Practice" by Howard Brown et al., and the accompanying bibliography in the latter (3:34-61); also H-MM nn. 318-376 and 1947-1953a.

62. See the article in NGDMM, as well as Willi Apel, *The History of Keyboard Music,* trans. and rev. Hans Tischler (Bloomington: Indiana University Press, 1972); Edward Higginbottom, "French Classical Organ Music and Liturgy," *Proceedings of the Royal Musical Association* 103 (1976-1977) 19-40; Eleanor Selfridge-Field, *Venetian Instrumental Music from Gabrieli to Vivaldi* (New York: Praeger, 1975); Alexander Silbiger, "The Roman Frescobaldi Tradition, c. 1640-1670," *Journal of the American Musicological Society* 33 (1980) 42-87; Peter Williams, *The European Organ, 1450-1850,* 2nd ed. (Bloomington: Indiana University Press, 1978); id., *A New History of the Organ* (Bloomington: Indiana University Press, 1980). On the liturgical use of the organ previous to this period, see Peter Williams, *The Organ in Western Culture, 750-1250* (New York: Cambridge University Press, 1993).

63. Besides the previously cited dictionaries and general works on this era, see H. Wiley Hitchcock, "The Latin Oratorios of Marc-Antoine Charpentier," *The Musical Quarterly* 41 (1955) 41-65; Günther Schmidt, "Grundsätzliche Bermerkungen zur Geschichte der Passionshistorie," *Archiv für Musikwissenschaft* 17 (1960) 100-125; Basil Smallmann, *The Background of Passion Music,* 2nd rev. ed. (New York: Dover, 1970).

64. Also see Leonard Ellinwood, "Tallis' Tunes and Tudor Psalmody," *Musica Disciplina* 2 (1948) 189-203; Robin Leaver, *Goostly Psalmes and Spirituall Songes: English and Dutch Metrical Psalms from Coverdale to Utenhove, 1535-1566* (New York: Oxford University Press, 1991); Millar Patrick, *Four Centuries of Scottish Psalmody* (London: Oxford University Press, 1949); Pierre Pidoux, *Le Psautier huguenot,* 2 vols. (Basel: Bärenreiter, 1962); W.S. Pratt, *The Music of the French Psalter of 1562: A Historical Survey and Analysis* (New York: Columbia University Press, 1959); Cecil Roper, "The Strassbourg French Psalters, 1539-1553," Unpublished DMA dissertation (Los Angeles: University of Southern California, 1972).

65. Also Ruth Ellis Messenger, *A Short Bibliography for the Study of Hymns* (New York: Hymn Society of America, 1964); as well as major sections in the various general bibliographies (e.g., Thompson) already cited (n. 4).

66. Also Katherine Smith Diehl, *Hymns and Tunes: An Index* (New York: Scarecrow Press, 1966).

67. For example, Konrad Ameln, Markus Jenny, and Walther Lipphardt, eds., *Das Deutsche Kirchenlied, Kritische Gesamtausgabe der Melodien,* 10 vols. (Basel: Bärenreiter, 1976-); Martin Luther, *Liturgy and Hymns,* ed. Ulrich Leupold (Philadelphia: Fortress Press, 1965); Isaac Watts, *Hymns and Spiritual Songs, 1707-1748,* ed. Selma Bishop (London: Faith Press, 1962); John and Charles Wesley, *John and Charles Wesley:*

Selected Prayers, Hymns, Sermons, Letters and Treatises, Frank Whaling, ed. (New York: Paulist Press, 1981).

68. For example, Maurice Frost, *English and Scottish Psalm and Hymn Tunes, c. 1543-1677* (London: SPCK and OUP, 1953); Robin Leaver, *The Liturgy and Music: A Study of the Use of the Hymn in Two Liturgical Traditions*, Grove Liturgical Study 6 (Bramcote Nottingham: Grove Books, 1976); Madeleine Forell Marshall and Janet Todd, *English Congregational Hymns in the Eighteenth Century* (Lexington, KY: University Press of Kentucky, 1982); Wilhelm Mützell, *Geistliche Lieder der Evangelischen Kirchen* (Hildesheim and New York: George Olms, 1975); Edna Parks, *Early English Hymns: An Index* (Metuchen, NJ: Scarecrow Press, 1972); J. Ernest Rattenbury, *The Eucharistic Hymns of John and Charles Wesley* (London: Epworth Press, 1948; reprint ed., Cleveland: O.S.L. Publications, 1991); Johannes Riedel, *The Lutheran Chorale—Its Basic Traditions* (Minneapolis: Augsburg Press, 1967); Erik Routley, *A General Introduction to Hymnody and Congregational Song* (Metuchen, NJ: Scarecrow Press, 1991); Howard C. Smith, *Scandinavian Hymnody from the Reformation to the Present* (Metuchen, NJ: Scarecrow Press, 1987).

69. Besides the appropriate reference work articles, as well as the relevant sections in Fellerer, Hayburn, etc., see Johannes Overath, ed., *Musicae Sacrae Ministerium: Beiträge zur Geschichte der kirchenmusikalischen Erneuerung im XIX. Jahrhundert* (Cologne: Luthe-Druck, 1962); also Ronald Damian, "A Historical Study of the Caecilian Movement in the U.S.," Unpublished DMA dissertation (Washington DC: Catholic University of America, 1984).

70. Aside from those already mentioned, some notables are Orlando Di Lasso (+ 1594), William Byrd (+ 1623), Orlando Gibbons (+ 1625), Girolamo Frescobaldi (+ 1643), Giacomo Carissimi (+ 1674), Henry Purcell (+ 1695), Dietrich Buxtehude (+ 1707), Arcangelo Corelli (+ 1713), François Couperin (+ 1733), Antonio Vivaldi (+ 1741), Georg Frideric Handel (+ 1759), Georg Phillipp Telemann (+ 1767), Wolfgang Amadeus Mozart (+ 1791), Franz Joseph Haydn (+ 1809), Franz Schubert (+ 1828), and Charles Gounod (+ 1893).

71. A more theological approach is provided by Jaroslav Pelikan's splendid *Bach Among the Theologians* (Philadelphia: Fortress, 1986).

72. Also, see the various denominational entries in *The New Grove Dictionary of American Music*, ed. H. Wiley Hitchcock and Stanley Sadie, 4 vols. (London: Macmillan Press, 1986); as well as the section on "American Psalmody and Hymnody" in Terry Miller's *Folk Music in America: A Reference Guide* (New York: Garland Publishing, 1986) 229-252. Other useful works include Allen Perdue Britton and Irving Lowens, completed by Richard Crawford, *American Sacred Music Imprints 1698-1910: A Bibliography* (Worchester: American Antiquarian Society, 1990); Albert Christ-Janer et al., *American Hymns Old and New* (New York: Columbia University Press, 1980); Buell E. Cobb, *The Sacred Harp: A Tradition and Its*

Music (Athens: University of Georgia Press, 1978); R. Paul Drummond, *A Portion for the Singers: A History of Music among Primitive Baptists since 1800* (Atwood, TN: The Christian Baptists Library, 1989); Leonard Ellinwood, *The History of American Church Music* (New York: Morehouse-Gorham, 1953); Henry W. Foote, *Three Centuries of American Hymnody* (Hamden, CT: The Shoestring Press, 1961 [1940]); Hamilton MacDougall, *Early New England Psalmody, 1620-1820* (New York: Da Capo, 1969 [1940]); and, Robert Stevenson, *Protestant Church Music in America* (New York: Norton, 1966).

73. Also, Ernesto Moneta Caglio, "Dom André Mocquereau e la restaurazione del Canto Gregoriano," *Musica Sacra: Rivista Bismestrale* 84 (1960) 2-17, 34-49, 98-117, 130-142, 162-172; 85 (1961) 8-20, 34-46, 68-87, 151-159; 86 (1962) 70-84, 108-118; 87 (1963) 4-16, 38-50, 75-85; Philipp Harnoncourt, "Katholische Kirchenmusik vom Cäcilianismus bis zur Gegenwart," *Traditionen und Reformen in der Kirchenmusik: Festschrift für Konrad Ameln zum 75. Geburtstag am 6. Juli 1974*, ed. Gerhard Schuhmacher (Kassel: Bärenreiter) 78-133; Jean-Yves Hameline, "Le son de l'histoire: chant et musique dans la restauration catholique," *La Maison-Dieu* 131 (1977) 5-47; Klaus Rohring, *Neue Musik in der Welt des Christentums* (Munich: Kaiser, 1975); Oskar Söhngen, *Die Erneuerungskräfte der Kirchenmusik unserer Tage* (Berlin: Evangelische Verlagsanstalt, 1949).

74. For example, William Bauman, "Church Music in America: Vatican II to '82," *Pastoral Music* 7:3 (1983) 30-33; Jean Beilliard and François Picard, eds., *La Musique sacrée après la réforme liturgique, décisions, directives, orientations* (Paris: Centurion, 1967); Virgil Funk, "Enculturation, Style and the Sacred-Secular Debate," *Sacred Sound and Social Change* 314-323; Joseph Gelineau, "The Music of Christian Communities, Twenty Years after the Council," *Music and Liturgy* 10 (1984) 82-90; Helmut Hucke, "Musical Requirements of Liturgical Reform," *The Church Worships*, Concilium 12 (New York: Paulist Press, 1966) 45-80; Bernard Huijbers, "Liturgical Music after the Second Vatican Council," *Symbol and Art in Worship*, Concilium 132 (New York: Seabury Press, 1980) 101-111; Francis P. Schmitt, *Church Music Transgressed: Reflections on "Reform"* (New York: Seabury Press, 1977).

75. The two best sources for official documentation for Roman Catholics in English are R. Kevin Seasoltz, *The New Liturgy: 1903-1965* (New York: Herder, 1966), and *Documents on the Liturgy 1963-1979* (Collegeville: The Liturgical Press, 1982). Also useful is the more comprehensive *Les Enseignements pontificaux, la liturgie (1740-1953), présentation et tables par les moines de Solesmes* (Paris, 1954). Additional documentation for U.S. Roman Catholics is found in Elizabeth Hoffman, ed., *The Liturgy Documents*, 3rd ed. (Chicago: Liturgy Training Publications, 1991). A sampling of the literature on these documents includes: Akademie für Musik und darstellend Kunst, *Die Kirchenmusik und das II. Vatikanische Konzil* (Graz: Styria, 1965); Ilario Alcini, *Pio X e la musica* (Rome: Associazione Italiana

di Santa Cecilia, 1956); Associazione Italiana di Santa Cecilia, *L'enciclia Musicae Sacrae Disciplina di Sua Santità Pio XII* (Rome: Associazione Italiana di Santa Cecilia per la Musica Sacra, 1957); A. Duclos, *Sa Santeté Pie X et la musique religieuse* (Rome: Desclée, 1905); Edward Foley, "Music in Catholic Worship: A Critical Reappraisal," *Liturgy 90* (February-March 1991) 8-12; Aloys Hanin, *La Législation ecclésiastique en matière de musique religieuse* (Paris: Desclée, 1933); Robert F. Hayburn, "St. Pius X and the Vatican Edition of the Chant Books," Unpublished DMA dissertation (Los Angeles: University of Southern California, 1964); J. Michael Joncas, "Re-Reading *Musicam Sacram*: Twenty-Five Years of Development in Roman Rite Liturgical Music," *Worship* 66 (1992) 212-231; Tómas de Manzarrata, *La música sagrada a la luz de los documentos pontificos* (Madrid: Editorial Coculsa, 1968); Johanna Schell, "Asthetische Probleme der Kirchenmusik im Lichte der Enzyklika Pius' XII Musicae Sacrae Disciplina," Unpublished doctoral dissertation (Berlin, 1961).

Two other unofficial documents from this period are the *Universa Laus Guidelines* and *The Milwaukee Symposia for Church Composers: A Ten-Year Report*. On the former, see "The Music of Christian Ritual: Universa Laus Guidelines 1980," *The Bulletin of Universa Laus* 30 (1980) 4-15; Felice Rainoldi, "Le document Universa Laus 1980 dans l'histoire de la musique de l'église," *La Maison-Dieu* 145 (1981) 25-48; and Claude Duchesneau and Michael Veuthey, *Music and Liturgy: The UL Document and Commentary*, trans. Paul Inwood (Washington, DC: The Pastoral Press, 1992). On the latter, see my "From Music in Catholic Worship to the 'Milwaukee Document,'" below, pp. 127-144.

76. In the U.S. these have included, **Episcopal:** *The New Hymnal* (1916-1918) *Hymnal* (1940) and *Hymnal* (1982); resources for the latter include Robert Klepper's *A Concordance of the Hymnal 1982* (Metuchen, NJ: Scarecrow Press, 1989); and, *The Hymnal Companion*, ed. Raymond Glover, 3 vols. (New York: The Church Hymnal Corporation, 1993-). **Lutheran:** *Common Service Book* (1917), *Service Book and Hymnal* (1958), *Lutheran Book of Worship* (1979), and *Lutheran Worship* (1982); resources for the LBW include Marilyn Stulken's *Hymnal Companion to the Lutheran Book of Worship* (Philadelphia: Fortress Press, 1979). **Methodist:** *The Methodist Hymnal* (1905), *The Methodist Hymnal* (1935), *Book of Worship* (1944), *Hymnal* (1960), *The United Methodist Hymnal* (1989); resources for the latter include Carlton R. Young, *The Companion to the United Methodist Hymnal* (Nashville: Abingdon, 1993). **Presbyterian:** *New Psalms and Hymns* (1901), *The Presbyterian Hymnal* (1927), *The Hymnal* (1933), *The Hymnbook* (1955), and *The Presbyterian Hymnal* (1990); resources for the latter include LindaJo H. McKim's *The Presbyterian Hymnal Companion* (Louisville: Westminster/John Knox Press, 1993).

77. The caution here is that historical works about liturgical music are also "theological," but usually implicitly. There is no such thing as purely "objective" history—all history is interpretive; any history of the liturgy

or liturgical music is, likewise, interpretive and consequently theological to some degree. For a discussion of the theological implications of historical or descriptive studies, see Don Browning, *A Fundamental Practical Theology* (Philadelphia: Fortress Press, 1991).

78. See my *Foundations of Christian Music,* chapters 2-4 for a further examination of this concept.

79. In the Babylonian Talmud, see Hagiga 2.12b, 'Erubin 2.21a, and Sanhedrin 11.91b.

80. See Hanoch Avenary, "A Geniza Find of Sa`adya's Psalm-Preface and Its Musical Aspects," *Hebrew Union College Annual* 39 (1968) 145ff.; Henry G. Farmer, *Sa`adyah Gaon on the Influence of Music* (London: Probsthain, 1943); also, Kalman Bland, "Medieval Jewish Aesthetics," *Journal of the History of Ideas* 54 (1993) 533-559; Amnon Shiloah, *The Dimension of Music in Islamic and Jewish Culture* (Brookfield, VT: Variorum, 1993); and, Eric Werner and I. Sonne, "The Philosophy and Theory of Music in Judeo-Arabic Literature," *Hebrew Union College Annual* 16 (1941) 251-319; 17 (1942-1943) 511-572.

81. See, for example, B. Cohen, "The Responsum of Maimonides concerning Music," *Jewish Musical Journal* 2 (1935) 3ff.; Henry G. Farmer, "Maimonides on Listening to Music," *Journal of the Royal Asiatic Society,* 3rd ser., 45 (1933) 867ff.

82. Judith Eisenstein, "The Mystical Strain in Jewish Liturgical Music," *Sacred Sound* 35-54.

83. For example, the writings from the Alexandrian school, especially Clement (+ c. 215) and Origen (+ c. 254). For a collection of the relevant texts, see Skeris, *Chroma Theoi* 54-93.

84. For this text, see Klaus Gamber, ed., *Textus Patristici et Liturgici,* vol. 1 (Regensburg: F. Pustet, 1964) 93-100; also C. Turner, "Niceta of Remesiana II. Introduction and Text of De Psalmodiae Bono," *Journal of Theological Studies* 24 (1922-1923) 225-250.

85. See, for example, A.D. Krestoff, "Musica Disciplina and Musica Sonora," *Journal of Research in Music Education* 10 (1962) 13-29; Ubaldo Pizzani, "Spunti escatologici nel 'De musica' di S. Agostino," *Augustinianum* 18 (1978) 209-218; also Robert O'Connell, *Art and the Christian Intelligence in St. Augustine* (Cambridge, MA: Harvard University Press, 1978) 178-188.

86. The best available translation is Anicius Manlius Severinus Boethius, *Fundamentals of Music,* trans., intro. and notes by Calvin Bower, ed. Claude V. Palisca (New Haven: Yale University Press, 1989); also, see Henry Chadwick, *Boethius: The Consolation of Music, Logic, Theology, and Philosophy* (Oxford: Clarendon Press, 1983).

87. Reproduced in this volume, pp. 87-126. Also Charles Cleall, *Music and Holiness* (London: Epworth Press, 1964); William Edgar, *Taking Note of Music* (London: SPCK, 1986); P. Froger, "Symbolisme de la musique liturgique," *La Maison-Dieu* 22 (1950) 146-153; Paul W. Hoon, "The Rela-

tion of Theology and Music in Worship," *Union Seminary Quarterly Review* 11:2 (1956) 33-43; Maria-Judith Krahe, "Psalmen, Hymen und Lieder, wie der Geist sie eingibt: Doxologie als Ursprung und Ziel aller Theologie," *Liturgie und Dichtung* 923-957; Winfried Kurzschenkel, *Die theologische Bestimmung der Musik: neuere Beiträge zur Deutung und Wertung des Musizierens im christlichen Leben* (Trier: Paulinus-Verlag, 1971); Gerardus van der Leeuw, "Music and Religion," *Sacred and Profane Beauty: The Holy in Art,* trans. David Green (New York: Holt, Rinehart and Winston, 1963) 211-262; Emil Martin, *Une Muse en péril: essai sur la musique et le sacré* (Paris: Fayard, 1968); Alfred Pike, *A Theology of Music* (Toledo: The Gregorian Institute of America, 1953); Erik Routley, *Church Music and the Christian Faith* (Carol Stream, IL: Agape, 1978); id., *Church Music and Theology* (Philadelphia: Fortress Press, 1965 [1959]); Victoria Sirota, "An Exploration of Music as Theology," *The Arts in Religious and Theological Studies* 5:3 (Summer 1993) 24-28; Oskar Söhngen, "Fundamental Considerations for a Theology of Music," *The Musical Heritage of the Church,* ed. Theodore Hoelty-Nickel (St. Louis: Concordia, 1954) 4:7-16; id., "Music and Theology: A Systematic Approach," *Sacred Sound,* pp. 1-19; id., *Theologie der Musik* (Kassel: Stauda Verlag, 1967); Jay W. Wilkey, "Prolegomena to a Theology of Music," *Review and Expositor* 69 (1972) 507-517.

88. Also the journal *Black Sacred Music: A Journal of Theomusicology,* which Spencer edits, published by Duke University Press.

89. Also Lois Ibsen al Faruqi, "What Makes 'Religious Music' Religious?" *Sacred Sound* 21-34; Helmut Hucke, "Le problème de la musique religieuse," *La Maison-Dieu* 108 (1971) 7-20; James Reilly, "What Is Liturgical Music?" *The Caecilia* 66 (1939) 325-328, 369-372; Nicolas Schalz, "La notion de musique sacrée: une tradition récente," *La Maison-Dieu* 108 (1971) 32-57; id., "Musique sacrée: naissance et évolution d'un concept," *La Maison-Dieu* 161 (1985) 87-104; Gino Stefani, "Il mito della `musica sacra': origini e ideologia," *Nuova Rivista Musicale Italiana* 10 (1976) 23-40; id., "Musica sacra e regía liturgica," *Nuova Rivista Musicale Italiana* 1 (1967) 744-757.

90. For example, Miriam Therese Winter, *Why Sing? Toward a Theology of Catholic Church Music* (Washington, DC: The Pastoral Press, 1984).

91. Also Walter E. Buszin, *The Doctrine of Universal Priesthood and Its Influence upon the Liturgies and Music of the Lutheran Church* (St. Louis: Concordia, 1946); Theodore Hoelty-Nickel, "A Philosophy of Lutheran Church Music," *The Musical Heritage of the Church* 6 (1963) 113-122; Markus Jenny, *Die Zunkunft des evangelischen Kirkengesangs* (Zurich: Theologischer Verlag, 1970). Two related historical studies are Charles Garside, "Some Attitudes of the Major Reformers toward the Role of Music in the Liturgy," *McCormick Quarterly* 21 (1967) 151-168; Markus Jenny, "The Hymns of Zwingli and Luther: A Comparison," *Cantors at the Crossroads* 45-63.

92. Some of Gelineau's further thinking and work is summarized in Charles Pottie's *A More Profound Alleluia: Gelineau and Routley on Music in Christian Worship* (Washington, DC: The Pastoral Press, 1984).

93. Also Eugenio Costa, "La réflexion postconciliaire sur le chant et la musique dans la liturgie," *La Maison-Dieu* 108 (1971) 21-31; Lucien Deiss, *Spirit and Song of the New Liturgy*, rev. ed. (Cincinnati: World Library, 1976); Claude Duchesneau, Paul Bardon, and Jean Lebon, *L'Important, c'est la musique! Essai sur la musique dans la liturgie* (Paris: Cerf, 1977); Frank Quinn, "Music in Catholic Worship: The Effect of Ritual on Music and Music on Ritual," *Proceedings of the Annual Meeting of the North American Academy of Liturgy* (1989) 161-176; and Mark Searle, "Ritual & Music: A Theory of Liturgy and Implications for Music," *Assembly* 12 (1986) 314-317.

94. Also see *Pastoral Music* 15:4 (1991), an entire issue on the communion rite. Some principles on the relationship between worship structures and music are explored in *The Milwaukee Symposia on Church Music* nn. 37-44. For a more extended study of the relationship between music and liturgical structures, see my "Musical Forms, Referential Meaning and Belief," below, pp. 145-172.

95. See, for example, the entire issue 12:6 of *Pastoral Music* (1988) on the "litany."

96. This form was a frequent focus of discussion at the Milwaukee Symposia for Church Composers, and the topic for the Music Study Group of the North American Academy of Liturgy meeting in 1989. One public exchange by Roman Catholics over the issue included Joseph Swain ("An Apology for the Hymn," *America* 156:19 [23 May 1987] 421-423), Kevin Irwin ("Musical Contretemps," *America* 156:23 [13 June 1987] 492), and the previously cited article by Frank Quinn, "Music in Catholic Worship: The Effect of Ritual on Music and Music on Ritual."

97. Also see the appropriate sections in works like Deiss' *Spirit and Song of the New Liturgy* or Gelineau's *Voices and Instruments in Christian Worship*, as well as Walter E. Buszin, *Theology and Church Music as Bearers of the Verbum Dei* (St. Louis: Concordia, 1959; and, Erik Routley, *Words, Music and the Church* (Nashville, TN: Abingdon Press, 1968).

98. More general works on inclusive language tackle some of the questions related to language for our worship song. For an introduction, see: Teresa Berger, "Liturgical Language: Inclusivity and Exclusivity," *Studia Liturgica* 18 (1988) 132-141; Mary Collins, "Inclusive Language: A Cultural and Theological Question," *Worship: Renewal to Practice* (Washington, DC: The Pastoral Press, 1987) 197-214; Frank Henderson, "ICEL and Inclusive Language," *Shaping English Liturgy*, ed. Peter Finn and James Schellman (Washington, DC: The Pastoral Press, 1991) 257-278; Elizabeth Johnson, *She Who Is: The Mystery of God in Feminist Theological Discourse* (New York: Crossroad, 1992); Gail Ramshaw-Schmidt, *Worship: Searching for Language* (Washington, DC: The Pastoral Press, 1988).

Works more specifically related to language for worship music include the introduction to the International Commission on English in the Liturgy's *Consultation on a Liturgical Psalter* (Washington, DC: ICEL, 1984); Gracia Grindal, "Inclusive Language in Hymns: A Reevaluation," *Currents in Theology and Mission* 16:3 (1989) 187-193; Erik Routley, "Gender of God: A Contribution to the Conversation," *Worship* 56 (1982) 231-239.

99. For example, Eugene Brand, "Word and Tone: A Challenge to the Composer," *Sacred Music* 93 (1966) 132-139; Deirdre Brown, "The Contemporary Composer and Liturgical Reform," *Worship* 61 (1987) 16-25; Carol Doran and Thomas H. Troeger, "Writing Hymns as a Theologically Informed Artistic Discipline," *Hymn* 36:2 (1985) 7-11; and my "On the 'Breath of Dawn' and Other Metaphors," *Pastoral Music* (April-May 1981) 23-25.

100. A good introduction to the field is provided by John Booth Davies, *The Psychology of Music* (Stanford: Stanford University Press, 1978) or the more recent John Sloboda, *The Musical Mind: The Cognitive Psychology of Music* (Oxford: Oxford University Press, 1985).

101. The first systematic attempt at a sociology of music was Max Weber's *Die rationalen und soziologischen Grundlagen der Musik*, dating from 1911 but not published until 1921 (an English edition, by Don Martindale et al., appeared as *The Rational and Social Foundations of Music* [Carbondale: Southern Illinois University Press, 1958]). Theodor Adorno (see his *Introduction to the Sociology of Music*, trans. E.B. Ashton [New York: Continuum, 1989 {1962}], and Hanns Eisler (whose works are collected in *Musik und Politik*, ed. Günther Mayer [Munich: Rogner & Bernhard, 1973]) are also important figures. More recently, see Kurt Blaukopf, *Musical Life in a Changing Society: Aspects of Musical Sociology*, trans. David Marinelli (Portland: Amadeus Press, 1992). An important journal on this topic is the *International Review of the Aesthetics and Sociology of Music*.

102. See the summary and bibliography on the historical interface between music and cultural anthropology in Alan Merriam's classic, *The Anthropology of Music* (Evanston: Northwestern University Press, 1964); more recently, see John E. Kaemmer, *Music in Human Life: Anthropological Perspectives on Music* (Austin: University of Texas Press, 1994).

103. On the distinction between comparative musicology and ethnomusicology, see Alan Merriam, "Definitions of 'Comparative Musicology' and 'Ethno-musicology': An Historical-Theoretical Perspective," *Ethnomusicology* 21 (1977) 189-204; also see the useful collection edited by Kay Kaufman Shelemay, *Ethnomusicology: History, Definitions and Scope* (New York: Garland Publishing, 1992).

104. A recent published example of such study is Kenneth George, "Music-Making, Ritual and Gender in a Southeast Asian Hill Society," *Ethnomusicology* 37:1 (1993) 1-27.

105. Mark Searle, "New Tasks, New Methods: The Emergence of Pastoral Liturgical Studies," *Worship* 57 (1983) 291-308.

106. Nathan Mitchell provides an introduction to Grimes' other major writings as well as an excellent overview of the field of ritual studies in *Liturgy Digest* 1:1 (1993).

107. See, for example, Charles Dreisoerner, *The Psychology of Liturgical Music* (Kirkwood, MA: Maryhurst Press, 1942); Karl Gustav Fellerer, *Soziologie der Kirchenmusik: Materialen zur Musik- und Religionssoziologie* (Cologne: Westdeutscher Verlag, 1963); my own "Ethnomusicology," *Pastoral Music* 14:6 (1990) 37-41; "Liturgical Musicology Redux," *Worship* 64 (1990) 264-268; and *Music in Ritual: A Pre-Theological Investigation* (Washington, DC: The Pastoral Press, 1984).

108. For example, n. 117 below on the increased publication of African-American, Hispanic and other ethnically identified hymnals in the past decade.

109. The hymns of Charles Wesley are an example of this in Methodism. The reverse is the development of indigenous hymnody, for example, as discussed by Robin Leaver, "Theological Dimensions of Mission Hymnody: The Counterpoint of Cult and Culture," *Worship* 62 (1988) 316-331.

110. See, for example, the section on "Cross-Cultural Music Making" in the *Milwaukee Symposia for Church Composers* (nn. 56-63) which relies upon this discipline in its challenge to traditional standards for evaluating worship music. One historical study explicitly addressing such cultural issues is Anscar Chupungco's "Liturgical Music and Its Early Cultural Setting," in *Worship and Culture in Dialogue,* ed. Anita Stauffer, Lutheran World Federation Studies (Geneva: Lutheran World Federation, 1994) 103-119; also in the same volume, see Mark Bangert, "Dynamics of Liturgy and World Musics: A Method for Evaluation" (183-203). An elaborated version of the Chupungco essay appears in Chupungco's *Worship: Progress and Tradition* (Washington, DC: The Pastoral Press, 1995) 67-86.

111. Also his *The Spirituals and the Blues* (Maryknoll, NY: Orbis Books, 1991 [1972]); Louis-Charles Harvey, "Black Gospel Music and Black Theology," *The Journal of Religious Thought* 43:2 (1986) 19-37; I-To Loh, "Contemporary Issues in Inculturation, Arts and Liturgy: Music," Unpublished paper presented at 12th international Societas Liturgica Conference (York, England: 14-19 August 1989); and, Gino Stefani, "Musica, liturgia, cultura," *Nuova Rivista Musicale Italiana* 14 (1980) 479-496.

112. An older guide which is still of some value here is Irene V. Jackson, *Afro-American Religious Music: A Bibliography and a Catalogue of Gospel Music* (Westport, CT: Greenwood Press, 1979).

113. Further works by Burnim include: "The Black Gospel Music Tradition: A Complex of Ideology, Aesthetic, and Behavior," *More than*

Dancing, ed. Irene V. Jackson (Westport, CT: Greenwood Press, 1985) 147-168; id., "The Black Gospel Music Tradition: Symbol of Tenacity," Unpublished Ph.D. dissertation (Bloomington: Indiana University, 1980); id., "Gospel Music Research," *Black Perspective in Music* (1980) 63-70; id., "The Nature of African American Music: A Chronology," *Currents in Theology and Mission* 21:2 (1994) 93-104; id., "The Performance of Black Gospel Music as Transformation," *Music and the Experience of God* 52-61. Also see Mark Bangert, "Black Gospel and Spirituals: A Primer," *Currents in Theology and Mission* 16:3 (1989) 173-179; Jacqueline Cogdell DjeDje, "Change and Differentiation: The Adoption of Black American Gospel Music in the Catholic Church," *Ethnomusicology* 30 (1986) 223-252; id., "An Expression of Black Identity: The Use of Gospel Music in a Los Angeles Catholic Church," *The Western Journal of Black Studies* 7:3, 148-160; Irene V. Jackson, "Music among Blacks in the Episcopal Church: Some Preliminary Considerations," *More than Dancing*; Portia Maultsby, "Afro-American Religious Music: 1619-1861," Unpublished Ph.D. dissertation (Madison: University of Wisconsin, 1974); id., "The Use and Performance of Hymnody, Spirituals and Gospels in the Black Church," *The Western Journal of Black Studies* 7:3, 161-171; Elkin Sithole, "The Role of Gospel Music in the Black Churches of Chicago," Unpublished Ph.D. dissertation (New York: Queen's University, 1976); Jon Michael Spencer, *Black Hymnody: A Hymnological History of the African-American* Church (Knoxville: The University of Tennessee Press, 1992); id., *Protest and Praise: Sacred Music of Black Religion* (Minneapolis: Fortress Press, 1990); Wyatt T. Walker, *Somebody's Calling My Name: Black Sacred Music and Social Changes* (Valley Forge, PA: Judson Press, 1979).

114. One such example of this work is Steven Harry Cornelius, "The Convergence of Power: An Investigation into the Music Liturgy of Santeria in New York City," Unpublished Ph.D. dissertation (Los Angeles: University of California Los Angeles, 1989).

115. For example, Wanda Jean Madsen, "Mexican Mission Music: A Descriptive Analysis of Two Seventeenth Century Chant Books," Unpublished DMA dissertation (Tulsa: University of Oklahoma, 1984); Linda Popp, "Music in the Early Evangelization of Mexico," *Missiology* 8 (1980) 61-69; and, Owen Francis da Silva, *Mission Music of California* (Los Angeles: Warren Lewis, 1941).

116. See Marilyn Stulken's "Multicultural Hymns for the Church Year," as an introduction to this material in *Liturgy* 11:3 (1994) 45-58.

117. The former include *Lift Every Voice and Sing* (1981), *Songs of Sion* (1981), and *Lead Me, Guide Me* (1987). The latter include *Celebremos* (1979), *Flor y Canto* (1989), *El Pueblo de Dios Canta* (1989), and *¡Cantad al Señor!*. Besides such hymnals for African-Americans and Hispanics, the Methodist Church published *Hymns from the Four Winds* (1983) for Asian-Americans.

118. A sometimes amusing collection of such opinions is Elwyn Wienandt's *Opinions on Church Music: Comments and Reports from Four-and-a-Half Centuries* (Waco, TX: Baylor University Press, 1974).

119. See, for example, Margaret Mary Kellcher's "Hermeneutics in the Study of Liturgical Performance, *Worship* 67 (1993) 292-318; also the report of her own field study in "The Communion Rite: A Study of Roman Catholic Liturgical Performance," *Journal of Ritual Studies* 5:2 (1991) 99-122.

120. Also Brett Stutton, "Speech, Chant and Song: Patterns of Language and Action in a Southern Church," *Diversity of Gifts: Field Studies in Southern Religion* (Urbana: University of Illinois Press, 1988).

121. For example, my and Mary McGann's "Why Do Congregations Sing?" *Proceedings of the North American Academy of Liturgy* (1990) 87-97; also the Lilly funded study of music programs in Episcopal and United Methodist churches in southern New England by Linda Clark (the description and findings were published in a series of reports issued from the Boston University School of Theology where Dr. Clark teaches). Prof. Don Saliers of Emory University is currently in the midst of a similar project. We look forward to the publication of his findings.

122. These findings by Mark Searle and David Leege were published at Notre Dame as two fascicles of the larger report: "The Celebration of Liturgy in the Parishes," *Notre Dame Study of Catholic Parish Life,* Report 5 (1985); and "Of Piety and Planning: Liturgy, the Parishioners and the Professionals," *Notre Dame Study of Catholic Parish Life,* Report 6 (1985).

123. See my discussion of this study in "When American Roman Catholics Sing," *Worship* 63 (1989) 98-112; also the entire issue of *Pastoral Music* entitled "Music and Song: Notre Dame Study of Catholic Parish Life," 10:6 (1986).

124. See J. Michael Joncas' introduction to this study, "Semiotics and the Analysis of Liturgical Music," *Liturgical Ministry* 3 (1994) 144-154.

2
The Auditory Environment[1] of Emerging Christian Worship

Introduction

ONE OF THE BASIC RESOURCES THAT MANY CHRISTIAN THEOLOGIANS, HISTOrians of music, and pastoral musicians employ for understanding or critiquing our tradition of liturgical music is the Bible. Very often, however, we impose categories or project our own presuppositions upon the Scriptures without exploring to what extent those categories or presuppositions are valid frameworks for approaching the Scriptures. For example, there is no generic Hebrew term for "music" in the Old Testament and, as was noted in the previous chapter, there is little that could properly be isolated as "music" in the New Testament. Even presuming to speak of "music" in the Bible, therefore, requires considerable nuance.

One significant reason why contemporary western categories are not always appropriate for employing Scripture as a source for reflection upon musical issues or ideas is that the Old and the New Testaments both emerged in the context of oral societies, whereas most European and North American societies are literate/visual societies. In order for the contemporary inquirer to employ the Scriptures as a source for reflecting upon liturgical-musical questions in our own day, or for the Christian to understand the emergence of Christian liturgical music, it is necessary to think cross-culturally. The first "Christians"[2]—most of them Jews—lived in a world very different from our own: a world dissimilar not only in time and geography, but distinctive in the ways that its inhabitants perceived and talked about reality. Any attempt to understand biblical, Jewish, or early Christian worship music, therefore, requires more than simply acquiring a new vocabulary or developing an ability to reconcile divergent texts about music in the ancient world. Rather, it compels us to think differently about music and its relationship to ritual. In doing so we will discover that, as noted above, some categories—such as distinctions between music and speech—are anachronistic frameworks that the ancients did not employ. Furthermore, many contemporary practices, such as our ability to celebrate worship without music, would be completely unintelligible to Christians and Jews of the first centuries of the Common Era. In order to enter into this world and comprehend the place and function of music in that world, we have to imagine and penetrate an auditory environment very different from our own.

Although there are many aspects of this ancient auditory environment that deserve our attention, few are more critical than the role of sound phenomena in divine revelation and worship. Whereas contemporary western society is visually oriented and believes what it sees, the first followers of Jesus, like their Jewish forebears, lived in a world where hearing was believing. Whether the interchange was a human affair or a divine-human dialogue, sound events were the prime mediator of presence and truth. This aural way of knowing deeply influenced the tonal landscape of emerging Christian worship which was as much a sonic event as an optic event.

As an preface to the other questions that we will raise about Christian or ritual music in this volume, therefore, we will first explore the tonal landscape of ancient Judaism and the New Testament. This investigation will provide a useful context for the other topics that will follow. In view of the outline provided in the previous essay, this study is more properly a cultural, then a theological reflection, rather than an historical piece.

Oral Societies

Although there are numerous ways in which to characterize the development of societies through various ages, in terms of communication it is possible to consider cultures in "three successive stages: (1) oral or oral-aural; (2) script; and (3) electronic."[3] The fundamental distinction between stages one and two—between an oral and what might be called a proto-literate society—is that the former does not use any form of phonetic writing.[4] Although an alphabet is not the only system that allows for phonetic transcription,[5] the presence of an alphabetic system does signal that a society has at least begun the transition out of its oral stage.

For those who wish to understand the nature of an oral society, Walter Ong offers an important caution: "the differences between oral-aural culture and our own technological culture are ... so vast and so profound as to defy total itemization."[6] These differences are underscored by Ong's own limited inventory of some of the characteristics of an oral society, in which explanation is possible only by drawing negative parallels with contemporary experience. For example, Ong suggests that the "one of the most striking and informative differences [between an oral culture and our own] is that an oral-aural culture is necessarily a culture with a relationship to time different from ours." In developing this concept, Ong relies almost exclusively on negative parallels to make his point: "[An oral-aural culture] has no records. It does have memory, but this is not by any means the same as records, for the written record is not a remembrance but an aid to recall. It does not belong to us as memory does. It is an external thing."[7]

Havelock proposes that one way to recognize the difference between our culture and an oral culture is by recognizing that in primary orality, relationships between human beings are governed exclusively by acoustics. He elaborates:

> The psychology of such relationships is ... acoustic. The relation between an individual and his society is acoustic, between himself and his tradition, his law, his government. To be sure, primary communication begins visually with the smile, the frown, the gesture. But these do not get us very far. Recognition, response, thought itself, occur when we hear linguistic sounds and melodies and ourselves respond to them, as we utter a variant set of sounds to amend or amplify or negate what we have heard.[8]

Although there are many other features of an oral society that one could enumerate,[9] this initial foray into cautions and characteristics alerts us to the radical differences between contemporary technological culture and the world of the ancient Near East.

Orality in Ancient Israel

In order for us to grasp something of the acoustic environment of ancient Israel we need to sketch in general terms when Israel was at the stage of primary orality and when, with the introduction of an alphabet and writing, it moved to the proto-literate stage. This necessitates the briefest of historical introductions to ancient Israel, followed by a similarly abbreviated overview of the history of alphabetic script in ancient Israel. These sketches will provide us with a framework for discussing the rise of writing within Israel, the movement from oral to written prophecy in Israel, the continuance of what might be termed "residual orality" in ancient Israel as it developed into a literate society, and allow some general comments about the dynamic nature of Hebrew language and thought. These historical-cultural reflections will allow us to gauge the auditory environment in Palestine in the first centuries of the Common Era at the birth of Christianity.

An Historical Framework

The history of Israel[10] commonly begins with the Patriarchal period, which de Vaux suggests can be roughly dated to the first half of the second millennium BCE.[11] A second phase of Israel's early history is connected to the sojourn in Egypt and Joseph's rise to power (Gn 37-50).[12] A third phase encompasses the Exodus and Conquest events. The former, possibly involving two separate exoduses,[13] can be dated in the middle of the thirteenth century BCE. The latter—which was as much a period of coexistence, peaceful infiltration, and interdependence between the residents of Canaan with the Hebrew settlers as it was a time of conquest[14]—spanned the period slightly before the exodus(es) until the mid-eleventh century BCE. The latter part of the period of the Conquest is roughly co-terminus with the age of the Judges. By the middle of the eleventh century BCE a series of cultural and political developments gave rise to the monarchy in Israel. At the death of Solomon (922 BCE) the kingdom was divided. The northern kingdom (Israel) fell to Assyria in 721 BCE; the southern kingdom (Judah) fell to Babylon in 587 BCE. A schematic of this history follows:

Patriarchal Period	c. 2000-1700 BCE
Sojourn in Egypt	c. 1700-1300 BCE?
entry of Semitic groups into Egypt	
the Joseph Story	

Exodus and "Conquest"	c. 1300-1050 BCE
the exodus(es)	c. 1250 BCE
the "conquest"	c. 1300-1050 BCE
Age of the Judges	c. 1200-1050 BCE
Monarchy	c. 1020-587 BCE
division of kingdom	922 BCE
fall of the Northern kingdom	721 BCE
fall of the Southern kingdom	587 BCE
the Exile	587-539 BCE

The Alphabet and Writing in Ancient Israel

It is possible that a Semitic alphabet[15] could have appeared as early as 1900 BCE.[16] The earliest extant Semitic texts are Proto-Canaanite, dating from the seventeenth century BCE, from the region now known as Syria.[17] Proto-Canaanite and Canaanite scripts were succeeded by Old Phoenician (or North Semitic) script in the eleventh century BCE. The Israelites borrowed either a Phoenician or a similar Palestinian script (a sub-species of Proto-Canaanite)—employed in Palestine before their arrival—sometime after the thirteenth century BCE.[18] Written Hebrew, properly speaking, has a single witness from the eleventh century BCE, and many more by the eighth century BCE.[19]

A schematic of this history,[20] follows:

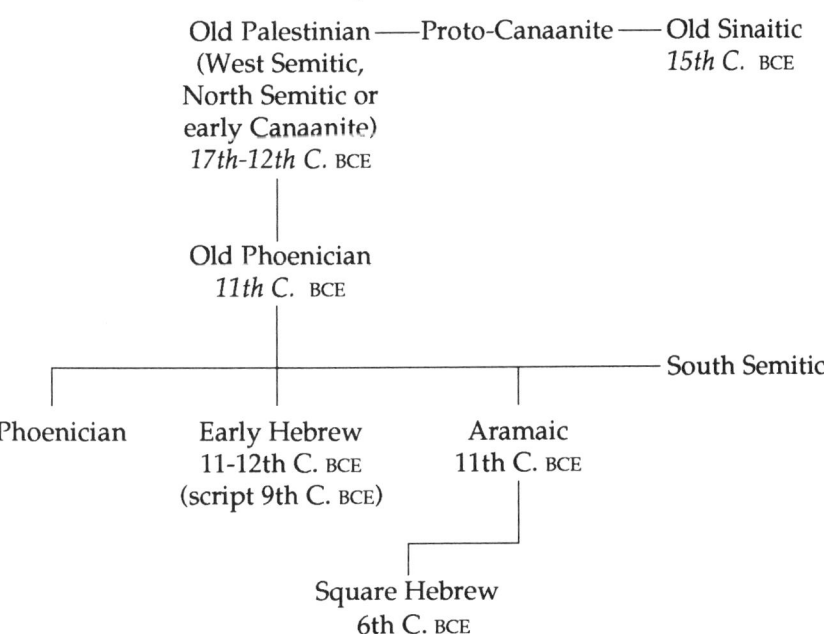

A comparison of this schematic with the preceding historical sketch suggests that writing entered the history of Israel very early. A first step in this process was a borrowing of either a Phoenician or a similar Palestinian script from the Canaanites, probably in the twelfth or eleventh century BCE. It is no coincidence that the refinement of Israel's national identity, symbolized in the rise of the monarchy, occurred in roughly the same period from which we have the first exemplars of Hebrew inscriptions.[21] It is possible that, just as guilds of professional scribes existed in Egypt and Mesopotamia at this time,[22] so did the emerging monarchy borrow this element of statecraft from Egyptian or Canaanite governmental models.[23] The emergence of Israel as a nation is intimately related to the emergence of the Hebrew language itself.

Writing, Scribalism, and the Deuteronomistic Movement

From the Old Testament we learn how widespread writing was among the Israelites. As de Vaux summarizes:

> Writing was in common use at an early date. Besides the professional scribes, like those employed at the court for administration (2 Sam 8:17; 20:25; 1 Kgs 4:3, etc.), and private secretaries like Baruch (Jer 36:4), members of the ruling class could write, judging by the stories of Jezabel (1 Kgs 21:8) and of Isaiah (Isa 8:1). But these were not the only ones: a young man of Sukkoth was able to give Gideon, in writing, the names of all the chiefs of his clan (Judg 8:14), and the commandment of Deut 6:9; 11:20 presumed that every head of a family could write.[24]

Although writing entered Israel's history early, it did not serve as a primary means of communication or a central vehicle for the development of new theologies in ancient Israel. Thus, while sections of the Pentateuch were put into writing in the tenth century BCE,[25] these elements did not originate as written texts and retained what might be called a residual orality.[26] This situation began to change, however, in the seventh century BCE.

In the eighth and seventh centuries BCE Assyria was a major military force in the Near East, dominating both the Northern and Southern Kingdoms. Under the influence of the Assyrian empire, which greatly valued the role of the professional scribe,[27] scribalism flourished throughout the Near East to the extent that this is sometimes characterized as a "scribal age."[28] In Israel this trend came to fruition in the emergence of the Deuteronomistic movement.

> It is hardly coincidental that the Deuteronomistic movement arose within this period. The written incorporation of historical traditions and legal codes by Deuteronomists parallels this increasingly prominent role of the scribe. This is evident in the Biblical portrayal of the Josianic Reform, which symbolizes the Deuteronomistic movement itself (2 Kgs 22). Here, it is the *written* word that is the basis for the king's conversion. Likewise, it is a scribe—Shaphan—who is accorded a primary place in the discovery (22.3), the handling (22.8) and the interpretation (22.14) of the scroll. From this point on the written traditions will be an increasingly important component in the cultic life of Jerusalem.[29]

Although the Deuteronomists are pivotal for giving written shape to the law, their influence on proto-literate Israel extends further, into prophetic literature. It is this development which becomes determinative for identifying the word of God with the written word in ancient Israel.

From Oral to Written Prophecy

Around the time of the Deuteronomistic movement a revolution was taking place in prophetic literature.[30] As M.B. Dick suggests, this revolution entailed the increased incorporation of written passages in prophecy, which in essence and origin was an oral medium. This conclusion is based on R. Coote's work on the Book of Amos[31] which demonstrated that one strata of Amos (Amos A) reflected the existence of orally delivered oracles whereas a second strata of the book (Amos B) suggested prophecy that was never orally delivered but was a written composition. Dick concludes that, because of the resemblance of Amos B to the Deuteronomist, it can be dated to the late seventh century.[32]

The work of the prophet Jeremiah stands at a pivotal moment in the transition from oral to written prophecy. The 36th chapter of Jeremiah describes the production of a written prophetic document.[33] What is unusual in this account, however, is that the process of oral prophecy and scribal transmission—separate processes in the previously described Book of Amos—now appear to converge. "Either during his lifetime or shortly thereafter, [Jeremiah's] oracles, and the accounts of many incidents within his life, were committed to writing."[34] Though the reasons for this convergence are yet to be agreed upon, the result of this process is that the written word is identified with the word of the Lord.[35]

By the post-exilic period, prophecy is more and more a written endeavor.[36] Dick suggests that the Book of Chronicles provides a *terminus ad quem* for this transition. "By the time of the Chronicler, a contemporary of Haggai and Zechariah (c. 520 BCE), prophecy was already presumed to be written."[37]

Residual Orality in Ancient Israel

The appearance of a Hebrew alphabet, the rise of scribalism, and the convergence of oral prophecy and scribal transmission in Jeremiah all attest to the gradual transformation of ancient Israel from a proto-literate to a craft- or even semi-literate society. Even the dominance of written prophecy in post-exilic Israel, however, does not mean the end of Israel as an oral society, for the transition from one stage of orality to another takes centuries to achieve.[38] Thus, whereas writing might have been widespread among the Israelites before the exile, de Vaux himself—who treats writing within the larger framework of education—concludes that most teaching was done by word of mouth.[39]

It was not only education that maintained an "auditory bias" in ancient Israel. Many of the characteristics of this pre-literate state endured for centuries. The primary source for discovering these characteristics is the Old Testament. Although it is true that the Old Testament was redacted by a society at least at the stage of craft-literacy, the texts themselves exhibit what Havelock calls "concealed oralism."[40] As he explains, concealed oralism is a way of acknowledging that "genuine echoes from a primary orality long forgotten have been retained intermittently in a text otherwise devoted to revising them, epitomizing them, and incorporating them in a theological framework devised by a written tradition."[41] Although there are a number of indicators of this "concealed oralism" in the Old Testament, a brief consideration of three of them should make the point.

1. *The Dominance of Auditory over Visual Imagery in Divine Manifestations*. It is generally true that auditory images dominate the stories of divine manifestation in the Old Testament. This can be demonstrated in a number of ways.

First, there is what might be called the preparatory nature of the visual manifestation of God in the Old Testament. As Kittel notes, accounts of seeing God in the Hebrew Scriptures simply provide the setting for the revelation of the word that follows as, for example, in the vision of the prophet Isaiah (6:1ff) or Ezechiel (1:1ff). "When God appears, it is not for the sake of the theophany, but in order . . . to cause Himself to be heard indirectly or directly. The decisive religious statement is: 'Hear the Word of the Lord' (Isa 1.10; Jer 2.4; Am 7.16)."[42]

Second, the divine presence is often visually obscured, so that God is never adequately or completely seen. As Samuel Terrien elucidates this point:

> Either there is too much light, in which case the storytellers emphasize the blinding quality of the experience, or there is too little light—the experience occurs in the gloom of night or in a cloud of total darkness—and the storytellers pile up synonyms for obscurity in order to stress divine invisibility.[43]

Thus, for example, in the previously noted divine "vision" of Ezechiel, the prophet describes the Lord's appearance (Ez 1:28b) in this way: "Upward from what resembled his waist I saw what gleamed like electrum; downward from what resembled his waist I saw what looked like fire; he was surrounded with splendor. Like the bow which appears in the clouds on a rainy day was the splendor that surrounded him" (Ez 1:27-28a). This is a description the prophet himself calls "the likeness of the glory of the Lord" (Ez 1:28b) more than it is a vision of God.

Third, a true vision of God is something both exceptional and dangerous in the Hebrew Scriptures.[44] Thus, when Moses realized that the Lord God was revealing self in the burning bush, "Moses hid his face, for he was afraid to look at God" (Ex 3:6). Later in Exodus God announced to Moses that, though God will "make all my beauty pass before you . . . but my face you cannot see, for no [one] sees me and still lives" (Ex 33:19-20). Although it is true that in some cultic contexts, "to see God" often had the positive meaning of experiencing the presence of God in the Temple (e.g., Ps 42:3; 84:8; Is 38:11), in other contexts, such as Exodus 33, it could be life-threatening. When Isaiah saw Yahweh in the Temple he feared for his life (Is 6:5) and when Amos saw the Lord in his fifth vision (Am 9:1) destruction and death ensued.[45]

Closely related to this pattern in which auditory imagery prevails over visual imagery in divine manifestation is the ban against visual depictions of God at the heart of Israel's law (Ex 20:4; Dt 5:8). The aniconic tradition in Israel is not only ancient, but also without a real parallel in the ancient Near East.⁴⁶ Although it is true that a variety of graphic designs, images, and decorations did grace various Jewish buildings,⁴⁷ "no certain image of Yahweh has so far been found at any Israelite site."⁴⁸ The one great exception to these generalizations about visions of God comes from Exodus 24:9-11. In this unusual passage God was seen directly by humans who actually ate and drank with God: "And they beheld the God of Israel. Under his feet there appeared to be sapphire tilework, as clear as the sky itself. Yet he did not smite these chosen Israelites. After gazing on God, they could still eat and drink." As if to emphasize the point, the passage twice reports that Moses and his companions saw God. Terrien suggests that this story is "without parallel in the Hebrew tradition" and was shocking to Hellenistic Jews who added the phrase "God is not seen, only the place where he stood" to verse 10 of this chapter.⁴⁹ Though this text is extreme, it does represent a pattern in stories of divine revelation that emerged from the southern tradition—and yet it is not clear that the story of Exodus 24:9-11 itself had such an origin. This pattern, as Terrien describes it, is one in which southern theologians increasingly interpreted divine presence and divine revelation through the *theologoumenon* of the glory.⁵⁰ This pattern, however, is a later development in the history of ancient Israel, while the emphasis on the preparatory, obscuring, and dangerous nature of visual encounters with the divine seems to be older and foundational.⁵¹

2. *The Importance of the Organs for Hearing and Speaking.* Another indicator of concealed oralism in the Old Testament is the importance that this collection of writings gives to the organs for hearing and speaking. There are three different ways in which the Old Testament stresses the organs for hearing and speaking.

First, these Scriptures emphasize that the ear and hearing are constitutive for an authentic definition of personhood. Although the Hebrew Scriptures refer to the ear as a physical attribute of humans, the text's figurative references to the ear "as a symbol of the complete process of hearing and, by extension, of understanding and obedience is far more significant."⁵² An introduction to the role of the ear and hearing in the Hebrew Scriptures is provided by Eliphaz who articulates how, starting from the ear, the whole person is activated (Job 4:12-14).⁵³ To "open someone's ears" (Is 50:4) is a basic expression for communicating with another. Other texts from the First Testament suggest that hearing determines one's behavior and state of being generally (for example, Gn 3:8-10). It is an organ not simply for acquiring auditory information, but for understanding and receptivity. In some instances the ear serves as a parallel for the heart (Prv 2:2; 18:15; 23:12), which is the seat of the whole inner life.[54] Thus, Solomon asks for a heart that hears so that he might be able to discern between good and evil (1 Kgs 3:10). In this instance the ear becomes the fundamental metaphor for Solomon's wisdom.[55] These and other examples demonstrate that hearing is constitutive of the whole, developed individual.[56]

Second, the Old Testament emphasizes that the ear and hearing are essential for an authentic relationship with God. Besides serving as a critical means for achieving personhood, the Scriptures emphasize that the ear and hearing provide a fundamental link between humans and God. In ancient Israel God was more often heard than seen. Besides the simple quantity or dominance of such passages, the Hebrew Scriptures further demonstrate that hearing provides an essential link between God and humanity. Without the capacity to hear—literally and metaphorically—humankind would be severely disabled in its ability to sustain a relationship with the God of Israel. The Hebrew Bible stresses that, from the beginning, God has initiated the dialogue: be that at the mythic beginning of time (Gn 1:26-30), the beginning of the covenant with Abraham (Gn 12:1-3), or when Yahweh took charge of the existence of Israel (Ex 23:22).[57] Not only does God speak, but God speaks a law that humans are called to hear and obey. The biblical expression for obeying is to "listen to" God, to God's voice (Gn 3:17; 28:7). Similarly, to obey God (Is 42:24) or to obey God's law (Jer 9:12) requires first that one hear God,[58] and then act. Since God has created the ear (Prv 20:12), humans have a great responsibility to use their ears wisely, allowing God to open them so that life can be aligned with reality.[59] This point is dramatically made in the daily confession known as the *shema* (Dt 6:4-9; 11:13-21; Nm 15:37-41), which begins "Hear, O Israel." Thus Kittel concludes that an essential feature of biblical religion is that,

> It is a religion of the Word, because it is a religion of action, of obedience to the Word. The prophet is the bearer of the Word of Yahweh which demands obedience and fulfillment. Man is not righteous as he seeks to apprehend or perceive God by way of thought and vision, but as he hears the command of God and studies to observe it.[60]

More than any other sense perception, hearing provides the vital link between the God of Israel and humankind.

A third indicator of concealed oralism in the Old Testament is the extended vocabulary employed in the Hebrew Scriptures for the organs of speech. Since the received word is incomplete without a response,[61] and the organs of speech articulate that response, so does the First Testament give these organ special attention. "Whereas the ear and the eye only have one word each in the Old Testament, a whole collection of parts of the body represent the instrument of speech."[62] The mouth (*peh*) is the main organ of speech mentioned in the Hebrew Scriptures. As the organ that expresses what the ear and eye has perceived, it distinguishes humans from all other creatures and stands quite near to humankind's essential being.[63] Besides the mouth, however, the Hebrew Scriptures also admit a host of other parts of the body that represent the instrument of speech[64]: *sāpā* which literally means lips (Ps 22:8), but also is a metaphor for language (Is 6:7); *lāsōn* is the tongue (Lam 4:4), but also is a figure for true (2 Sm 23:2) or false (Ps 12:3) speech; *hek* or palate is literally the seat of the sense of taste (Ps 119:103); *gārōn* is at once the throat (Jer 2:25), but also an organ of speech (Is 58:1).

3. *The Dynamic Nature of the Hebrew Language and Hebrew Thought.* A third indicator of concealed oralism in the Old Testament is what Boman calls the dynamic nature of the Hebrew language and thought. This dynamism is demonstrated by the dynamic character of Hebrew verbs of inaction. According to Boman, Hebrew verbs always tend to express movement or activity.[65] This tendency toward movement or activity is most striking in verbs of inaction such as standing (*natsabh*), sitting (*vashabh*), or stretching out (*shakhabh*). Though indicating a position of repose or inactivity, in the Hebrew mind such experiences of stasis were related to the motion that preceded them. Boman concludes that "motionless and fixed being is for the Hebrews a nonentity; it does not exist for them."[66] Boman draws a similar conclusion about verbs of condition and quality such as to be/become angry (*'aneph*), or to be/become bright (*'ôr*),[67] as well as the verb "to be" (*hayah*).[68] Tresmontant concurs when considering the nature of understanding (*bina*) in the prophetic writings. He explains:

> What the prophets call understanding, *bina*, is not a faculty, an *organon* endowed with certain *a priori* categories, a power that would pass into action under certain circumstances. Under-

standing is action, the act of intellection of subsistent truth. Hebrew, a concrete language, never speaks of understanding except in such a context of truth's fruition.[69]

Boman concludes that for the Hebrews, the world itself possessed an active character, and was always in motion.[70]

Orality in Emerging Christianity

The Hellenistic Context

Almost four centuries before the birth of Christ, Alexander the Great (+ 323 BCE) conquered the whole of the eastern Mediterranean world. Besides conquering nations, Alexander also transformed the Near East by imposing his own culture and language upon the peoples he subdued throughout the Mediterranean. Although his empire was divided among his generals after his death, the influence of Alexander's Hellenizing campaign continued for centuries. This was true even in Palestine where the Jews did not reestablish their political independence until almost 150 years after the death of Alexander. Although they attempted to assert their cultural independence from Hellenism as well, this effort was short lived and ultimately unsuccessful. Rome conquered the Jewish monarchy in 63 BCE and continued the process of Hellenization. Thus it was in a Jewish milieu under the political and cultural influence of the Greco-Roman world that Christianity emerged.

The culture that Alexander exported from Greece was one in which seeing rather than hearing was celebrated as the most important human sense. This development occurred between the time of Homer (before 700 BCE,) and Plato (+ 347 BCE). Although Greek culture at the time of Homer was not without writing, and at the time of Plato was not without epic poetry or oral performance, in the latter period the emphasis was clearly shifting from the ear to the eye. It was not Plato who initiated this change. In his writings there is a general absence of argument on the subject and he simply seems to take for granted the preeminence of vision.[71] Plato does, however, become the great prophet of visualization,[72] and after him there is little doubt that vision is held to be the most excellent of the senses. The influence of Plato and the philosophy that emerged from a society that valued seeing over hearing was extensive and pervasive. Ultimately it provided a framework for western civilization that would allow one to assert that seeing is believing.

Despite this powerful Hellenistic influence, the ancient world in general—and Palestine in particular—were places in which hearing continued to dominate. Although segments of the culture communicated significantly through literary means,[73] the culture of late western antiquity was what Paul Achtemeier calls "a culture of high residual orality."[74] One irrefutable symbol of this residual orality was the continued practice of reading aloud. "The oral environment was so pervasive that no writing occurred that was not vocalized . . . even solitary readers, reading only to themselves, read aloud."[75] Thus it appears that the Hellenized world that provided the context for the emergence of Christianity, maintained a distinctive auditory environment in which orality was highly valued.

Hellenized Judaism, in particular, continued as a culture with high residual orality. Though there are many symbols of the continued emphasis on orality in Hellenistic Judaism around the time of Christ, one of the most important of these is the growing importance during this period of the oral Torah (*Torah she-b'al peh*). The Pharisees were a small group within Palestinian Judaism that emerged during the period of the second Temple. They distinguished themselves from other Jews by claiming:

> when God revealed the Torah to Moses at Mount Sinai, God gave the Torah in two parts. One part was in writing . . . the other part was not written down, but was meant to be handed on through memorization and repetition of the precise language that had been memorized from one generation to the next. This other half of the Torah is called, therefore, the oral Torah, or the Torah which is memorized.[76]

Between ca. 200 BCE and 100 CE the Pharisees strongly asserted their right to rule all the Jews by virtue of their possession of this oral Torah.[77] Eventually the Pharisees succeeded in wresting spiritual leadership in Palestinian Judaism away from the Sadducees who did not believe in these claims about the oral Torah. The Pharisees' growing influence with its reassertion of the oral component of the law effectively underscores the sensitive auditory environment of first-century Palestinian Judaism and its continued emphasis on orality.

The Jesus Experience

Just as one can not consider the oral nature of emerging Judaism apart from its cultural context, so one cannot understand the auditory aspects of the Jesus experience apart from Palestinian Judaism at the beginning of the Common Era. Jesus was a Jew and was part of a culture and religious tradition that valued hearing as much if not more than seeing—especially in the transmission of religious truths. This auditory awareness, common to all Palestinian Jews of the period, seems to have been especially true for Jesus because of particular geographic and linguistic circumstances. Greek was the language that, more than any other in the Ancient Near East, served as a vehicle for the ascendancy of sight over sound in western thought. One can surmise, however, that because Jesus was a Jew from rural Palestine who only spoke Aramaic, the Hellenistic tendency to prize the visual over the auditory was significantly muted.

We have already noted how teaching in Judaism was essentially an oral enterprise.[78] As a teacher, Jesus was inevitably engaged in this auditory venture. It is true that some rabbis did employ writing as a way to communicate their teachings, and yet there is no evidence that Jesus ever did so, even though he could read (Lk 4:16ff.) and write (Jn 8:6). Jesus' reliance on oral instead of written communication may have been a conscious choice. The basis for any such choice would have been an awareness of oral communication's "greater power for reaching and transforming the people of the day."[79]

Was Jesus unique in this regard, or could his preaching style simply be understood to be similar to that other rabbis of his day?[80] The latter position would seem to ignore a radical difference between the speech of Jesus and that of other Jewish teachers—a difference that has its own theological significance.[81] According to Wilder, Jesus' speech was naïve, not studied: "It is *extempore* and directed to the occasion, it is not calculated to serve some future hour. This utterance is dynamic, actual, immediate, reckless of posterity; not coded for catechesis or repetition."[82]

If Wilder's analysis is accurate then Jesus, unlike other rabbis of first-century Palestine, "was not schooling his followers in a learned mode that could be passed on to future generations. Rather, he spoke to the immediate crisis of the day in a free and spontaneous style."[83] And it was a particular crisis of his day that demanded this new style of speech-act.[84]

As an eschatological prophet,[85] Jesus was aware that the kingdom was in the process of being revealed.[86] Even though there were those in Palestinian Judaism whose primary expressions of eschatological hope were written, "there was another stratum of society whose hopes were expressed in a more 'activist,' even 'revolutionary' manner."[87] Jesus' eschatological message, understood in this context, was a dynamic and revolutionary speech-act that eschewed writing. "The act of writing presupposes continuities and a future... [but for Jesus] and his generation, history was fractured, time's course was in dissolution, continuities were broken. Jesus' word was for the present, the last hour."[88] Thus his examples are realistic and vivid—deftly chosen from existential experience.[89] This immediacy of language well serves the eschatological message in a style that is unique and memorable. As Wilder summarizes:

> The incomparable felicity and patterning of his sayings is indeed evident, but this formal perfection is not a matter of mnemonics; it is the countersign of the most effective communication of the moment. Naturally his words and parables were remembered and retold, often with great accuracy, so lucid and inevitable was his phrasing. But here as always the new speech of the Gospel was not a matter of words on a table but a word in the heart, not a copybook for recitation but winged words for life.[90]

Jesus the rabbi embodied the Jewish predilection for orality over visualization: the speech-act over writing. As an eschatological prophet, he not only relied upon a heightened auditory environment, but transformed it through revolutionary forms of speech that could not be contained by writing. And, as the word made flesh, he proclaimed and embodied the word so uniquely that the kingdom was revealed in a singular and unrepeatable articulation.

The Oral Kerygma. Jesus' revolutionary style of preaching evoked a similar revolution in the language of his disciples. Although the early community was concerned to hand on Jesus' teaching, its members did not persuade people to believe in Jesus by repeating his teachings (*didaché*), but through preaching (*kerygma*)—an act having more in common with town criers or auctioneers than traditionally understood rabbinic discourse.[91] "Although Christianity from the very beginning had a scripture, the Hebrew Scriptures, the faith of the earliest Christians was evoked by and focused on a person, Jesus of Nazareth. Jesus, in the earliest Christian communities, was known not in bible texts but in missionary preaching, oral tradition and charismatic experience."[92]

It is from this perspective that Ernst Fuchs can suggest that primitive Christianity itself was a speech-phenomenon[93] that did not first concern itself with written forms. Rather, in the memory and example of Jesus, the first disciples went about proclaiming the good news, and in so doing contributed to a heightened auditory environment in which Jesus was proclaimed. It is this oral performance that lies at the heart of the early Christian message, and generated the new religious form of truth known as the Gospel. It was only through this auditory kerygma—what Frederick Crowe calls "gospeling the gospel"[94]—that belief was possible.[95]

Residual Orality in the New Testament

With increasing frequency scholars are approaching the New Testament not simply as a collection of literary works but as attempts by various communities to translate into writing what was essentially an auditory phenomenon. The Gospel of Mark, for example, is dominated by the oral form of storytelling.[96] Not only the Gospel of Mark, however, but all of the New Testament documents "are oral to the core, both in their creation and in their performance."[97] Rooted in the free oral dialogue of Jesus and his disciples, that was remembered and repeated for believers, the stories and parables were eventually written down.

> But even when the face-to-face rhetorical forms of the beginnings gave way to the conventionality of written records and letters, these are still characterized by a perennially dramatic element which goes back to the very nature of the Christian religion. The Christian styles tend to evoke or restore the face-to-face encounter.[98]

Like the Hebrew Scriptures, the New Testament preserves many traces of residual orality. This "concealed oralism" is much more prominent in the New Testament than in the Hebrew Scriptures as the time between the oral event and written form for the former is far more condensed than that same process for the latter. While there are a number of indicators of the New Testament's concealed orality, a brief consideration of three of them should make the point.

First is the emblematic role of parables in the New Testament. As Schillebeeckx and others have noted, Jesus not only taught in parables but himself was a parable.[99] As Jesus announced the kingdom, so were his parables intimately wed to that announcement.[110] Parables were certainly one of the most characteristic story forms employed by Jesus. Kelber reminds us that the "oral propriety of parabolic stories requires little argument."[101] Parables are oral forms that presume and require the speech-event for their power. Even when they are translated into written forms, they retain various oral characteristics. One of these is the presence of certain mnemonic devices.[102] In the Gospel of Mark, for example, both the parable of the sower and that of the mustard seed employ the mnemonic device of contrast, which renders these stories "orally impressionable."[103] Paul Ricoeur has suggested that another characteristic of many parables is what he terms extravagance.[104] According to Kelber, this concept of extravagance further illuminates the mnemonic process of parables. As he explains, "over and above the mnemonic patterning, it is the element of excess and irregularity that eases remembering. The trivial facilitates identification, but oddness makes these stories memorable. For one what remembers is not the pane in the window, but the crack in the pane."[105]

The residual orality of the New Testament is also demonstrated by the dominance of auditory over visual imagery for revelation and faith. Although the verbs of seeing outnumber the verbs of hearing in the New Testament, this does not mean that seeing is the more important of the senses. It is true that at some moments seeing is more highly esteemed than hearing (Jn 8:38) in the redemptive enterprise. The sense of sight takes on particular significance in the Gospel of John.[106] In general, however, the visual does not replace the auditory in the New Testament at moments of revelation or faith, where "there can be no doubt as to the primacy of hearing."[107] Even when the New Testament depicts revelatory events in visual terms, such events usually acquire their true significance through what is heard. For example, the appearance of the angel acquires its true significance through the accompanying message at the annunciation (Lk 1:28-37); the baptism of Jesus acquires its true significance with the voice after Jesus' baptism (Mk 1:11); and, the transfiguration acquires its true significance with the revelatory word (Mt 17:5). As Amos Wilder summarizes:

> The New Testament speaks of the divine apprehension in terms of all the senses, not only hearing and sight but touch

and smell (the last in the form of incense and fragrant odours). Yet the hearing mode is primary. The spirit may be rapt in vision, but it is with the heart that [one] hears the word of faith and with [one's] mouth that [one] confesses and is saved (Rom 10.8-10). Language, then, is more fundamental than graphic representation, except where the latter is itself a transcript in some sense of the word of God.[108]

A further testimony to the oral genesis and foundation of the New Testament is the existence of numerous parallel passages that are yet markedly different from each other. No example of this is more striking than that of the institution narratives.[109] Although there is a core of material that is common to the four institution narratives recorded in the New Testament—both in structure[110] and in text[111]—there is yet enormous diversity between these citations.[112] This diversity can best be explained by what Jeremias calls "a living process of growth in the tradition."[113] At the basis of these varying texts was an historical, oral event. This event, in turn, served as the basis for the liturgical practice of emerging Christianity. It was the liturgical context—the cultic speech-event of emerging Christianity—that gave rise to the parallel yet diverse institution accounts imbedded in the New Testament. The institution narratives are one example of residual orality, in which oral transmission and enactment generated written texts. The residual orality of the institution narrative continues to be affirmed by various segments of Christianity which over the centuries have employed variations on the biblical texts in ritual enactment.[114]

Summary

This brief introduction to the dominance of auditory over visual imagery in divine manifestations, the importance of the organs for hearing and speaking, and the dynamic nature of the Hebrew language and Hebrew thought as revealed through the Old Testament suggests that, despite the fact that writing might have been widespread in ancient Israel, there continued what might be called an "auditory bias" in Israel. This observation finds a corollary in the work of Jack Goody who asserts that "the division between 'literacy' and 'orality' is never a question of crossing a single frontier, a simple binary shift."[115] Rather, as Goody notes, even literary composition requires oral or sub-oral processes. Thus, whereas the Old Testament was redacted by a society at least at the stage of craft-literacy, the texts exhibit the kind of concealed oralism which allows us to assert the auditory bias of Hebrew life and thought.

At the dawn of Christianity, this heightened auditory environment endured, despite Hellenizing influences that valued seeing over hearing. For Jesus, in particular, the spontaneous word-event was a fundamental characteristic of his ministry. Announcing the immediacy of the good news in a manner "reckless of posterity"[116] typified his public ministry and that of his followers. Despite the emergence of written forms like the Gospel, a primacy of audition continued to characterize developing Christianity. For them, hearing was believing.

Though there have been few explicit references to music in this essay, some acknowledgement and understanding of the broader sonic environment of the ancient Near East, Judaism, and emerging Christianity is essential before broaching such a topic. As has been noted before, and will be noted again, twentieth-century western concepts of music do not necessarily provide an adequate framework for understanding what another culture or another time might consider music or musical. This is especially true when people from a visually dominated tradition attempt to raise musical questions about an oral society. Appreciating something of the nature of an auditory environment in general, and the auditory environment of the movement or culture under investigation in particular, are first steps in gaining such understanding.

Notes

1. "Auditory environment" and "acoustic environment" are terms that are meant to demonstrate a concern not simply or essentially for an individual sound or musical event, but for the physical, historical, and cultural environment that shapes the perception and understanding of such individual sounds or musical events. The terms are somewhat analogous to those of "soundscape" or "sonic environment" coined by F. Murray Schafer. See, for example, the definitions Schafer offers in his glossary of *The Tuning of the World* (New York: Alfred Knopf, 1977) 274-275, and passim.

2. Even this term must be used with caution and did not appear in the ancient world until around the year 80 CE, possibly in the environs of Antioch.

3. Walter Ong, *The Presence of the Word* (New Haven: Yale University Press, 1967) 17. Eric Havelock offers a refinement on this three part

schema by suggesting that the first stage of a culture in communication terms is that of primary orality, followed by the proto-literate, the craft-literate, the semi-literate, and the fully literate stages. Eric Havelock, *The Muse Learns to Write: Reflections on Orality and Literacy from Antiquity to the Present* (New Haven and London: Yale University Press, 1986) 65.

4. The common use of the term "writing" as applied to any and every form of symbolization, without distinction between phonetic transcription and other forms of communication which are more properly considered pictographic or hieroglyphic, blurs the boundaries between the various stages of a society's development. Havelock, *The Muse Learns to Write* 65.

5. Jack Goody, *The Interface between the Written and the Oral* (Cambridge: Cambridge University Press, 1987) 38-41.

6. Ong, *The Presence of the Word* 23.

7. Ibid.

8. Havelock, *The Muse Learns to Write* 65-66.

9. The following list is distilled from Ong, *The Presence of the Word* 22-35 and Havelock, *The Muse Learns to Write* 63-78: (1) in an oral society communication, even between individuals, has an aspect of social phenomenon; (2) oral societies rely on the narrative format for memorizing and transmitting fundamental truths; (3) tradition is taught by action, not by idea or principle; (4) the oral audience participates not merely by listening passively but by active participation—they clap, dance, and sing collectively in response to the chanting of the singer; (5) an oral society has no history in the modern sense of that term; (6) an oral society nourishes memory skills beyond those cultivated in present-day technological societies; (7) in oral societies ritualization becomes the means of memorization; and (8) in oral societies words are more celebrations and less tools than in literate cultures. For a cautionary note on comparing literate to non-literate societies, see Ruth Finnegan, "Literacy versus Non-Literacy: The Great Divide?" *Modes of Thought: Essays on Thinking in Western and Non-Western Societies*, ed. Robin Horton and Ruth Finnegan (London: Faber & Faber, 1973) 112-144.

10. See the accessible outline by Addison Wright and Roland Murphy in NJBC 75:5-144; this outline provides the basis for the historical reconstruction that follows.

11. Roland de Vaux, *The Early History of Israel*, trans. David Smith (Philadelphia: Westminster Press, 1978) 266.

12. Although it appears that certain Semitic groups entered Egypt sometime in the middle of the second millennium BCE, the historicity of the Joseph story is disputed. See, for example, Siegfried Herrmann, *A History of Israel in Old Testament Times*, 2nd ed. (Philadelphia: Fortress Press, 1981) 56.

13. de Vaux, *The Early History of Israel* 363-387.

14. See, for example, David Noel Freedman and David Graf, eds. *Palestine in Transition*, The Social World of Biblical Antiquity, series editor James W. Flanagan (Sheffield: Almond Press, 1983): especially Marvin L. Chaney, "Ancient Palestinian Peasant Movements and the Formation of Premonarchic Israel" 39-90.

15. These were what Goody calls "consonantal alphabets" in counterdistinction to alphabets consisting of consonants and vowels, which did not appear until around 750 BCE in Greece. Goody, *The Interface* 40-41.

16. B.L. Ullman, *Ancient Writing and Its Influence*, Medieval Academy Reprints for Teaching 10 (Toronto: University of Toronto Press, 1980 [1932]) 11.

17. Goody, *The Interface* 41.

18. Ibid. 43 and 45.

19. Ibid. 45.

20. This schematic is distilled from Goody's more complex table on the genealogy of the alphabet. *The Interface*, Table 2, p. 48.

21. The Afeg Tablet from the eleventh century, and the Gezer Calendar, probably of the late tenth century, the Davidic period. Goody, *The Interface* 45.

22. Norman K. Gottwald, *The Hebrew Bible* (Philadelphia: Fortress Press, 1985) 567-568.

23. Joseph McIntyre, "Jeremiah 36 and the Emergence of Scribal Prophecy," Unpublished MA Thesis (Chicago: Catholic Theological Union, 1990) 10.

24. Roland de Vaux, *Ancient Israel*, 2 vols. (New York and Toronto: McGraw-Hill, 1965) 1:49.

25. Namely, the J tradition; see Raymond Brown's chronology of approximate dates of the collection of composition of the works of the Old Testament in the *NJBC* 66:23.

26. Walter Ong defines residual orality as "habits of thought and expression ... deriving from the dominance of the oral as a medium in a given culture." *Rhetoric, Romance and Technology* (Ithaca, NY: Cornell University Press, 1971) 27-28.

27. The Assyrian monarch Asshurbanipal (668-626 BCE), for example, not only employed numerous scribes and assembled an impressive library, but himself mastered the art of writing. James Mullenberg, "Baruch the Scribe," *Proclamation and Presence* (Richmond: John Knox Press, 1970) 216.

28. Ibid. 217.

29. McIntyre, "Jeremiah 36" 11.

30. M.B. Dick, "Prophetic *Poipsis* and the Verbal Icon," *Catholic Biblical Quarterly* 46 (1984) 230.

31. R.B. Coote, *Amos Among the Prophets: Composition and Theology* (Philadelphia: Fortress Press, 1981).

32. Dick, "Prophetic Poiesis" 230.

33. McIntyre, "Jeremiah 36" 4; the following analysis of the role of Jeremiah relies on McIntyre's work.

34. Ibid. 5.

35. McIntyre hypothesizes, "oral cultures seem to be uncertain about how to treat written documents . . . it is evident that Jeremiah 36 is intended to resolve that question. It seems to address the theological issue of preserving a written tradition . . . I contend that the final form of Jeremiah 36 resolves this situation. It identifies the word of the Lord with the written word of Jeremiah." Ibid. 47-48.

36. Dick, "Prophetic *Poipsis*" passim.

37. Ibid. 230-231.

38. Havelock, *The Muse Learns to Write*. In a related comment Ruth Finnegan notes: "In practice, interaction between oral and written forms is extremely common, and the idea that the use of writing automatically deals a death blow to oral literary forms has nothing to support it." *Oral Poetry: Its Nature, Significance and Social Context* (Cambridge: University Press, 1977) 160.

39. de Vaux, *Ancient Israel* 1:49.

40. Havelock, *The Muse Learns to Write* 47.

41. Ibid. 47; Werner Kelber makes a similar assertion when he suggests that "The objectifying, controlling power of the written medium, while taking the life out of spoken language, can freeze oral forms and preserve them in fossilized profiles." *The Oral and the Written Gospel* (Philadelphia: Fortress Press, 1983) 44.

42. Gerhard Kittel, "akouw," TDNT 1:218.

43. Samuel Terrien, *The Elusive Presence*, Religious Perspectives 26 (San Francisco: Harper & Row, 1978) 69.

44. Kittel, *TDNT* 1:218.

45. Michael Barré, "Amos," NJBC 13:23.

46. Terrien, *The Elusive Presence* 163.

47. See, for example, Joseph Gutmann, *No Graven Images: Studies in Art and the Hebrew Bible* (New York: Ktav, 1970).

48. Richard Clifford, "Exodus," NJBC 3:33.

49. Terrien, *The Elusive Presence* 135.

50. Ibid. 136-138.

51. Some have also suggested that there was an ancient strata in Israel's history that put emphasis on vision rather than hearing in divine revelation. As Sanders, for example, notes: "Anciently a prophet was called a 'seer' (1 Sam 9.9). The emphasis on word rather than vision may be connected with the Hebrew rejection of Idolatry and, indeed mistrust of any visual aids to religious faith such as are found in most religions, including Christianity itself." J.N. Sanders, "Word," IDB 4:869.

52. R.C. Denta, "Ear," IDB 2:1.

53. Thus Wolff concludes, "Just as the auditory reception of the word by the wise man through the ear changes the whole state of the body, so

the hearing determines a man's behavior and state of health generally." Hans Walter Wolff, *Anthropology of the Old Testament*, trans. Margaret Kohl (Philadelphia: Fortress Press, 1974) 76.

54. *Encyclopedic Dictionary of the Bible*, ed. Louis Hartmann (New York: McGraw-Hill, 1963), s.v. "ear" and "heart".

55. Wolff, *Anthropology* 76.

56. G. von Rad, *Weisheit* 309 as cited in Wolff, *Anthropology* 76.

57. Xavier Léon-Dufour, *Dictionary of Biblical Theology*, 2nd ed. (New York: Seabury Press, 1973), s.v. "communion".

58. *Encyclopedic Dictionary of the Bible*, s.v. "ear".

59. K.H. Maahs, "Ear," *The International Standard Bible Encyclopedia*, ed. Geoffrey Bromiley, 4 vols. (Grand Rapids: Eerdmans, 1982) 2:2.

60. Kittel, "akouw," TDNT 1:218.

61. "According to the Hebraic meaning of the word *truth*, to listen, to receive the word of God, is not only to lend it an attentive ear but also to open one's heart to it; it is to be put into practice, that is, to obey." Léon-Dufour, *Dictionary*, s.v. "listen."

62. Wolff, *Anthropology* 77.

63. K.H. Maahs, "Mouth," *The International Standard Bible Encyclopedia* 2:428.

64. Much of what follows comes from Wolff, *Anthropology* 77-78.

65. Thorlief Boman, *Hebrew Thought Compared with Greek*, trans. Jules Moreau (Philadelphia: Westminster Press, 1960) 28-31.

66. Ibid. 31.

67. Ibid. 31-35.

68. Ibid. 38-49.

69. Claude Tresmontant, *A Study of Hebrew Thought*, trans. Michael Francis Gibson (New York: Desclée Company, 1960) 125.

70. Boman, *Hebrew Thought* 49-51; Boman's discussion of the dynamism of Hebrew thought contrasted with Greek thought needs to be read with caution. As will be demonstrated, Greek thought before Plato (+ 347 BCE) was also dynamic; and Hebrew thought after the influence of Alexander the Great demonstrates certain Hellenized influences. Thus, Boman's analysis of what we have called concealed oralisms in the Hebrew Scriptures is especially demonstrative of a type of thinking prominent before the exile.

71. Evelyn Fox Keller and Christine R. Grontkowski, "The Mind's Eye," *Discovering Reality*, ed. Sandra Harding and Merrill Hintikka (Dordrecht, Boston, and London: D. Reidel Publishing, 1983) 209.

72. Eric Havelock, *Preface to Plato: A History of the Greek Mind* (Cambridge, MA: Belknap Press of Harvard University Press, 1963) vii. Also Keller and Grontkowski who comment: "So evident was it to him [Plato] that vision enjoys an elevated status over the other sense that he was able merely to assert is preeminence, at least implicitly, without feeling it

necessary to argue the point. In his only extensive analysis of the senses per se, he entirely separates the discussion of vision from the discussion of the other four senses [*Timaeus*, 61d-68e]. He describes the creation of the sense of sight in the same context as the creation of soul and intelligence in human beings; all of the other sense are described in the context of the creation of man's material nature. He also says, in *Timaeus*, that 'the first organs they (the gods) fashioned were those that gave us light' [45b]. He comments elsewhere on the intrinsic nobility of this construction, as for example, in *Phaedrus*, when referring to 'the keenest of all the senses' [250d] and in the *Republic* when he observes: 'Have you noticed how extremely lavish the designer of our senses was when he gave us the faculty of sight?' [507c]" p. 210.

73. Pliny the Elder, for example, speaking about the history of paper, noted how a shortage of paper could completely upset life in the Roman Empire. *Natural History* XIII.27.89, as edited by H. Rackham in 10 volumes, Loeb Classical Library (Cambridge, MA: Harvard University Press, 1945) 370:153.

74. Paul Achtemeier, *"Omne Verbum Sonat*: The New Testament and the Oral Environment of Late Western Antiquity," *Journal of Biblical Literature* 109 (1990) 12.

75. Ibid. 15-16.

76. Jacob Neusner, *The Way of Torah*, 3rd ed. (North Scituate, MA: Duxbury Press, 1979) 13; also, his *The Memorized Torah: The Mnemonic System of the Mishnah* (Chico, CA: Scholars Press, 1985).

77. Jacob Neusner, *From Politics to Piety: The Emergence of Pharisaic Judaism* (New York: Ktav Publishing House, 1979) 11.

78. de Vaux, *Ancient Israel* 1:49.

79. Harold Coward, *Sacred Word and Sacred Text: Scripture in World Religions* (Maryknoll, NY: Orbis Books, 1988) 36.

80. For such a perspective, see Birger Gerhardsson, *The Origins of the Gospel Traditions* (Philadelphia: Fortress Press, 1979).

81. Amos Wilder, *Early Christian Rhetoric: The Language of the Gospel* (Cambridge, MA: Harvard University Press, 1971) 15.

82. Ibid. 13.

83. Coward, *Sacred Word* 37.

84. Wilder, *Early Christian Rhetoric* 4.

85. See, for example, E.P. Sanders, *Jesus and Judaism* (Philadelphia: Fortress Press, 1985) 8 and passim.

86. Joachim Jeremias, *The Parables of Jesus*, rev. ed. (New York: Charles Scribner's Sons, 1963); for a summary and critique of Jeremias' position, see Norman Perrin, *Jesus and the Language of the Kingdom* (Philadelphia: Fortress Press, 1976) 91-107.

87 Adela Yarbro Collins, "Eschatology and Apocalypticism," NJBC 81:41.

88. Wilder, *Early Christian Rhetoric* 14.
89. C.H. Dodd, *The Parables of the Kingdom*, rev. ed. (New York: Scribner's, 1961) 9-10.
90. Wilder, *Early Christian Rhetoric* 15.
91. C.H. Dodd, *The Apostolic Preaching and Its Developments* (Grand Rapids, MI: Baker Book House, 1980) 7-8.
92. Coward, *Sacred Word* 34.
93. "Die Sprache im Neuen Testament," *Zur Frage nach dem historischen Jesus* (Tübingen, 1960) 261, as cited by Wilder, *Early Christian Rhetoric* 10.
94. Frederick Crowe, *Theology of the Christian Word* (New York: Paulist Press, 1978) 35.
95. Gerhard Friedrich, "kerygma," TDNT 3:716.
96. Kelber, *The Oral and the Written Gospel*, especially 44-89.
97. Achtemeier, "*Omne Verbum Sonat*: The New Testament" 19.
98. Wilder, *Early Christian Rhetoric* 16.
99. Edward Schillebeeckx, *Jesus*, trans. Hubert Hoskins (New York: Vintage Books, 1981) 155.
100. Dominic Crossan, *The Dark Interval* (Niles, IL: Argus Publications, 1975) 124.
101. Kelber, *The Oral and the Written Gospel* 58; much of what follows relies upon Kelber, 57-64.
102. Such as alliteration, paranomasia, appositional equivalence, proverbial and aphoristic diction, contrasts and antitheses, synonymous, antithetical, synthetic and tautologic parallelism, etc. Kelber, *The Oral and the Written Gospel* 27. For a further discussion of mnemonic devices in oral speech, see Marcel Jousse, *Etudes de psychologie linguistique: le style oral rhythmique et mnémontechnique chez les verbo-moteurs* (Paris: Gabriel Beauchesne, 1925).
103. Kelber notes that the display of opposites appeals to the imagination and holds the attention as few rhetorical devices do. *The Oral and the Written Gospel* 59.
104. Paul Ricoeur, "Biblical Hermeneutics," *Semeia* 4 (1975) 32; Dominic Crossan calls this an "antitraditional" story element, in *In Parables: The Challenge of the Historical Jesus* (New York: Harper & Row, 1973) 118; Robert Funk calls it the "imaginative shock" in the story, in *Language, Hermeneutic, and the Word of God: The Problem of Language in the New Testament and Contemporary Theology* (New York: Harper & Row, 1966) 193; Wilder calls it the "trait of hyperbole" in these stories, in *The Language of the Gospel* 85.
105. Kelber, *The Oral and the Written Gospel* 61.
106. Wilhelm Michaelis, "orao," TDNT 5:361-364.
107. Michaelis, "orao," TDNT 5:348.
108. Wilder, *Early Christian Rhetoric* 11.

109. 1 Cor 11:23-25; Mk 14:22-24; Mt 26:26-27; Lk 22:19-20; while not a parallel passage, an independent version of Jesus' word of interpretation over the bread can be found in Jn 6:51c.

110. See Gregory Dix, *The Shape of the Liturgy*, 2nd ed. (London: Dacre Press, 1975 [1945]) 48-50.

111. Joachim Jeremias, *The Eucharistic Words of Jesus*, trans. Norman Perrin (Philadelphia: Fortress Press, 1977) 189-196.

112. Ibid. 160-173.

113. Ibid. 105.

114. The current official text of the Latin Rite of the Roman Catholic Church, for example, is a variation on various biblical texts.

115. Goody, *The Interface* 106.

116. Wilder, *Early Christian Rhetoric* 13.

3
The Cantor in Historical Perspective

Introduction

IN THE YEARS SINCE THE SECOND VATICAN COUNCIL, THE ONCE DEFUNCT ministry of the cantor has achieved new levels of musical and liturgical acceptability. From the narrowing confines of the *schola cantorum* and the limits of Gregorian intonations, this almost extinct agency has risen to a position reminiscent of a former preeminence. Still, the theological and ministerial significance of the role of the cantor has yet to be fully understood or articulated.

This may be due in large part to our inability to recognize the cantor (and other musicians as well) as prayer leader rather than mere musical adornment. The cantor's primary responsibility is to engage the assembly in the dialogue of praise, to call forth the psalm response or "Amen" from the community, and not simply to supply musical background to some more important ritual action. This emphasis on prayer leadership rather than musical accompaniment, on engaging the community in praise rather than enthralling with vocal gymnastics, is fundamental to our Judaeo-Christian heritage.

History does not even suggest the existence of a primitive Christian musician as much as the presence of a prayer leader who exercised leadership in a style that we would consider musical.[1] The early church did not know of the designation "cantor," that is, one selected for musical leadership in the assembly,[2] just as the pre-Christian synagogue did not know of such an office. As will be demonstrated, however, both traditions did know the ritual experience of chanting: the action of declaiming publicly prayers, creedal formulae or readings in musical or semimusical forms, which usually presumed some kind of congregational response. Eventually the tradition began to distinguish between the sung and the spoken, between chanting and reading.[3] As this occurred in Judaism and Christianity, a professional singer emerged.

This essay argues that in both traditions the cantor developed from a form of volunteer prayer leadership that clearly emphasized the prayer component over the musical. It was only after centuries of ritual development that the singer or musician *per se* appeared. It is hoped that this consideration of our musical heritage within the framework of prayer leadership will provide a clearer understanding of the role of the cantor and other musical ministries in contemporary worship.

The Jewish Tradition

Hazzan ha-knesset

Though some continue to suggest that the Christian cantor developed out of a well-established synagogue parallel (that is, the *hazzan ha-knesset*), this view was refuted as early as the turn of the century by Ismar Elbogen.[4] More recently, Leo Landman has reiterated that "the *hazzan ha-knesset* is not to be mistaken for a cantor."[5] Besides the etymological evidence, which suggests that *hazzan* is probably borrowed from the Assyrian *hazzunu*, which translates as "director" or "overseer,"[6] there is also extensive Talmudic data that reveals a host of nonmusical responsibilities for the *hazzan ha-knesset*.[7] In this regard "Epiphanius [+ 403] was in a certain sense right when he compared the *hazzan* with the deacons who actually had the role of administrators."[8] Thus, we must look beyond the *hazzan ha-knesset* for a precursor to the Christian cantor.

Mithpallel

According to Abraham Idelsohn, one important principle differentiated the precentors found in ancient civilizations from those of Judaism.

> In Judaism the idea became prevalent, through the influence of the prophets, that God is near to everybody, and that everybody is worthy of approaching God. The relationship between God and Israel, as between parent and children, entitled everyone to pray to God without priestly mediation.[9]

Idelsohn believed this to be a critical perspective in the development of Jewish prayer: that every individual possessed the right to prayer. If any individual was called upon to pray for another, that person's stance was as a community member—from within—not as a mediator from above. Mediation did not lay in the hands of a professional priesthood (though priests eventually were to lead public sacrifices). As evidence of this, even women were selected to mediate in the name of the community.[10]

The mediator or intercessor was called *mithpallel*, literally "lead oneself to prayer." This was an especially gifted community member who possessed the charism of prayer leadership. The uniqueness of this role is reflected in the Hebrew appellation: for, whereas the act of leadership would normally presume a transitive verb, *mithpallel* indicates a reflexive form,[11] etymologically supporting the idea that such intercessors were not in a position of hierarchical leadership. Rather, as they were invested with the prayer of the community, they became the community, interceding on its own behalf.

Ma'amadot

Another witness to democratic prayer leadership in the history of Judaism is reflected in an institution which some believe to be of considerable influence in the development of the synagogue.[12] Each *ma'amadot*, in weekly rotations, sent representatives to the Temple to "stand by" the priests and Levites during the daily sacrifices. Since only a representative group (*anshe ma'amadot*) was allowed to attend, the rest of the *ma'amadot* "stood by" at home where, in union with their representatives in Jerusalem, they fasted, prayed, and read those sections of the Torah which related to sacrifice.[13] This ancient institution further reflects a democratic perspective on prayer leadership which was to influence the emergence of Christian ministries in general and the cantor in particular.

The *ma'amadot* (literally "standing men" or "bystanders") was a Second Temple division of the Israelites into twenty-four groups or watches.

Sheliach tsibbur

With the gradual development of the synagogue, a central core of prayer and ritual emerged. Although no single text of these prayers existed and diverse practices occurred side by side, we can yet speak with some certainty about a core of *shema, amidah,* and word in the pre-Christian synagogue.[14] These were ordinarily the constitutive elements of synagogue worship at the time of Christ.

Concurrent with the gradual standardization of this service, we can recognize a phenomenon which prepares the way for specifically "musical" ministries in another age. Because of the unique Jewish perspective on prayer leadership, the execution of the synagogue service was not relegated to an ordained or permanent clergy,[15] and through Talmudic (c. 200-500 CE) and early Geonic (c. 500-1000 CE) times, volunteers functioned as leaders of the service. Such a volunteer was already in the oldest sources called *sheliach tsibbur* (literally "messenger of the people").[16] These volunteers were chosen by the elder of the synagogue, the *rosh ha-knesset* or *archisynagogos*: a kind of superintendent who was responsible for overseeing the worship and maintaining order.[17] The volunteers, who could be any member of the congregation, were responsible for reciting the *amidah*, leading the *shema*, declaiming the Scriptures, and improvising prayers as they were needed.

Interestingly enough, the role of the assembly was never usurped by this messenger, who did not substitute for the action of the community. Nor was the intercession of the *sheliach tsibbur* necessarily more effective because of any personal piety.

> Rather, it was significant and potent because he had been delegated by the community to serve as its spokesman. God would listen to him because God was committed to the covenant of Israel. Nevertheless, it did not hurt if the community chose a man of exemplary piety and charism to represent it.[18]

Although it was true that anyone could be called upon as emissary, the fact that this action was regarded with such esteem eventually influenced the development of standards for selection of such leadership. A list of qualifications, for example, was fixed by Rabbi Judah ben Illai in the second century CE, which required the emissary to be

> . . . a man who has heavy family obligations, who has not enough to meet them, who has to struggle for a livelihood but who nonetheless keeps his house clean, who has an attractive

appearance, is humble, pleasant to and liked by people, who has a sweet voice and musical ability, who is well versed in the scriptures, capable of preaching, conversant with the halakah and haggadah and who knows all the prayers and benedictions by heart.[19]

With increasing frequency vocal ability became a determining factor in selecting the honorary precentor. Idelsohn goes so far as to admit that a sweet voice was regarded as the "most essential element,"[20] quoting in support of this position a famous rabbinic passage which considers a sweet voice to be a "heavenly gift, bestowed upon a person . . . to inspire the people to devotion."[21] The gift of a fine voice more and more obliged a community member to be the *sheliach tsibbur*.[22]

Eventually the tension between piety and performance surfaced: a tension still reflected in the *Shulhan Arukh* from the fifteenth century, which comments: "If there is a choice between an old man with a sweet voice but who is an ignoramus and a young boy of only thirteen years of age, possessing no sweet voice, but who understands what he reads, the boy is to be preferred."[23] Such preference faded in practice, however, and vocal ability increasingly became a determinative factor in this selection.

This emphasis on performance skills was accompanied by two other important developments. First, with the destruction of the Temple and the rise of the synagogue as the worship center in Judaism, there followed a predictable complexification of the synagogue liturgy. This is well reflected in the growing desire on the part of the sages to standardize developing prayer forms.[24] This tendency was rendered even less intelligible by a gradual decline in the knowledge of Hebrew among the general populace during the Talmudic period.

A second factor contributing to the demise of the volunteer precentor was the gradual amplification of existing prayers with intricate poetic forms known as *piyyutim*. Such forms emerged, at least in part, as a reaction to Novella 146 promulgated under Emperor Justinian (+ 565), which prohibited scriptural exegesis and midrashic homilies in the synagogue. To circumvent this law, the Jews introduced "didactic homiletic poetry as substitutes for exegesis within the liturgy."[25]

Thus, with increased emphasis on musical skill as the *sine qua non* of honorary precentorship, the growing complexification of worship (accentuated by a decline in the knowledge of Hebrew), and the gradual introduction of *piyyutim*, it is small wonder that by the sixth century CE there appeared the professional *sheliach tsibbur*. The natural choice for this role ordinarily seems to have been the previously mentioned *hazzan ha-knesset* who was constantly present in the synagogue, traditionally responsible for safeguarding the sacred scrolls,[26] and who was already called upon to chant portions of the service by special request.[27] This transformation of *hazzan ha-knesset* to permanent *sheliach tsibbur* was not, however, simply an act of expediency since the outstanding virtue and popularity of many leading *hazzanim* of the period made them the obvious choice.

The Christian Tradition

These developments within Judaism help us to contextualize the emergence of the cantor within Christianity. Although canonical recognition of the cantor does not occur until the mid-fourth century CE,[28] there is scattered but substantial evidence from earlier periods that enables us to plot this development in a framework not unlike that of Judaism. Questions of democratic prayer leadership, tensions between piety and performance, and the gradual complexification of worship all contribute to the emergence of this recognized ministry even before its Jewish counterpart.

New Testament Considerations

The difficulty in projecting anything about liturgy or liturgical ministries in the primitive period—and project is all one can due—is due, in large part, to the limited and ambiguous information at our disposal concerning worship at this time. We know that "official separation between Judaism and Christianity did not take place until the end of the first century and was instigated primarily by Judaism, not Christianity."[29] Consequently the early church continued to worship in a Jewish context with some continuity of form, place, and ministry. On the other hand,

> The irruption of the eschaton, which was already taking place in the old aeon, made it impossible simply to adopt the worship of Judaism. Not only had Jesus himself breached and abrogated the traditional cultic order, a fact that the primitive community could not escape; it was the present reality of God's eschatological activity that demanded new forms of worship.[30]

Consequently, this period was at once one of continuity and disruption.

Aware of the ambiguity of this period, I nevertheless believe that the form of volunteer prayer leadership which crystallized in the *sheliach tsibbur* was not only well known to Jewish-Christians but was also so resonant with their emerging images of ministry that it could not easily be rejected. Intimacy with the one whom Jesus called Abba was the invitation and privilege of every baptized believer, and such an intimacy would by its very nature seem to predicate essentially democratic forms of prayer leadership, parallel to the *sheliach tsibbur*. Such a contention is even more plausible when considering the primitive community's acquaintance with such a role. The early Christians were continuous and visible members of the synagogue after the resurrection and would consequently have been led in prayer by such precentors. Furthermore, the New Testament gives evidence that Jesus, as well as Paul, assumed such a role.

The *birkat ha-minim*, the malediction directed towards the "Nazarenes" which was added to the *amidah* in the last decades of the first century, substantiates the early communities' continued visibility in the synagogue service.[31] To have made such an expansion of this central statutory prayer was a dramatic measure which is well explained by the continued attendance of Christians at the synagogue service. Their presence is corroborated by the New Testament, which often depicts the members of the early community within the synagogue. Paul, Silas, and Barnabas often frequented this institution,[32] and the content of their preaching, coupled with a presumed fervor of delivery, certainly could have been prototypical of that which precipitated the introduction of the *birkat ha-minim*.

All the more should this presence be accepted as usual in light of the precedent set by Jesus. All four Gospels record Jesus teaching in the synagogue.[33] Furthermore, the synoptics explicitly cast Jesus in the role of the *sheliach tsibbur* when he is in the synagogue of Nazareth: invited by the *archisynagogos* to read and preach, while attended by the *hazzan ha-knesset* who ministered the scroll.

> He came to Nazareth where he had been reared; and entering the synagogue on the Sabbath as he was in the habit of doing, he stood up to do the reading. When the book of the Prophet Isaiah was handed him, he unrolled the scroll and found the passage where it was written, "The spirit of the Lord is upon

me . . ." Rolling up the scroll, he gave it back to the assistant [*hazzan ha-knesset*] and sat down. (Lk 4:16-20)

It is highly unlikely that this story and its parallels would have been retold if the Christian community had been ill-disposed toward the synagogue. Wolfgang Schrage, commenting on the New Testament attitude toward this institution, remarks that

> there are only a few instances where one may detect alienation from what is done in the synagogue, especially by the synagogal authorities. Closer analysis shows that it is not the institution itself which is the target of criticism and attack; it is the misuse of the institution by the scribes and pharisees.[34]

It could finally be said that a Christian continuance of the *sheliach tsibbur* is supported by the underlying theological perspective of this role which was so resonant with emerging Christianity. Implicit in the service of the *sheliach tsibbur* was the belief that each individual had access to God through prayer, and so the community was never distanced from the prayer action. This implicit theological tenet was carried to the extreme of disqualifying for synagogal use

> any formula which addressed the congregation in the "you" style, since anyone who employs such a formula is, as it were, excluding himself from the congregation. The prayer leader of the synagogue is not an officiating "minister" apart from the people and elevated over them. He is rather their "emissary" . . . and for this reason he is obliged to refrain from any expression which would be interpreted as if he were disassociating himself from the congregation.[35]

In primitive Christianity as well, no matter how the disciples might have rejected some elements of Judaism, it would have been difficult to reject this concept of ministry which was so central to their Semitic consciousness and resonant with the spirit of emerging Christianity.

A similar perspective in prayer leadership is articulated by Paul, who emphasizes that any leadership in psalms, sermons, revelations, gifts of tongues, or interpretations must be for the *common good*. Paul further emphasizes the need for intelligibility in communal gatherings, preferring prophecy to tongues:

> Seek eagerly after love. Set your hearts on spiritual gifts— above all, the gift of prophecy. He who speaks in a tongue is

not talking to men but to God. No one understands him
because he utters mysteries in the Spirit. The prophet on the
other hand speaks to men for their upbuilding, their encouragement, their consolation. He who speaks in a tongue builds
up himself, but he who prophesies edifies the church. (1 Cor
14:1-4)

This passage is reminiscent of the rabbinic requirement that the *sheliach tsibbur* be capable of clear and intelligible declamation.[36] Paul's writings on this point are consistent with the traditions of *mithpallel, ma'amadot,* and *sheliach tsibbur,* articulating a theological frame consonant with the continuation of a similar style of prayer leadership in the Christian community. Although it is true that the forms of Jewish worship eventually gave way to distinctive Christian cult, the underlying principle of volunteer prayer leadership, exercised in a manner which we would consider "musical," continued.

The Christian Transformation of the Sheliach Tsibbur

Having posited this historical-theological underpinning for the continuation of something like the *sheliach tsibbur* in primitive Christianity, it remains for us to see how such a counterpart might have served the emerging cult and then to specify how such a generic service of prayer leadership could have led eventually to a distinctly musical ministry. Since the *sheliach tsibbur* was less an office than a action, less an instituted ministry than an occasion to serve the assembly, it is possible that any prayer leadership required in the primitive community could have been fulfilled by one so selected. This projection would seem to be supported by the silence of the New Testament sources on the identity of the leader of prayer. Although we know, for example, that the community gave thanks over bread and wine from the earliest times,[37] we are never told who presided or whether such presidency was continuously invested in one individual. As Raymond Brown summarizes:

> The only thing of which we can be reasonably sure is that
> someone must have presided at the Eucharistic meals, and
> that those who participated acknowledged his right to preside. How one got the right to preside and whether it endured
> beyond a single instance we do not know; but a more plausible substitute for the chain theory is the thesis that sacramental "powers" were part of the mission of the Church and

that there were diverse ways in which the Church designated individuals to exercise those powers—the essential element always being Church or community consent (which was tantamount to ordination).[38]

Such an evaluation of the New Testament evidence (or lack thereof) with regard to eucharistic presidency in the primitive community supports the existence of a style of prayer leadership consistent with that of the *sheliach tsibbur*.

This phenomenon of a prayer-action led by an unspecified minister is the rule for the primitive community, and so we know that some speak in tongues (1 Cor 14:2), some prophesy (1 Cor 14:3), some interpret (1 Cor 14:5), and others respond "Amen" to another's thanksgiving (1 Cor 14:16). Furthermore, some "sing" (Eph 5:19, Col 3:16), whereas others read (Justin, 1 *Apol.* 76.3).[39] What is distinctive in each of these references is that no office is connected with these prayer-actions. We know that there were prayers, songs, and readings, but we do not know who led them. This consistent lack of evidence, coupled with the previously discussed wide-ranging acquaintance of the primitive community with the *sheliach tsibbur* in Jewish worship, plus the very acceptance of such a role by Jesus and Paul in the synagogue, suggests that such volunteer prayer leadership continued in the emerging Christian cult.[40]

Towards a Distinctive Musical Ministry

To say that some form of the *sheliach tsibbur* continued in Christian worship is one thing, but to progress from this volunteer prayer leader to the cantor as recognized member of the minor clergy is quite another. This move requires, first of all, a demonstration of music's place in Christian worship. Second, it means establishing that this musical component acquired an independent existence in worship and needed a specially designated person to perform it. Finally, it is necessary to explain how this specially designated individual assumed a continuing and canonically recognized place in the church.

New Testament Period

The ambiguity surrounding questions of musical leadership in primitive worship is parallel to the obscure place of music in such worship. Numerous attempts have been made to study musical aspects of the New Testament period.[41] As previously noted, however, the difficulty with attempting to isolate or study any musical elements in this era stems from the fact that music was not an independent element in the emerging cult. Rather, what we in the twentieth century might consider music was, at the onset of Christianity, part of a broader auditory environment which only centuries latter assumed an independent identity and spawned musical ministries properly speaking. For the ancients, "singing and speaking are very close ... the two verbs themselves are coupled or used interchangeably, and in numerous literary descriptions, we cannot tell whether speech or song is in question."[42] This ambiguity exists in ancient Judaism where "to say" and "to sing" are so interchangeable that it is almost impossible to distinguish between them.[43] Joseph Gelineau summarizes:

> Hebrew and Greek have no separate word for music. The frontier between singing and speaking was far less precise. As soon as speech turned to poetry, or when public or ceremonial speaking was involved, rhythmic and melodic features were incorporated which today would be classified as musical, or at least pre-musical."[44]

To believe that in poetic or ceremonial situations speech migrated towards the musical is especially understandable in a Jewish milieu where the auditory was of singular importance in revelation. Walter Ong suggests a primacy accorded to the word of God in Judaism, and "thus in some mysterious way to sound itself."[45] It is the word which instigates the created order (Gn 1:3ff.); it is through the word that God summons Abraham (Gn 22:1) and Jacob (Gn 31:11); and it is through obedience to the voice of God that the Israelites become a holy nation (Ex 19:5). This auricular sensitivity reaches a particular intensity in the prophets, where the word of God is not an inert record but clearly a living, on-going reality.[46] Such sensitivity is more than continued in the New Testament, where

> "the Word of God ... [is] even more the center of its teaching ... As in no other religion the Word here is the proper name of a person ... It is his divine name. The visually grounded titles such as the "light of light" ... are second level designations, less meaningful than "word."[47]

Further New Testament evidence of this aural sensitivity is found in the fragments, couplets, and stanzas that have been identified at one time or another as hymnic.⁴⁸ Scholarly opinion has by no means converged around this material, and Gerhard Delling is typical in his caution that any identification of New Testament material as hymnic "must remain hypothetical." He continues: "The pieces in the New Testament which take the form of praise are in general so little controlled by any clearly discernable laws that for the most part judgment to their character as hymns can only claim limited validity."⁴⁹ Yet for all of his caution, even Delling accepts "many hymn-like passages in primitive Christian literature"⁵⁰ and concedes that some New Testament passages (e.g., 1 Tim 3:16) are plainly old hymns.⁵¹

Concerning the New Testament period, therefore, we must conclude that the existence of distinctive songs or musical excursions in the cult are only hypothetical. However, in the light of what we have already demonstrated about Jewish auricular sensitivity, the tradition of cantillating statutory elements in the synagogue,⁵² the Pauline admonitions to address one another "in psalms and hymns and inspired songs" (Eph 5:19; see Col 3:16), and the tenuous but extensive hymnic material in the New Testament,⁵³ we are compelled to agree with Gelineau that there must have been an "intensely lyrical quality in the life of the Apostolic Church."⁵⁴ Such pervasive lyricism, however, is yet to be distinguished as an independent element in the cultic life and, consequently, presumed no specially designated individual for its execution.

Second to Third Century

It is only in the late second and into the third century that one finds clear references to singing in the Christian assembly. In the apocryphal *Acts of Paul* (c. 190)⁵⁵ we find a reference to the "singing of David's psalms and hymns" in the context of the assembly of believers.⁵⁶ This is the first of many texts that clearly speak of psalm-singing.

Tertullian (+ c. 225) makes numerous references to singing in the assembly, mentioning in *De Anima* that "the Scriptures are read and psalms are sung, sermons are given and prayers offered."⁵⁷ He also suggests that married people should challenge one another in psalm-singing,⁵⁸ that the more fervent usually added "alleluia" to their prayers "and those kinds of psalms to which the company may respond by using the closing words,"⁵⁹ and at lucenarium "each is asked to stand and sing as he is able a hymn to God, either from Holy Scripture, or through his own improvising."⁶⁰

What is noteworthy in these passages is the lack of suggestion of any permanent musician or cantor. Rather, one gets the impression, especially from the *Apologeticum*, that a volunteer style of prayer leadership is operative, much like that of the *sheliach tsibbur*. The responsorial element in *De Oratione* seems indisputable,[61] and so presumes some leadership role.

Clement of Alexandria (+ 215) attests to the usage of "psalms and hymns during meals and before bed,"[62] and Cyprian (+ 258) similarly speaks of psalmody at the evening meal.[63] Origen employs wide-ranging musical imagery—for example, referring to Christ as the "chorus leader"[64]—and although he does not specifically mention psalm-singing,[65] he does speak of singing praise to God in a worship context and of addressing "hymns of praise to the supreme God alone and to his only-begotten Son."[66]

These third-century references, together with a substantial amount of musical imagery in other patristic sources, seem to sustain the illusion of Gelineau's "lyricism," but now with clearer references to what was sung and when singing was appropriate. Here again, however, we have no mention of any established role or office of singer. Hippolytus (+ c. 236) has informed us that there were deacons, subdeacons, and readers;[67] Cornelius of Rome (+ 253) in his letter of 251 to Fabius attests to the presence of acolytes, exorcists, and doorkeepers;[68] *Didaskalia* (c. 225) knows of deaconesses;[69] and Tertullian considers widows to be part of the clergy.[70] Yet in none of these listings, church orders, or correspondence do we hear of the singer, psalmist, or cantor.

One exception could be an epitaph from Hadrian in Bythinia which Leclercq claims "is certainly anterior to the peace of the church, probably appearing in the second or third century."[71] The epitaph commemorates an eighteen year old man who was known for "chanting the praises of the most high God, and training all the faithful to chant the sacred psalms and the reading of the holy books."[72] If this epitaph originated in the second or third century, it could be our earliest known reference to someone leading the assembly in psalm singing. Leclercq's contention, however, that this "young cantor held the offices of *psaltes* and *anagnostes*"[73] is overdrawn. The epitaph speaks of no office but only of action, not of a "chanter" but of "chanting." Also, the epitaph attests to the intimate relationship between singing and reading, between psalms and lections—and not, as Leclercq suggests, because in this era there was "not always sufficient hierarchical personnel to fulfill the diverse functions of the church,"[74] but because the community as yet saw little distinction between the sung and the publicly declaimed. As such, a division between singers and public speakers, or specifically between cantors and readers, is as yet unnecessary. Reader was the only designation known for those responsible for the cantillated, be that psalms or lessons.[75]

Fourth Century and Beyond

This lack of differentiation of cantor from reader continued for many centuries. Ambrose (+ 397) knows of the lector singing psalms in worship,[76] and Augustine (+ 430) gives an account of a lector singing psalms in the Church of North Africa.[77] In his *Confessions* Augustine relates the story of Athanasius, bishop of Alexandria (+ 373), who "had the reader of the psalm modulate his voice so little that it was more like speaking than singing."[78] Sozomen (early fifth century) reported that Marcian was both a lector and a cantor,[79] Victor of Vita (late fifth century) reported that a reader was killed with an arrow through the throat while singing the alleluia during an attack of Arian Vandals,[80] and the tenth-century Typikon of Constantinople indicates that both the reader and the psalmist are responsible for chanting portions of the liturgy.[81] It is natural that the reader should assume a prominent role in leading the singing, especially the psalms, since the psalms were initially considered a prophetic book to be read, and all public reading of Scripture presumed what we might consider a "musical" rendering.[82] Numerous other texts suggest that others besides readers led the singing. Athanasius appointed a deacon to sing when his church was being attacked by Arian soldiers;[83] *Apostolic Constitutions* indicates that a "choir" of boys sang the Kyrie in the presence of the assembly;[84] and a fifth-century epitaph records that one Jonathan, a Jewish convert, was an archdeacon who sang the Songs of David.[85]

In spite of this fusion of roles, however, a distinctive musical ministry finally emerged in the fourth century as evidenced by a series of independent texts. Eusebius of Caesarea (+ c. 340), for example, in one of his commentaries on the psalms notes the presence of the psalm-singer (*psalmodias*).[86] The most important references are the canons of the Council of Laodicea (c. 344-360): "No other shall sing in the assembly except the canonical singers, who ascend to the ambo and chant from a parchment" (can. 15);

"The readers and singers have no right to wear the orarium, or to read or sing thus vested" (can. 23); "No one of the clergy, from presbyters to deacons, and so on in ecclesiastical rank from subdeacons, readers, singers, exorcists, doorkeepers or any of the order of ascetics, ought to enter a tavern" (can. 24).[87]

Another important text is the forged recension of the Ignatian Epistles (middle of the fourth century) which gives the following list of ministers: presbyters, deacons, subdeacons, readers, psalm singers, door keepers, grave diggers, exorcists, confessors, deaconesses, virgins, and widows.[88] The *Apostolic Constitutions* make numerous references to the "singer": "Further we do not allow the rest of the clergy to baptize, that is, for example, neither readers nor singers nor porters"; "Let us pray for . . . the readers, singers, virgins, widows, and orphans"; "for these are your high priests, as the presbyters are your priests, and your present deacons instead of levites; as also your readers, your singers, your porters, your deaconesses, your widows, your virgins, and your orphans."[89]

Another possible testimony to the existence of a singer during this period is the *Apocalypse of Paul*, which could date from the last decades of the fourth century,[90] and includes the following citation:

> There was standing alongside the altar one whose face shone like the sun and who held in his hands a psaltery and harp and who sang saying, "Halleluia!" . . . And I asked the angel and said, "Who, sir, is there with such great power?" And the angel said to me, "This is David."[91]

Although not providing an explicit reference to the cantor or psalmist, the metaphoric reference to David could be interpreted as such.

Cyril of Jerusalem (+ 386) makes a reference to psalms (*psalmodoi*) in his catechetical lectures which date from around the year 348.[92] This might be a reference to a specific office and not simply the act of singing psalms.[93] In the *Mystagogical Catechesis* of Cyril, ordinarily dated toward the end of his life, there is another reference: this time to the "chanter" (*psallontos*) who invited the neophytes to sing the psalm "Taste and see."[94] In the last decades of the fourth century there are also references from John Chrysostom (+ 407),[95] Jerome (+ 420),[96] and the Third Council of Carthage (c. 397), which notes that lectors and psalmists are clerics.[97]

It is notable that this first evidence of a distinctively musical ministry occurs in a century of such ecclesiastical upheaval and expansion. It was the age of Constantine (+ 337) and the Edict of Milan (313) which brought newly won legality to Christianity: the church flourished, property was restored, imperial loans were inaugurated, and clergy were exempted from public office.[98]

As this was a time of ecclesiastical expansion, so was it one of ritual complexification. The eucharistic perspective of *Apostolic Tradition* (chapter 4), with its servant Christology and pneumatic ecclesiology in which the community was identified with the servant-son, gave way to a developing Roman prayer which emphasized the presence of Christ as priest and victim, downplayed the role of the community, and presented an almost monophysitic Christology in court rhetoric. This change in liturgical perspective and evolution in liturgical language in the west is mirrored by euchological language in the east which increasingly emphasizes fear and awe.[99]

Concurrent with such linguistic developments, the fourth century also generated new canonical evidence (like the above cited canons of Laodicea) which increasingly limited ritual functions to specified and fixed offices. The episcopacy assumed new civil as well as ecclesiastical importance, and bishops acquired the accompanying imperial trappings from their civil counterparts: the *lorum, mappula, campagi, camalaucum,* and probably the gold ring.[100] These and numerous other political-ecclesiastical developments accentuated the clerical distinction that increasingly solidified after the Constantinian recognition of Christianity.[101]

Thus there develops a situation not dissimilar to that of Judaism: worship becomes more complex, fewer volunteers or non-specialists are capable of executing the various functions with ease, and consequently individuals are selected to fulfill such functions on a regular basis in light of some particular charism or training. In the process, action becomes office.

With the rise of the Christian office of cantor, as in Judaism, the state of the art flourished. From simple chants, cantillated readings, and antiphonal invitations there eventually emerged a body of solo literature so above the ability of the congregation that eventually no musical invitation was even extended to them by the medieval cantors. Intricacies in monophonic development, embellished melismas, and ornate improvisations moved Augustine to remark, "He who sings a *jubilus* speaks no words, but it is a song of joy without words; it is the voice of a heart dissolved in joy which tries as far as possible to express the feeling, even if it does not understand the meaning."[102] Moved by the beauty of the art, however, Augustine was yet cautious of such bravura, and wrote in his *Confessions*:

> When I call to mind the tears shed at the songs of the church ... and how even now I am moved not by singing but by what is sung ... then I acknowledge the great utility of this custom ... Yet, when it happens to me to be more moved by the singing than by what is sung, I confess myself to have sinned criminally, and then I would have rather not have heard the singing at all.[103]

Eventually the church appeared to be moved as much by the singing than by what was sung. As in Judaism, the pleasant voice, the *jubilus*, the stirring art prevailed. So the Christian cantor came unknowingly to abandon the tradition of the *sheliach tsibbur*: no longer emissary from within the community but performer, over and above the congregation—substituting and inspiring, but seldom leading the assembly at prayer. Essentially the cantor in Christianity forsook the role of prayer leader for that of musician. It is such a development that we must now reverse.

Notes

1. On the difficulties in employing language of "music" in discussions of early Christian worship, see the previous chapter on "The Auditory Environment of Emerging Christian Worship."

2. See, for example, Erich Reimer's study of the term "cantor" and its usage in *Handwörterbuch der musikalischen Terminologie*, ed. Hans Heinrich Eggebrecht (Wiesbaden: Steiner, 1978), s.v. "musicus-cantor." As Reimer notes, the Latin *cantor* is used to designed the psalmist only by the second half of the fifth century CE. I am grateful to Peter Jeffery for this reference.

There is no evidence of the designation *psaltes* before the Council of Laodicea (c. 344-360), or of *psaltanagnostes* before Gennadius of Constantinople (+ 471). Where *psalmodos* appears in patristic sources before Laodicea—for example, in Clement of Alexandria (+ 215), *Protrepticus* 8, or Origen (+ 254) *Contra Haereses* 8.17—it refers to David and not to any liturgical functionary of the early church. See G.W.H. Lampe, *A Patristic Greek Lexicon* (Oxford: Clarendon Press, 1961) 1540.

3. Alexander Schmemann, *Introduction to Liturgical Theology*, 2nd ed. (New York: St. Vladimir's Seminary Press, 1975) 127.

4. Ismar Elbogen, *Der judische Gottesdienst* (Leipzig: G. Fock, 1913) 485-492. This confusion is probably due to the fact that the *hazzan ha-knesset* eventually assumed the cantorial responsibilities in the synagogue.

5. Leo Landman, *The Cantor: An Historical Perspective* (New York: Yeshiva University, 1972) 4.

6. In the tables of El Amarna, *hazanuti* refers to those governors stationed by the Egyptian conquerors in the occupied cities of Palestine according to Abraham Millgram, *Jewish Worship* (Philadelphia: The Jewish Publication Society of America, 1971) 518.

7. These include the carrying out of physical punishments prescribed by the law courts (B. Makkoth 23a), teaching children (B. Shabbath 11a), and serving as custodian of the synagogue building (J. Sukkah 3.3).

8. Elbogen, *Der judische Gottesdienst* 486.

9. A.Z. Idelsohn, *Jewish Music in Its Historical Development* (New York: Shocken Books, 1967 [1929]) 101-102.

10. Ibid. 102; also, Bernadette Brooten who, although not specifically treating the role of the *sheliach tsibbur* (to be discussed below), does comment: "Seen in the larger context of women's participation in the life of the synagogue, there is no reason not to take the titles [archēgos {leader}, elder, mother of the synagogue, and priest] as functional, nor to assume that women heads or elders of synagogues had radically different functions than men heads or elders of synagogues. Of the functions outlined for each title, there are none which women could not have carried out." Bernadette Brooten, *Women Leaders in the Ancient Synagogue*, Brown Judaic Studies 36, ed. Jacob Neusner et al. (Chicago: Scholars Press, 1982) 149. That this perspective was to change radically is illustrated by Rav's harsh statement recorded in the Talmud: "The voice of a women is indecency" (B. Berakoth 24a).

11. Idelsohn, *Jewish Music* 102.

12. On the various theories for the emergence of the synagogue, see above, p. 19, n. 29.

13. S. Zeitlin, "The Origin of the Synagogue," *Studies in the Early History of Judaism*, vol. 1 (New York: Ktav Publishing House, 1973) 77.

14. Joseph Heinemann, *Prayer in the Talmud* (Berlin and New York: Walter De Gruyter, 1977) especially chapter 1.

15. "It is true that the priest is the first to read from the Torah, but it would seem that this custom derives from the priest's ancient role as teacher of Torah to the people. There is, however, no *halakah* which grants him preferential privileges in conducting public worship, such as leading the *amidah* or the reading of the *shema*. Nor is being a priest enumerated among the desirable characteristics which a prayer leadership should possess (as in Taanith 3.2)." Heinemann, *Prayer in the Talmud* 117, n. 30.

16. Elbogen, *Der judische Gottesdienst* 488.

17. Ibid. 483.

18. Gerald Blidstein, "Sheliach Tsibbur: Historical and Phenomenological Observations," *Tradition* (Summer 1971) 71.

19. B. Taanith 16a.

20. Idelsohn, *Jewish Music* 105.
21. Peskita Rabbathi 23, as cited in Idelsohn, *Jewish Music* 501, n. 8.
22. See Pesikta de-Rav Kahana 97a, as cited in Hanoch Avenary, "Music: The Emergence of Synagogue Song," *EJ* 12:571.
23. Shulkan Arukh, Orah Hayim 53:4-5, as cited in Millgram, *Jewish Worship* 520.
24. See Heinemann, *Prayer in the Talmud* 37-68; also, Lawrence Hoffman, *The Canonization of the Synagogue Service* (Notre Dame: University of Notre Dame Press, 1979).
25. Eric Werner, "The Music of Post Biblical Judaism," in *Ancient and Oriental Music*, ed. Egon Wellesz, vol. 1 of *The New Oxford History of Music* (London: Oxford University Press, 1957) 324. In another place Werner suggests that Novella 146 was no more than an apparent cause for this development and believes that the Jews were primarily stimulated by the developments of Christian hymnody and weary of the dull settings of their own worship, *Sacred Bridge* 1:235.
26. Elbogen, *Der judische Gottesdienst* 485-486.
27. J. Berakoth 9.1.
28. Canons 15, 23 and 24 of the Council of Laodicea, cited on pp. 77-78.
29. Ferdinand Hahn, *The Worship of the Early Church* (Philadelphia: Fortress Press, 1973) 33.
30. Ibid. 35.
31. "The Birkath ha Minim makes it unmistakably clear that the Sages at Jamnia regarded Jewish Christians as a menace sufficiently serious to warrant a liturgical innovation. It worked simply, but effectively, as follows. In the synagogue service a man was designated to lead in the reciting of the Tefillah. As he approached the platform, where stood the ark containing the Scrolls of the Law, the congregation rose. The leader would recite the Benedictions and the congregation, finally, responded to these with the Amen. Anyone called upon to recite the Tefillah who stumbled on the 12th Benediction [the Birkath ha Minim] could easily be detected. Thus the Birkath ha Minim served the purpose of making any Christian who might be present in a synagogal service, conspicuous by the way in which he recited or glossed over this benediction." William Davies, *The Setting of the Sermon on the Mount* (Cambridge: University Press, 1964) 276. For a more recent discussion, see W. Horbury, "The Benediction of the Minim and Early Jewish Christian Controversy," *Journal of Theological Studies* 33 (1982) 19-61. As to whether or not this "malediction" was directed specifically or exclusively at Christians, see Reuven Kimelman, "*Birkat Haminim* and the Lack of Evidence for an Anti-Christian Prayer in Late Antiquity," *Jewish and Christian Self-Definition*, vol. 2: *Aspects of Judaism in the Graeco-Roman Period*, ed. E.P. Sanders, A.I. Baumgarten, and Alan Mendelson (London: SMC Press, 1980) 226-244, 392-403.

32. Paul and Barnabas: Acts 13:5, 13:14, 14:1; Paul and Silas: Acts 17:1, 17:10; Paul: Acts 17:17, 18:4, 18:19.

33. Mk 6:2; Mt 13:54; Lk 4:16; Jn 6:59; also, Matthew twice remarks that Jesus visited many synagogues throughout Galilee in 4:23 and 9:35.

34. Wolfgang Schrage, "Synagoge," *TDNT* 8:833.

35. Heinemann, *Prayer in the Talmud* 105.

36. B. Megillah 24b.

37. See, for example, 1 Cor 10:16-17, 11:23-24; Acts 2:42, etc.

38. Raymond Brown, *Priest and Bishop: Biblical Reflections* (New York: Paulist Press, 1970) 41-42.

39. 1 Timothy 4:13 and Revelation 1:3 might be earlier references to this action, which von Campenhausen and others project back to the earliest strata of Christian worship. Hans von Campenhausen, *The Formation of the Christian Bible* (Philadelphia: Fortress Press, 1977) 123.

40. Paul Bradshaw concurs that there was "an apparent continuation of the *sheliach tsibbur* in Christian worship," although Bradshaw does not agree that this would have been the model for leadership in the eucharistic practice of the early community. Paul Bradshaw, *Liturgical Presidency in the Early Church*, Grove Liturgical Study 36 (Nottingham, England: Grove Books, 1983) 8.

41. See above for the review of some of this literature, pp. 6, 80-81.

42. E. Lippman, "The Sources and Development of the Ethical View of Music in Ancient Greece," *The Musical Quarterly* 40 (1963) 195.

43. Herman L. Strack and Paul Billerbeck, *Kommentar zum Neuen Testament aus Talmud und Midrasch*, vol. 4 (Munich: C.H. Beck, 1922-1955) 394-395.

44. Joseph Gelineau, "Music and Singing in the Liturgy," *The Study of Liturgy*, ed. Cheslyn Jones et al., rev. ed. (New York: Oxford University Press, 1992) 497.

45. Walter Ong, *The Presence of the Word* (New Haven: Yale University Press, 1967) 12.

46. Ibid.

47. Ibid. 13; also the discussion of the auditory environment of the New Testament above, pp. 53-55.

48. For a review of the literature on this topic, see above, n. 37, pp. 20-21.

49. Delling, "Humnos," *TDNT* 8:500.

50. Gerhard Delling, *Worship in the New Testament*, trans. Percy Scott (Philadelphia: Westminster Press, 1962) 82.

51. Ibid. 88.

52. Avenary, "Music: The Emergence of Synagogue Song."

53. Ralph Martin comments: "Religious speech tends to be poetic in form; and meditation upon the person and place of Jesus Christ in the Church's cult is not expressed in a cold, calculating way, but becomes

rhapsodic and ornate" *Carmen Christi* (Cambridge: University Press, 1967) 19.

54. Gelineau, "Music and Singing in the Liturgy" 497.

55. Cited by Tertullian in *De Baptismo* 17, and so dated by Schubart and Schmidt as composed between 180-190 CE. See *Acta Pauli*, ed. and trans. Wilhelm Schubert and Carl Schmidt (Hamburg: J.J. Austin, 1936) 130. Schneemelcher suggests a similar date of composition in Edgar Hennecke, *New Testament Apocrypha*, vol. 2, ed. Wilhelm Schneemelcher, English trans. ed. R. Mcl. Wilson (Philadelphia: Westminster Press, 1976) 351. Quasten projects a date before 190 CE in Johannes Quasten, *Patrology*, vol. 1 (Utrecht and Antwerp: Spectrum Publishers, 1966) 313.

56. *Acta Pauli* 7.10 (Schubart and Schmidt, p. 50).

57. 9.4 (PL 2:2660 = CSEL 20:310); as this outline confirms that found in Justin Martyr 91 *Apol.* 67:3-5) with the exception of the element of psalm-singing, and whereas the palms were cantillated as were other scriptural readings, each according to its own mode, it is not inconceivable that psalm-singing was a part of Justin's service as well.

58. *Ad Uxorem* 2.9 (PL 1:1416-1417 = CSEL 70:124).

59. *De Oratione* 27.17 (PL 1:1301 = CSEL 20:198).

60. *Apologeticum* 39.18 (PL 1:540 = CSEL 69:95).

61. Whereas E.T. Moneta Caglio concludes that responsorial psalmody did not exist in the east much before the end of the third century, and was introduced into the west by Ambrose, this perspective is based on too sharp a distinction between responsorial forms that employed only a single word (e.g., "Alleluia") and those that employed phrases. See E.T. Moneta Caglio, *Lo Jubilus e le origini della salmodia responsoriale*, Jucunda Laudatio 14-15 (1976-1977) 5-30, 58-59.

62. *Stromata* 7.7 (PG 9:469 = GCS 3:37).

63. *Ad Donatum* 16 (PL 4:222-223 = CSEL 3:16).

64. *Chorostates* in *Contra Celsum* 5.33 (PG 11/1:1229 = SC 147:100).

65. Except for a reference to the one who recites "spiritual psalms" (*psalmous pneumatikous*) and sings to God in his heart, *In Ps.* 32.2 (PG 12:1304).

66. *Contra Celsum* 8.67 (PG 11/1:1618 = SC 150:328).

67. *Apostolic Tradition* 4; see, *La Tradition apostolique de Saint Hippolyte*, ed. Bernard Botte, Liturgiewissenschaftliche Quellen und Forschungen 39 (Münster: Aschendorff, 1963) 10.

68. Eusebius, *Ecclesiasticae Historiae* 6.43 (PG 2:621 = SC 41:156).

69. *Didaskalia* 2.26.6; see, *Didaskalia et Constitutiones Apostolorum*, ed. F.X. Funk, 2 vols. (Torino: Bottega d'Erasmo, 1964) 1:104.

70. *De Monogamia* 11.1 (PL 2:943 = CSEL 76:65).

71. Henri Leclercq, "Chantres," *Dictionnaire d'archéologie chrétienne et de liturgie*, vol. 3 (1914) 345.

72. Ibid.

73. Ibid.

74. Ibid.

75. *Apostolic Constitutions* (c. 380) appears to be breaking new ground when it indicates that someone besides the reader of the lessons should sing the psalms. *Apostolic Constitutions* 2.57.6 (Funk 1:161).

76. *Exc. Sat.* 1.61 (CSEL 73:241.1). For a more complete discussion of Ambrose's vocabulary in this matter, see Leeb, *Die Psalmodie bei Ambrosius* (Vienna: Herder, 1967) 41-52.

77. *In Ps.* 138 (PL 37:1784 = CCL 40:1990).

78. *Confessions* 10.33.50 (PL 32:800 = CSEL 33:364).

79. *Historia Ecclesiastica* 4.3 (PG 67:1116) = GCS 50:141).

80. *De Persecutione Vandalica* 1:13 (PL 58:497).

81. See *anagnostes* and *psaltes* in the liturgical index of Juan Mateos, *Le Typikon de la Grand Eglise*, Orientalia Christiana Analecta 166 (Rome: Pont. Institutum Studiorum Orientalium, 1963) 283 and 328.

82. Avenary, "Music: The Emergence of Synagogue Song" 577.

83. *Apologia de Fuga Sua* 24 (PG 25:676).

84. *Apostolic Constitutions* 8.6.4 (Funk 1:478); Egeria (c. 384) also makes reference to children singing the Kyrie in response to the deacon's invitation, *Ethérie: Journal de voyage*, trans. Hélène Pétré (Paris: Cerf, 1971) n. 24 = p. 192.

85. Eric Werner, "The Conflict between Hellenism and Judaism in the Music of the Early Church," *Hebrew Union College Annual* 20 (New York: Ktav Publishing House, 1968) 432; see Leclercq, "Chantres," for further epitaphic evidence, pp. 351-364.

86. *Ad Ps. 65* (PG 33:657-659).

87. *Canones Apostolorum et Conciliorum*, ed. H. Bruns (Torino: Bottega d'Erasmo, 1959) 75-76 (Mansi 2:567).

88. Pseudo-Ignatius, *Ad Antiochenos* 12 (PG 5:908).

89. *Apostolic Constitutions* 3.11.1 (Funk 1:200), 8.10.10 (Funk 1:490), and 2.26.3 (Funk 1:103) respectively. In a parallel to this last passage, *Didaskalia* does not mention readers and singers, but only "deacons, presbyters, widows, and orphans" 2.26.3 (Funk 1:102). For further references to the singer in *Apostolic Constitutions* see 8.12.43 (Funk 1:512); 8.13.14 (Funk 1:516); 8.28.8 (Funk 1:530); 8.31.2 (Funk 1:532); 8.47.26 (Funk 1:570); 8.47.43 (Funk 1:576); 8.47.69 (Funk 1:584).

90. R.P. Casey argues for a composition date around 388; the arguments are rehearsed in Everett Ferguson, "Psalm-Singing at the Eucharist: A Liturgical Controversy in the Fourth Century," *Austin Seminary Bulletin* 97 (1983) 58-60.

91. Translated by E. Best in *New Testament Apocrypha* 2:778.

92. PG 33:804.

93. This is the opinion of Brian Sparksman, in "The Minister of Music in the Western Church: A Canonical-Historical Study," unpublished

J.C.D. dissertation (Washington, DC: The Catholic University of America, 1981) 68-69. Unfortunately Sparksman does not distinguish clearly enough between the catechetical lectures offered earlier in Cyril's career and the *Mystagogical Catechesis* from the end of his life when discussing this terminology and the possible existence of the office of psalmist in Jerusalem at the end of the fourth century.

94. *Mystagogical Catechesis* 5.20 (PG 33:1124).

95. In his homily 36 on 1 Corinthians, which is difficult to date (but possibly from after 391), he mentions "the one who chants" (*ho psallon*) (PG 61:315).

96. In letter 52, written in 394, he mentions the *psaltes*. *Selected Letters of St. Jerome*, English trans. by F. A. Wright, The Loeb Classical Library (London: William Heinemann, Ltd., 1933) 202.

97. Canon 21 (Mansi 4:883-884).

98. See Eusebius, *Ecclesiasticae Historiae* 9.9 (PG 2:823 = SC 55:64), 10.2 (PG 2:845 = SC 55:79), 10.5 (PG 2:884 = SC 55:106), 10.6 (PG 2:892 = SC 55:110), 10.7 (PG 2:893 = SC 55:112).

99. See, for example, the Homilies of Cyril of Jerusalem (+ c. 386), John Chrysostom (+ 407) and especially Theodore of Mopsuestia (+ 428). For specific references to their works and a review of the literature on this topic, see Robert Taft, "The Liturgy of the Great Church: An Initial Synthesis of Structure and Interpretation on the Eve of Iconoclasm," *Dumbarton Oaks Papers* 34 (1980) nn. 110 and 113.

100. Theodor Klauser, "Der Ursprung der bischoflichen Insignien und Ehrenrechte," *Bonner Akademische Reden*, vol. 1, 2nd ed. (Krefeld: Scherpe, 1948) 11-13.

101. Bernard Cooke, *Ministry to Word and Sacraments* (Philadelphia: Fortress Press, 1976) 557.

102. *In Ps.* 99.4 (PL 37:1272 = CCL 39:1394).

103. 10.33.50 (PL 32:800 = CSEL 33:264).

4
Martin Luther:
A Model Pastoral Musician

Introduction

"NEXT TO THE WORD OF GOD, THE NOBLE ART OF MUSIC IS THE GREATEST treasure in the world."[1] Such unabashed enthusiasm for the muse might not seem surprising had it sprung from the pen of Johann Sebastian Bach or even some new breed pastoral musician. That these words originated with Martin Luther, however, could catch the uninformed by surprise. Yet this statement does not exist as singular testimony to Luther's propensity for hyperbole, but rather as a summation of theological and pastoral pursuits—writing, composing, and celebrating—which affirm his belief that next to the word of God, music is the greatest treasure of all.

Many fascinating aspects of the musical Luther could occupy us here. A biographical sketch of the Reformer's own training and performing, for example, could supply us with valuable background for understanding why he composed the way he did. On the other hand, the study of Luther's perception of music as gift, the primacy he gives to hearing, and his belief in the close relationship between music and word could provide sufficient basis for sketching a theology of music in Lutheran mode.[2] What seems more valuable, however, and what in some way touches upon these others, is a brief study of Luther as pastoral musician: as a proponent and composer of music from the people and for the people, as especially evidenced in his chorales.[3] It is hoped that such an investigation might not only increase our appreciation for this monumental figure, but also inform and guide contemporary composition, that it might achieve a similar integrity and success.

Although a single essay does not allow for an extensive study of Luther's music, it is nonetheless hoped that the following progression might at least introduce those central elements which underline Luther's pastoral musicianship. First, we will briefly consider the main melodic and textual sources for the chorales which, in themselves, seem to indicate a pastoral perspective. Second, we will survey some of the specific compositional elements of Luther's music and discover how these served his fundamental attentiveness to the congregation. Third, we will attempt a similar analysis of the texts. Finally, having theoretically summarized some of the pastoral elements in Luther's chorales, we will attempt to concretize our analysis through a brief study of the chorale "A Might Fortress" (*Ein feste Burg*, LBW 228 and 229).[4]

The Sources

In a helpful overview of the sources of Lutheran Church lieder, Friedrich Blume writes:

> Luther and his co-workers consciously made use of pre-Reformation traditions in their creation of a repertory of German lieder ... Liturgical chants of the Catholic church, pre-Reformation German sacred lieder, and German folk and fraternal songs were the sources of the largest number of texts and melodies; they were assimilated in extremely different ways. Both text and melody might be used, in which case the text was merely "improved in a Christian manner" (i.e. a manner suitable to the Reformation) or simply translated from Latin into the vernacular; or new texts might be written for melodies whose special popularity made their fullest use desirable; or—vice versa—texts that had been taken over or translated might be supplied with new melodies or melodies originally associated with other texts; or, finally, texts and melodies could pass through several of these methods of revision and combination one after another. The supply of lieder newly composed or only loosely based upon older examples, though significant in quality, was small in number.[5]

Given this perspective, it is not surprising that there is little clarity about what it means to call Martin Luther a composer of church music.[6] This confusion is not diminished when limiting the discussion to Luther's chorales. There are at least thirty-seven texts ascribed to Luther and an even larger number of tunes.[7] Furthermore, some authors include one or more of the Mass chants (e.g., the *Gloria in excelsis*) in their listing of chorales, whereas others do not. For the purpose of our discussion here, we will limit ourselves to the thirty-seven texts ascribed to Luther in the critical edition of his works, and repeated in the English edition of his complete works.[8] Furthermore, we will forgo any discussion to the variant melodies of these chorales: all of our references will be to the first tune listed in the Weimar edition.

Konrad Ameln provides a helpful, introductory outline of the sources or "inspirations" of Luther's chorales.[9] The first type of sources are what Ameln calls the "Gregorian chorale," or those Latin chants from the ordinary and proper of the Latin Mass which punctuated the liturgical year.[10] One example is the Pentecost hymn or sequence entitled "Come Holy Ghost" (*Veni Sancte Spiritus*) which served as the basis for Luther's hymn of the same name (*Kom Heyliger Geist*, LBW 163). Second, Luther relied upon popular unison hymns of the Middle Ages called *cantios*.[11] It was a *cantio* entitled "In the Midst of Life We Are in Death" (*Media Vita in Morte Summus*) which the Reformer shaped into a chorale of the same name (*Mitten wyr im leben sind*, LBW 350). Third, there are the religious folk songs which Ameln considers to be the most powerful sources for the chorales, though these are also the most difficult to trace.[12] "All Praise to Thee, O Jesus Christ" (*Gelobet seystu Jhesu Christ*, LBW 48), for example, is known to be based upon a popular folk hymn of fourteenth-century origin which was sung on Christmas as a congregational response to the sequence. It is not clear, however, whether Luther retained the original folk melody or wrote his own. Finally, Ameln notes that what we would consider "secular" folk songs—a distinction which would be less clear to people of the day—were an important source for Luther. Often only the melody was retained, with a new text being supplied.[13] Luther's "To Me She's Dear, the Worthy Maid" (*Sie ist mir lieb die werde Magd*), however, seems to be a situation in which both "secular" text and tune provided the model for Luther.[14]

Besides considering specific examples of textual and melodic influences, it is also informative to take a broad look at the sources of all the chorales together. Here we discover, for example, that only five out of the thirty-seven chorales have texts that could be considered original: the rest consist of translations, paraphrases, or adaptations of biblical texts, liturgical texts, and previously existing song texts. A similar picture emerges when summarizing the musical resources behind the chorales. Most of the tunes were based on secular folks songs (e.g., "Death Held Our Lord in Prison" = *Christ lag ynn Todes Banden*, LBW 134) or Latin chants (e.g., "Come, God Creator Holy Ghost" = *Kom Gott Schepfer heyliger Geyst*, LBW 284). The rest show such a clear affinity with a specific style of composition that they can be said to have relied upon other sources, although such sources are not always identifiable. "Dear Christians, Let Us Now Rejoice" (*Nun freut euch*, LBW 299), for example, is clearly in the style of some folk music of the period, although it is not certain whether one tune alone served as the basis for this chorale.

The point of this source tracing and comparison is not so much to prove something about any single piece of music, but rather to begin developing a wider consciousness about Martin Luther the pastoral composer. Although it is possible to analyze his writings to discover how Luther thought an effective pastor should shape worship and song for the people,[15] it is more informative—and in many ways more accurate—to see how the Reformer himself realized his principles in the concrete. Thus this initial foray into the sources seems to illustrate that, true to his word, Luther believed that music was a gift: but not only a gift from God to people and one which must answer only to the criteria of art, but also a reciprocal gift of praise from people to God, which therefore must allow the people accessibility. This accessibility Luther reinforced through familiarity. The consistent and predominant employment of familiar texts and tunes reveals Luther to be a traditional yet imaginative talent in a clearly pastoral mode.

The Music

Now that we have at least entertained the suggestion of Luther's pastoral musicianship in light of the musical and textual sources, it is for us to explore how the Reformer specifically employed both borrowed and original materials in his chorales. We begin with a consideration of the musical forms he employed.

Forms

One of the structural devices Luther employed most consistently was some variation of the barform. In its simplest form, the barform consists of a first musical phrase (A) which is repeated (A) and followed by a second musical phrase (B). The resulting structure is AAB. This form, which at least in principle can be traced back to the ancient Greeks and is detectable in some segments of Gregorian chant, became one of the favorite musical structures of the Minnesingers and Meistersingers who dominated the popular music scene in medieval Germany.[16] A well-known example of the barform is Luther's hymn, "Dear Christians, Let Us Now Rejoice," or "Dear Christians, One and All" (*Nun freut euch, lieben Christen gmeyn*, LBW 299).

Besides the simple AAB structure, there are a number of variations on this form which Luther employed.[17] One of these is the repetition barform, in which material from the first musical phrase (A) is integrated into the second musical phrase (B). An example of the repetition barform is found in the hymn "Death Held Our Lord in Prison," or "Christ Jesus Lay in Death's Strong Bands" (*Christ lag ynn todes banden*, LBW 134). Here we find that the last five notes of A are repeated, becoming the last five notes of B: thus the name, repetition barform.

Luther employed other variations on the barform. For us, more important than an exhaustive listing of these variations is a basic awareness of the fundamentals of this form, Luther's consistent use of it, and what such a form helped to achieve. Regardless of its specific configuration or variation, the barform is marked by continuous melodic repetition. This repetition is, in effect, a kind of built-in rehearsal. Learning is reinforced through the repetition of the first two phrases of the chorale (AA), and in a variation like the repetition barform, there is some reiteration of central musical fragments again at the end of B.

This "self-rehearsing" form is employed in fifteen out of the thirty-seven chorale melodies attributed to Luther. Although that number might not seem especially significant at first—only 41 percent—the number grows in significance when one considers that out of the remaining twenty-two chorales, sixteen rely heavily upon previously existing melodies. It is in the context of new melodic material that Luther consistently employs the barform; and there are only six (15 percent) out of thirty-seven chorales that either do not employ the barform or do not employ pre-existent material. Consequently, we begin to understand the formal manipulation of Luther's melodic material, both old and new, as an indicator of the Reformer's pastoral intent: generally employing either well known melodies, or a well known formal structure which itself reinforces the new melody.

Range. Besides considering the form or structural design of the chorales, we can also detect clear pastoral intentions by examining other compositional building blocks in Luther's chorale melodies. The range employed in these chorales, for example, is quite instructive. Range or ambitus refers to the gamut of notes within the capacity of a voice or instrument. It can also refer to the gamut of notes that a specific piece of music requires of a given voice or instrument. When examining the chorales of Luther, we find that most often his hymns require the range of a 9th, i.e., an octave plus one note. This range of a 9th is employed in fourteen out of thirty-seven chorales. The next most frequently employed range is that of an octave (7 times); then a 7th (5 times), a 6th (6 times), a 10th (4 times), and finally an 11th (1 time). Graphically, this results in the following curve:

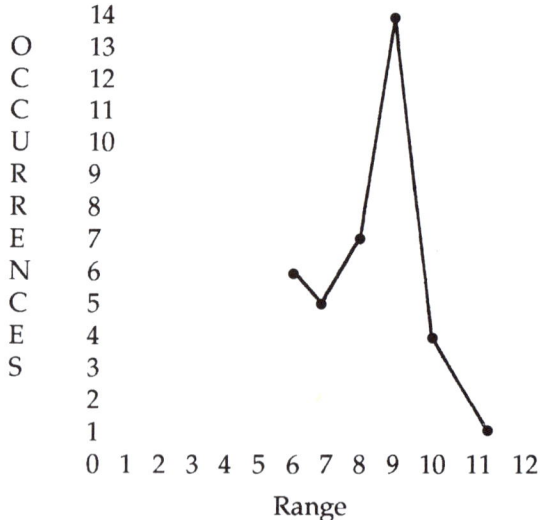

Most often Luther employed the range of a 9th in his chorales (57 percent of the time), which is a very friendly range for congregational singing. The more demanding range of a 10th is seldom used (11 percent of the time), and the difficult range of an 11th virtually never appears (3 percent of the time). Rather than making serious vocal demands on the congregation, therefore, we see that in matters of range, Luther seems to take into account the limited vocal abilities of an average assembly. It is statistically clear that the Reformer tended toward the more restricted range of a 6th or a 7th (employed 30 percent of the time) in his composing than the congregationally more demanding 10th or 11th (employed 14 percent of the time).

This is not to suggest that Luther set out to mathematically balance the number of times he employed a given range in his various chorales. On the other hand, this simple analysis does reveal that the Reformer's congregational attentiveness shaped his composition, clearly placing it within the range of an ordinary assembly.

Mode

A similar picture emerges when analyzing the various modes which Luther employed in his music. Here the word "mode" designates the arrangement of tones in an octave, which in turn forms the basic tonal substance of a composition.[18] Most in the U.S. are well acquainted with two modes: the major mode and the minor mode.

The musicians of the Middle Ages, however, did not think of music in terms of major or minor modes (or keys) as we do, but used another system of scales or modes. This system was based upon the location of the half-steps within the octave. In what we call a major scale, for example, the half-steps occur between the third and fourth tones, and the seventh and eighth tones. A simple minor scale, on the other hand, has half-steps between the second and third tones, and the seventh and eighth tones. Some modes in this system seem easier to sing, while others appear more difficult to sing: all because of the placement of the half-steps in the scale.

The Lydian mode, for example, has half steps between the fourth and fifth tones, and the seventh and eighth tones.[19] This mode, therefore, includes the interval of an augmented fourth[20] which can be such a difficult interval to sing that its late medieval nickname was "*diabolus in musica*" or "the devil in music."

A survey of the modes employed by Luther indicates that the Reformer employed the Lydian mode only once: for the German "Sanctus" or "Isaiah 'twas the Prophet" (*Jesaja dem Propheten das geschah*, LBW 528 alt.). Furthermore, this was an adaptation of a pre-existent melody from a Gregorian *Sanctus*. Thus the occurrence of this mode in the chorales of Luther is somewhat akin to the existence of the range of an 11th in his works: both occur only once and under the influence of borrowed material.

Much more usual was Luther's employment of the Dorian mode, which is very similar to our "minor" scale, with half steps between the second and third tones and the sixth and seventh tones. It is used in twelve of the chorales. The second most frequently employed mode was the Ionian, which is similar to our "major" scale and occurs in nine of the chorales. Thus those two modes which sound relatively close to the major-minor system—a system which was definitively established in Northern Europe in the seventeenth century, and whose two central modes were already becoming the most popular modes in the sixteenth century, and which avoided the most difficult intervals—were employed in the majority of Luther's chorale tunes (57 percent). Here again, one could suggest that ease and accessibility, now in tonal language, were important guiding principles for the composing Luther.

This attentiveness to the needs of the congregation which we have suggested through our discussions of form, range, and mode is also evident in other aspects of Luther's composition. His preference for conjunct or stepwise movement over disjunct movement in the chorale melodies certainly makes for easier congregational involvement, as does his penchant for syllabic settings (one syllable per note) instead of neumatic (one syllable per few notes) or melismatic (one syllable to many notes) settings for his texts. Further investigation of these and other elements would seem to support the pattern already noted: one that distinguishes Martin Luther as a gifted congregational composer. It was not only professionals or the naturally skilled who were invited into this music, just as it was not only the professionals or skilled who were invited into being church. Ecclesial identity and ministry belonged to the whole of the baptized, according to Luther, as did their sung praise.

The Texts

That Luther's pastoral intent can also be deduced from a textual analysis of his chorales was already intimated in our initial discussion of sources. There we noted, first of all, that out of the thirty-seven chorales only five have texts that could be considered original—and some of these five have well-known textual referents. Therefore, as with the music, so with the texts did a clear continuity through familiarity exist. Besides the mere employment of texts familiar in theme if not in language, however, there are other specific and significant patterns that Luther wove through his liturgical lyrics which further reveal his congregational empathy.

Literary Style

Aside from his employment of the vernacular, it is also clear that in terms of literary style, Luther shaped his texts for broad comprehension, liturgical durability, and easy access. Luther explicitly outlined some of his philosophy of text writing in a letter to George Spalatin in 1523, in which he tried to enlist Spalatin's help in developing texts for congregational song. Luther wrote:

> I would like you to avoid any new words or the language used at court. In order to be understood by the people, only the simplest and the most common words should be used for singing; at the same time, however, they should be pure and apt; and further, the sense should be clear and as close as possible to the psalms.[21]

In his discussion of the simplicity and directness of the language and vocabulary of Luther's hymns, Leupold has observed that "like the ancient poets he knew so well, Luther used few adjectives and formed brief, pungent lines consisting almost exclusively of verbs and nouns."[22] Leupold's point is clearly illustrated by citing the first ten titles of these hymns as they appear in Leupold's edition, whose English translations well mirror the original German.

> A *new* **song** here shall be begun
> *Dear* **Christians**, let **us** now rejoice
> From **trouble** *deep* I cry to **thee**
> Ah **God**, from **heaven** look down
> Although the **fools** say with their **mouth**
> Would that the **Lord** would grant us **grace**
> Come, the **heathen's** *healing* **light**
> **Jesus we** now must laud and sing
> *All* **praise** to **thee**, O **Jesus Christ**
> *Happy* who in **God's fear** doth stay[23]

Out of the sixty-seven words that comprise these ten titles, only six (9 percent) are adjectives (here italicized), and six are prepositions. Seventeen of these words (25 percent), however, are verbs (here underlined) and twenty-two (33 percent) are nouns or pronouns (here in boldface): a number which would increase to twenty-five (37 percent) if we included the possessive forms of nouns and pronouns. This simple word-survey of random titles thus bears out Leupold's observation that adjectives are clearly secondary in the language of these hymns, and that nouns (plus pronouns) and verbs predominate.

Furthermore, it is almost without exception that each line—each musical phrase—encompasses a single, compact unity of meaning. One need not scan ahead in a text of Luther for some focus for praise while struggling through thickets of prose. On the contrary, virtually every line can bear the weight of congregation attention, and may even invite a lingering fermata of reflection. Consider, for example, the opening verse of "From Heaven on High or "From Heaven Above" (*Vom himel hoch da kom ich her*, LBW 51). The translation, which follows the original German, is by George MacDonald (+ 1905).[24] The original is offered for comparison.[25]

> From heaven on high I come to you.
> *Vom himel hoch da kom ich her*
>
> I bring a story good and new;
> *ich bring euch gute newe mehr,*
>
> Of goodly news so much I bring,
> *der guten mehr bring ich so viel,*
>
> Of it I must both speak and sing.
> *davon ich singen und sagen wil.*

Note the concision and clarity of each line, which communicates a unit of meaning without necessarily spilling over into the next line. Thus Leupold remarks:

> The carrying over of one or more words from one line to the next, so as to bridge the break between verses, is quite uncommon. There is never a break in the middle of the verse . . . [which] again agrees with the nature of mass singing. The crowd sings a verse at a time, and so each verse must make sense as a unit.[26]

This is thoughtful and demanding writing, which Luther has achieved with such apparent effortlessness that it usually escapes our very notice.

Meter

Allied to this compact literary style is Luther's employment of meter, which aided the accessibility and memorability of his texts. Meter, in this context, simply refers to the number of syllables Luther used in each line of his verse. Although we may not be accustomed to think in terms of the textual meter, but rather only of the musical meter,[27] the textual meters employed by Luther can be quite instructive.[28]

The vast majority of the time Luther employs a seven or eight syllable line. We see this in the previously cited hymn, "From Heaven on High," which consists of four lines of eight syllables.[29] In all, twenty-five out of the thirty-seven chorales employ only seven or eight syllable lines (68 percent). Furthermore, in almost every other chorale the seven or eight syllable line plays a dominant role. The significance of this use of textual meter becomes clear when we recall our previous discussion of Luther's literary style. There we noted that the Reformer tended toward clarity and concision in his texts: with a predominance of nouns and verbs, capsulizations of single units of meaning in each line, and little textual carry-over between one line and the next. Considering the requirements of this style, it is little wonder that Luther continuously employed seven and eight syllable lines which—in a configuration of nouns and verbs—allow for the development of a single thought but little else. This textual metric complements Luther's literary style, whereas a shorter configuration of syllables could have required the composer to carry over a thought from one line to the next, and more syllables could have invited the insertion of non-essential modifiers. In this regard it would not be inappropriate to compare Luther's use of textual meter to his use of range: both allowed sufficient latitude for development of essentials, without placing unnecessary demands on the assembly.

This pattern of textual metrics also seems to complement a previously noted element in Luther's musical style, i.e., his propensity for syllabic rather than neumatic or melismatic settings. Fewer syllables per musical line could have meant that each syllable would have been wedded to more than one note, requiring more neumatic or melismatic writing. As we have noted, however, Luther clearly preferred syllabic writing. Consequently, Luther's deployment of meter appears as a further manipulation of the compositional building blocks to serve his pastoral purposes.

It could also be beneficial for us to study the patterns of textual rhyme Luther employed: patterns which often coincided with melodic rhyme in the chorales and served as valuable mnemonic devices. A more extensive study could also explore Luther's use of word painting, the interplay between stressed and unstressed syllables in his lyrics, and more. These would help confirm what already is becoming clear: that Martin Luther wrote scripturally based, well-crafted, people-centered texts which comprehensibly spoke the message of salvation and enabled praise. To be able to instill this consistency with beauty is true art at the service of worship—and such is the very definition and demand of all liturgical music.

A Mighty Fortress

Now that we have offered this brief, general analysis of Luther's chorale writing, and have demonstrated how these chorales could be interpreted as concrete explications of the Reformer's pastoral intentions, it is for us to be concrete as well. The vehicle for this concretization will be Luther's celebrated hymn "A Mighty Fortress" (*Ein feste Burg*, LBW 228 and 229). We reproduce the music and English text of the hymn as it is found in Leupold's edition,[30] with the original German from the critical edition of Luther's works.[31]

Sources

As to the sources of this chorale, we find that—as is so often the case—the text is scriptural: here a paraphrase of the 46th psalm. Musically the source is a little more difficult to determine. Some suggest that the melody shows a strong affinity to a famous Meistersinger tune, whereas others contend that it relies upon a Gregorian melody. Which ever the case—and it conceivably could be both—the strong suspicion here is that Luther employed a pre-existent melody as the basis for this chorale.

Music

Turning to the music, we find that "A Mighty Fortress" is structured as a barform. The first musical phrase (A) which encompasses the first two lines of the music is repeated (:), followed by a new section (B) which comprises the last three lines. The basic structure for this chorale, therefore, is AAB. Moreover, within this fundamental barform structure we find a further variation known as repetition-serial-barform. This variation is detectable in two additional elements added to the basic barform structure: (1) a "serial" or string of unrelated musical phrases, and (2) the "repetition" of an earlier musical phrase.

Ein feste burg ist unser Gott, Ein gute wehr und waffen.
Er hilfft uns freh aus aller not, die uns ist hat betroffen.
Der alt böse feind mit ernst ers ist meint,
gros macht und viel list sein grausam rüstung ist,
auff erd ist nicht seins gleichen.

If each musical unit is assigned a lower case letter, the first line of the hymn appears as a single unit (a) and the second line as another unit (b). These two units together comprise the first musical phrase (a + b = A). Since the first musical phrase is repeated in the barform, AA = a-b-a-b. Line three begins a new musical element (c), and the end of the line begins another (d). Line four includes the new musical idea (e) and the beginning of the final new musical element (f). The last musical unit (i.e., the last nine notes of the hymn) are identical to the second line (b). Thus, the B section of this chorale encompasses five musical units: c-d-e-f-b. The first four of these are the "serial" (c-d-e-f) and the final unit is the repeated element (b). Schematically this repetition-serial-barform appears as:

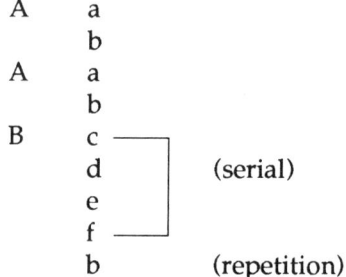

Five of the eight musical units that constitute this chorale are repeated each verse (i.e., a and b). Consequently "A Mighty Fortress" could be considered a true "self-rehearsing" hymn. Aside from the form, one further notes that the range of this chorale is an octave: one of the most commonly employed by Luther. The mode is Ionian, which along with Dorian predominates in his chorale compositions. The ratio of conjunct or stepwise to disjunct motion in the melody is over 4 to 1, with only about 22 percent of the intervals involving a leap of more than a whole step. Finally, as to the wedding of text and tune, we find a predominantly syllabic setting, with no melismas and only an occasional neumatic passage.

Text

Finally, we turn to the text whose scriptural basis we have already noted. As Leupold has suggested, we find here succinct writing with few adjectives, clear images, and compact language. There are, for example, only two three-syllable words in

MacDonald's faithful translation ("wickedness" and "policy"), and the original German has only one three-syllable word (*"betroffen"*). Furthermore, each phrase expresses a relatively complete thought, and there is little carry-over between phrases.

The meter is slightly irregular (87.87.55.567), with some preferences for lines of seven or eight syllables, so characteristic of Luther. More interesting is the relationship between the rhythmic stresses in the music and the accompanying text. Even in MacDonald's translation, the indefinite articles, conjunctions, and prepositions usually occur on eighth notes, whereas the more important nouns and verbs fall on the quarter notes. Moreover, many of the latter stand at the end of a musical phrase or half phrase, followed by an eight rest, thus receiving even more stress.

There is also a limited amount of musical and textual rhyme, which MacDonald has tried to maintain in his translation. The rhymed phrases "castle strong" and "every wrong," for example, have identical musical settings, as do the words "weapon" and "heap on." The dovetailing of these textual and musical rhymes further contribute to a tighter wedding of text and tune.

Summary

In theory as well as in practice, "A Mighty Fortress" appears to be a paradigm of liturgical "people-music" (*Volkmusik*). Scripturally founded and melodically traditional, this chorale employs a self-rehearsing form within a singable range and accessible mode, articulated with syllabic ease in conjunct motion. Furthermore, this well-wrought tune is imaginatively wed to a thoughtful and succinct psalmic paraphrase, parcelled out in digestible yet tastefully arranged morsels. The chorale is memorable without being repetitious, accessible without being bland, syllabic without being pedestrian, and concise without being curt. It is, in other words, that delicate combination of the usual in a most unusual way which appears entirely effortless in its art, but whose craft is affirmed by its ageless singability.

Conclusion

The conclusions of the study exist not so much in words but in music—not in the saying, but more in the singing. The chorales of Martin Luther have endured for over four hundred years, and are as effective today as they were in the sixteenth century. The question of why they have endured and why they still move congregations to praise, though beyond any exact formulation, are yet valuable for us to ponder.

Today in the arena of worship composition there continues that eternal tension between musical integrity and liturgical appropriateness; between the stirring of the muse and the submission of that muse to the service of worship. It is a difficult tension to resolve, and for each composer there exists various solutions. The import of Martin Luther as a musical paradigm is, to some degree, his ability to demonstrate that resolution is possible without sacrificing either art or the community's participation in the same. This is not to suggest, of course, that all of the Reformer's chorales are so exemplary, for the abandonment of some of them even in his own lifetime disproves that point. Many of these works, however, are clearly exemplary, which in part explains why they have influenced other hymn writers for almost half a millennium, generating a form of praise that continues to dominate much of western Christian music.

In these days of so much musical-liturgical energy, we need to look to the future for sounds and forms that will serve our worship well in this post-Christian era of reform and evangelization. We would do well, however, to look also to the past, to the work and genius of another visionary in reform and evangelization, and there discover again something of the true meaning of "pastoral" in praise. Only then might we avoid that cycle of error which results from ignoring our history, and enter anew the song of the Lamb.

Notes

1. Martin Luther, *Preface to George Rhau's Symphoniae Iucundae*, trans. Walter Buszin in "Luther on Music," *Musical Quarterly* 32 (1946) 83; a translation of the full preface is found in *Luther's Works*, vol. 53: *Liturgy and Hymns*, ed. Leupold 321-324.

2. For bibliography on this topic, see above, p. 30-31, n. 87.

3. Since the seventeenth century this term has come to denote the tunes and texts that comprise the congregational song or hymn of the Protestant church in Germany. Originally the German term *Choral* signified a plainchant melody sung unaccompanied and in unison (*choraliter* in Latin). Eventually, chorale became a synonym for the vernacular hymn in Protestant Germany.

4. Where possible, references will be given to chorales as they appear in the *Lutheran Book of Worship* (LBW).

5. Blume, *Protestant Church Music,* 14-15; also his further discussion of this topic, 15-35.

6. A useful introduction to the question of Luther's role as a composer is provided by Blume, *Protestant Church Music* 35-51; also Nettl, *Luther and Music,* 28-29.

7. See, for example, *D. Martin Luthers Werke,* vol. 25 (Weimar: Hermann Böhlaus Nachfolger, 1923) 487-531.

8. Namely, the Weimar edition cited above, and *Liturgy and Hymns* 211-309.

9. Though less nuanced than that of Blume, Ameln's schema is a good starting point for grouping the sources. Konrad Ameln, *The Roots of German Hymnody of the Reformation Era* (St. Louis: Concordia, 1964) 3-19.

10. Blume comments: "The most important pieces of the abundant Catholic repertory of hymns were taken over with their melodies and left in their customary *de tempore* place." *Protestant Church Music* 15.

11. Blume describes these as occupying "a place between the more or less song-like hymns and sequences and the sacred and secular German lieder. This group of Latin or macaronic Latin-German *cantiones* and songs had generally enjoyed a long medieval tradition and had frequently been used by the people in pre-Reformation worship. In the fifteenth century they had experience a rich flowering as congregational songs, as household devotional lieder, as processional and pilgrimage *cantiones,* and probably also as school songs." Ibid. 17-18.

12. In this category Blume groups "pre-Reformation German sacred lieder, pilgrim songs and *Leisen,* sacred songs of the Minnesinger and Meistersinger, songs of penitence (*Geisslerlieder*—songs of the flagellants), Crusade songs, and sacred folk songs, for which the Germans had long been famous; they were taken over unchanged by the new church or were merely improved in small details 'in a Christian manner'." Ibid. 19.

13. See Blume's discussion of "The *Contrafacta.*" Ibid. 29 35.

14. Blume comments that this lied "resembling the Meistersinger type in text and melody, was probably not written without a direct model; it stands in complete isolation among Luther's lieder." Ibid. 42.

15. Schalk, *Luther on Music* provides a useful introduction to the Reformer's thought, especially chapter two.

16. Luther, *Liturgy and Hymns* 219; also, John Barker, "Sociological Influences upon the Emergence of Lutheran Music," *Miscellenea Musicologia: Adelaide Studies in Musicology* 4 (1969) 163-164.

17. For a more detailed discussion of the barform and its variations in the works of Martin Luther, see Riedel, *The Lutheran Chorale,* 41-49.

18. On the wide range of meanings of this term, see *The New Harvard Dictionary of Music,* s.v. "mode."

19. Or by playing the white keys on a piano between F and f.

20. F to B on the piano.

21. Martin Luther, *Letters II*, ed. and trans. Gottfried Krodel, *Luther's Works*, vol. 49 (Philadelphia: Fortress Press, 1972) 69.

22. Luther, *Liturgy and Hymns* 198.

23. Ibid. viii-ix.

24. Ibid. 290.

25. *D. Martin Luthers Werke* 35:524.

26. Luther, *Liturgy and Hymns* 198.

27. It is indicated by the "time signature" at the beginning of the piece, e.g., a work in 3/4 time.

28. For an outline of the many and varied textual meters employed in the LBW, see that volume, pp. 949-954.

29. Noted as 8.8.8.8.

30. Luther, *Liturgy and Hymns* 284.

31. *D. Martin Luthers Werke* 35:518.

5

Toward a Sound Theology

Introduction

WHILE IT WAS PIUS X (+ 1914) WHO COINED THE PHRASE "INTEGRAL PART of the solemn liturgy,"¹ the Constitution on the Sacred Liturgy (1963) placed this phrase at the heart of musical-liturgical reform in the twentieth century by noting:

> The musical tradition of the universal Church is a treasure of inestimable value, greater even than that of any other art. The main reason for this preeminence is that, as sacred song closely bound to the text, it forms a necessary or integral part of the solemn liturgy.²

Since the reappropriation of Pius X's famous phrase in 1963, musicians and liturgists have struggled to understand its meaning. Innumerable lectures have been given, articles penned, discussions organized, and conventions mounted on the topic. What is surprising in these various undertakings, however, is that seldom does anyone question the basic presupposition behind the phrase and ask whether music actually is integral to worship. And even if one accepts the premise that music is integral to worship, few have attempted to explore why this is so. As a result, most commentators on the subject—be they musicians or liturgists—find themselves addressing questions of how music is integral to worship rather than questions of whether or why music is integral to worship.

Although not wanting to suggest that any of these questions are unimportant, the impulse to resolve questions of how music is integral to worship without inquiring whether music actually is integral to worship, or why this might be so, can be problematic. It can be problematic because it allows one to enter the arena of pastoral application without ever examining the underlying principles favorable to long term-pastoral effectiveness; it can be problematic because it seems to encourage the exploration of musical-liturgical technique without establishing the bases or consequences of such technique; and it can be problematic because it permits the discussion of liturgical music to remain at the level of performance without addressing the role of music as enacted theology and formative vehicle for belief.

Ultimately our inattentiveness to questions of whether or why music is integral to worship has resulted in an inadequate theology of liturgical music[3] for the church. The post-conciliar era has witnessed many advances in the theology of the liturgy.[4] It is disappointing that there is so little comparable work on the theology of music or liturgical music. Even such premier documents as *Music in Catholic Worship*, which offers a splendid introduction on the "theology of celebration," offers no parallel reflections on a "theology of liturgical music." The little that has appeared on a theology of music has mostly arisen in Protestant circles.[5] Although these reflections are enormously useful, they do not always provide an adequate framework for reflecting on the place of music in the renewed rites of Roman Catholic worship. It is the goal of this essay to sketch a basic outline for a theology of liturgical music attuned to the sacramental framework of the Roman Catholic Church in the post-Vatican II era.

Before one can construct a theology of liturgical music it is first necessary to understand something of the nature of music apart from any explicit religious or ritual usage. Specifically this means examining the nature of sound, and outlining key psychological and sociological effects of its acoustic properties. Second, it is necessary to address the dynamic relationship between music and ritual. This requires outlining the ways in which, apart from Christian liturgy, music weds itself to ritual. It further requires uncovering what, if anything, music does for ritual and why it is such a common ritual component. Finally, with these pre-theological examinations behind us, we can turn to theological reflection. In particular we will discover how the acoustic properties of sound and music resonate with the kernel of Judaeo-Christian revelation, and how the dynamic between music and ritual well serves this revelation. Ultimately we will propose that sacramental language is the most effective for expressing the power and potential of liturgical music.

The Sound Phenomenon

Sound or Noise

Although the goal of this essay is to outline a theology of liturgical music, it is not simply music and its commonly defined components of melody, rhythm, harmony, texture, form, tempo, and dynamics that are the raw material for later theological reflection. Rather, it is sound itself—the acoustic experience of which music is a most refined genre—that provides the beginning point for such reflection.

Sound can be defined as "a vibratory disturbance in the pressure and density of a fluid, or in the elastic strain in a solid, with frequency in the approximate range between 20 and 20,000 cycles per second, and capable of being detected by the organs of hearing."[6] While this and other definitions note the physical attributes of the sound phenomenon, it also indicates that sound is not simply a physical phenomenon but, more importantly, a perception of a physical phenomenon. "Sound, as such, does not really exist in the world around us. What does exist is vibration . . . In other words, there is no sound until we hear it."[7]

Ultimately it is the way in which we hear that allows us to distinguish between music and noise, which are both sound events. In particular it is our instinct to posit the presence or absence of intention at the source of the "vibratory disturbance" that enables us to distinguish between sound as communication and sound as random natural phenomenon. John Booth Davies, for example, convincingly argues that it is impossible to distinguish between noise and music or speech in purely physical terms.[8] Just as important as the vibratory disturbance that defines the physical properties of any sound is the response to such phenomenon by the listener.

For example, the creaking of a door at night during a power outage might be the result of the wind or of some uninvited stranger intruding into our home. Both wind and intruder could create the same sound. Regardless of whether the wind or stranger moved the door—regardless of the intention behind the movement and the resulting sound—the distinction between random noise or communication of danger lies in the perception and response of the listeners. It is their perception of the acoustic phenomenon that determines whether this is a sound requiring some action or simply a noise to be ignored. Thus it is not only the physical phenomenon, but also the response to that phenomenon and to a lesser degree the intentionality behind the phenomenon that enable us to distinguish between noise and communication.

"Sound Effects"

Human beings experience the world around them through a rich variety of senses. Each type of sensory perception allows a different mode of knowing and, therefore, a different kind of knowledge. If we could only touch a clove of garlic and not see it hanging in an Italian deli, hear it as it separates from the bulb, smell it as it simmers in olive oil, or taste it in a delicate pasta sauce we would have incomplete and even faulty information about garlic. Each sense provides us with a different perspective in our perception of the world—a perspective shaped both by the material that is perceived as well as our own physiology of perception.

As a particular type of sense perception, hearing allows for distinctive kinds of knowing. This is true both because of the nature of sound as well as the physiology of human hearing. Though not an exhaustive list, it is possible to outline some of the essential influences of sound phenomenon and the physiology of hearing on the way we know in terms of five categories.

(1) *Sound as an Experience of Impermanence.* One of the most frequently cited characteristics of sound events like music is their transitory nature.[9] Hearing can be considered a sophisticated way of marking time with the ear: registering a sequence of sounds which eventually fade and come to an end. Sound events like music or speech are impermanent events which exist for the listener only in the doing of them—only for the duration of the performance. Thus sound events like music are fundamental experiences of change: one note or syllable or lapping wave in sequence after another. Sound events cannot stay the same. Hans Jonas concludes that "transience is thus of the very essence of the *now* of hearing, and 'present' is here a mere following in the stream of onmoving process."[10] It is especially music as the most sophisticated sound event produced by humans that is marked by imper-

manence, change, sequence, and passing time. Susanne Langer suggests that music makes time audible and renders its form and continuity sensible.[11]

(2) *Sound as an Experience of the Intangible*. Closely related to the impermanence of the sound event is the intangibility of the sound phenomenon. The paradox of all sound phenomena like speech or music is that they are perceivable but elusive, recognizable but uncontainable. When sculptors, painters, or architects ply their craft they employ materials that before, during, and after the process can be touched, weighed, and measured. But when orators or musicians ply their art, no comparable material has been transformed. Although they may sometimes employ instruments, as the painter uses a brush or the sculptor a chisel, the real stuff of their art is simply air: controlled, manipulated, articulated, and punctuated, but air nonetheless. And air is a virtually imperceptible reality. This experience of the apparent intangibility of sound phenomenon is heightened by the fact that sound phenomena are perceptible by only one sense. Whereas oil paints, sandstone, and steel can be seen, touched, and—if one wishes—tasted, sound is usually only heard. Music in particular is not only perceived as insubstantial but itself seems to have an "ambivalence of content."[12] This elusiveness in form and content is part of the reason why music is so often used for communicating with the spirit world.

(3) *Sound as an Experience of Activity*. Sound events are perceived as active, dynamic experiences in comparison, for example, to the visual which can more easily give the subject the illusion of having taken part in a passive, disengaged activity. This, again, is due to the nature of sound and to the physiology of hearing. Because sound events are fundamentally temporal events and perdure only as long as the sound is being generated, they have an inherent dynamism about them. Such dynamism is less easily predicated of the plastic arts since some artifacts, such as a painting, continue to exist long after the artistic process is finished. Furthermore sound waves, traveling at approximately 750 miles per hour or 1120 feet per second at 15 degrees Celsius, move fast enough to communicate movement and yet slow enough to be perceived as moving. Thus we can watch someone shoot a starter gun in the distance and hear the shot milliseconds later. Human physiology contributes to the illusion that sound events are dynamic events.[13] The human ear, for example, is able to distinguish two clicks separated by only

two or three thousandths of a second whereas the human eye can only distinguish the flashing of a light at between a fifteenth and a sixtieth of a second. Beyond this point the human observer no longer experiences a flashing light but continuous illumination. Humans have more developed physiological capacities for hearing than for seeing. As Davies summaries, "the 'length of the present' for the ear is of shorter duration than for the eye."[14]

(4) *Sound as an Invitation to Engagement.* As Plato (+ 347 BCE) recognized, sound events like those of the epic poets of his generation, were not neutral occurrences which an impassive listener could take or leave.[15] Rather, sound events like poetry or music are essentially acts of engagement. For example, Plato believed that poetry was so engaging that listeners were unable to distinguish themselves from the poetic event. The sound event disabled the listener from detaching self from the sound and, therefore, rendered the listener unable to distinguish between subject and object; between poem and listener; between poem and poet. Sound events, from this perspective, are not only active events in and of themselves, but dynamic to the extent that they engage the other and captivate the listener. Thus some have suggested that sound events like human song are fundamentally unitive:[16] uniting singer with the song, listener with the song, singer with the listener, the listener with other listeners, and even in a new way the listener with her or himself. To be in the presence of a sound event is to be engaged in that sound event and to be engaged with both the producer of the sound and with the others who hear it. One aspect of human physiology that underscores not simply the dynamic but also the engaging nature of sound is the human ear. Unlike the human eye, the ear has no natural covering: there is no "earlid." The ear is born open to every sound. Thus the ear is the metaphor for human beings born open to engagement, not just with sounds but with the people who produce them. Consequently the ear could be considered a physiological metaphor for relationship.

(5) *Sound as an Experience of the Personal.* The assertion that sound events are not only dynamic but invitations into engagement leads us to a final assertion about the sound event: that they are not simply experiences of something other, but of another. Sound encounters are keyed to be personal encounters. Walter Ong explains this phenomenon in terms of "acoustic space":

> Habits of auditory synthesis give rise to a special sense of space itself. For besides visual-tactile space there is also acous-

tic space (which, through voice and hearing, has its own associations with the kinesthetic and tactual not quite the same as the kinesthetic and tactual associations of sight). We can apprehend space in terms of sound and echoes (abetted by tactile associations). Space thus apprehended has qualities of its own.[17]

One of the characteristics of acoustic space is that it is fluid space. It is a sphere without fixed boundaries. Acoustic space does not, like visual space, contain a thing but is a sphere delineated by activity.[18] And such acoustic activity is translated by the human imagination as evidence of animation, of life, and particularly of human presence. Acoustic space, therefore, is what we might call "filled space."

> Because of its association with sound, acoustic space implies presence far more than does visual space... Noises one hears, for example in a woods at night, register in the imagination as presences—person-like manifestations—far more than do movements which one merely sees. In this sense acoustic space is precisely not "pure" space. It is inhabited space.[20]

It is in the acoustic arena that Martin Buber's relational paradigm of the "I-Thou" becomes fully possible.[20] Buber believed that the two ways of being in the world can be expressed as either "I-it" or "I-You."[21] Relationship is an experience of I-You, an experience of reciprocity, of engagement and response. This is precisely the dynamic which is embodied in acoustic space.

> Whoever says You does not have something for his object. For wherever there is something there is also another something; every It borders on other Its; It is only by virtue of bordering on others. But where You is said there is no something. You has no borders. Whoever says You does not have something; he has nothing. But he stands in relation.[22]

It is only the word, only dialogue in Buber's perspective, that enables the I-You to be spoken and that enables us to become truly aware.[23]

Music in Ritual

Types of Ritual Music

There are few rituals known to us that do not employ music. Whether celebrating the harvest, mourning the dead, or welcoming heroes back from the fray, human beings have consistently invested their rituals and ceremonies with the lyricism of the human voice and the sounds of instruments. Though there are numerous ways in which music weds itself to various rituals, the following four categories are an attempt to classify types of ritual music according to the juxtaposition of three distinct yet complementary musical-ritual ingredients: (1) the music itself; (2) any text employed with the music; and (3) any ritual action accompanying the music and/or text.[24] This exploration of the interplay of music and ritual will enable us, in the following section, to explore why music and ritual are so easily wed.

Music Alone. Although we may not have many experiences of textless, instrumental music in our rituals, this can be a powerful form of ritual music. One poignant example is the playing of taps at a military funeral. In this form there is no text, properly speaking, to give the music its ceremonial import, nor is there any accompanying action to which the music must be joined. Rather, this is what could be called pure ritual music, where the act of music making itself—even devoid of lyrics—is the ritual. Although the surrounding words and actions provide the context for this ritual music, the playing of taps is a self-contained unit of meaning which finds expression in the music alone.

Music Wed to Ritual Action. A second type of ritual music combines instrumental music with ritual action. A familiar example of this for citizens of the United States is the arrival of the president to the strains of "Hail to the Chief." Although a text does exist for this music, it is virtually unknown by the public. What is known is the context: when the music begins the president is to appear. Here ritual music is so intimately connected with a particular ritual action that comedians and satirists can parody the presidential presence merely by playing a few bars from this familiar tune. Thus textless music—like "Pomp and Circumstance" at the procession of high school graduates—is so fused with a specific ritual action that together they form a single unit of meaning.

Music United to a Text. A third type of ritual music consists of a text joined to music without any accompanying ritual action. A most familiar example of this genre in the United States is the singing of the national anthem. Although a specific posture (standing) is normally assumed during the rite, there is no activity during the ritual other than the singing of the song. Here text is identified with an invariable tune, and music is never submitted to the art of contrafactum. Together text and music form a unit which ritually is experienced only and essentially as an act of singing.

Music Wed to a Text, Accompanying an Action. This final category of ritual music brings together all three elements—music, text, and action—in a single ritual moment. Examples of this genre are readily found in dance music where tune, text, and prescribed steps converge in "Swing your partner" or "Put your right foot in." Probably the most common example of this type of ritual music in our culture occurs during a birthday ritual, when lights are extinguished, the cake ablaze with candles is carried toward the "celebrant," and the attending assembly sings the ritual song, "Happy Birthday."[25] Such examples from our own culture are related to the ritual prescriptions of traditional societies, where rites of initiation or burial are accomplished, at least in part, through strictly defined songs with equally defined dance movements.

The "Why" of Ritual Music

The four categories of ritual music illustrate how music weds itself to various rituals. Sometimes this means supporting some ceremonial action, or serving to heighten a text. Other times the music itself, without the benefit of accompanying text or ceremony, assumes a central role in the rite. In such circumstances the music does not so much wed itself to the rite, for at that moment the music actually defines and becomes the ritual. This experience of "pure ritual music," and to a lesser degree the experience of texted music without an action, offer us a valuable insight as to why music is so easily united with human ritual.

Although there are many ways that one could define ritual, the following is a useful and progressive definition: ritual is patterned, shared, public behavior, expressing a meaning and purpose that cannot be put into words alone, in the face of some reality larger than ourselves. What is especially noteworthy in this and similar definitions is the emphasis on ritual accomplishing something achievable by no other human activity. Ritual is not a substitute for some other human practice, but a distinctive human enterprise that "expresses, reaches, conveys, intends (and) effects something which otherwise would remain void."[26]

Ritual is able to accomplish this because, in the language of Susanne Langer, it is a presentation and not a discursive event.[27] More precisely, ritual is a presentational-symbolic event.

> The ritual does not belong to the realm of mere [discursive] thought, it is not a doctrine or an ideal entity, it does not pertain exclusively to the domain of the logos. It belongs, rather, to the realm of gesture, of external and corporeal manifestation.[28]

Presentational symbols are essential components of ritual actions: the multivalent means by which rituals transform those experiences that no other medium can adequately express. This offers us the key for understanding the essential relationship between music and ritual.

Rituals achieve the inexpressible by means of symbols; and although all art is symbolic, opening up levels of reality which can be broached in no other way,[29] the "most highly developed type of such purely connotational semantic is music."[30] Music is nondiscursive symbol,[31] has little capacity for fixed definitions, and is not easily explained as a language.[32] It is not primarily representational and is well suited for accomplishing the task of expressing, reaching, conveying, intending, and effecting what otherwise would never be.

In fact, music so easily serves ritual and so readily weds itself to various rites that sometimes, as noted above, the music itself becomes the ritual. Thus, without benefit of any movement, dance, text, gesture, action, or artifacts, the music itself defines the ritual moment. This ability is not unrelated to the various characteristics of sound that undergird the power of music in and out of the ritual context. As an encounter with impermanence and "audible time," as a powerful event created by seemingly intangible forces, as a point of entry into experience and dynamism, as an invitation to engagement or relationship, and as an experience of the personal, music creates that acoustic space which—as much as any other environment—enables ritual precisely to express meaning and purpose that cannot be put into words alone, in the face of some reality larger than ourselves.

Such reasoning supports what has been attested to and believed from time immemorial. Traditional societies have known that beautiful sounds convey feelings and thoughts more powerfully, more completely, and more exactly than does any word,[33] and consequently is universally tied to their rituals. Thus, music's "most important and frequent use is . . . in religious rituals."[34] The primitive belief in the power of music to energize and validate rituals is probably best demonstrated by the widespread belief that music was actually a divine gift.[35]

Toward a Theology of Christian Ritual Music[36]

The Properties of Sound and Judaeo-Christian Revelation

Constructing a theology of ritual music requires, first of all, that we recall the properties of sound discussed above and note how the sound phenomenon, by its very nature, serves the revelation of God as understood in the Judaeo-Christian tradition.

The Judaeo-Christian God as Historical. One of the most celebrated and distinctive aspects of the God of the Hebrew and Christian Scriptures is that this God intervenes in history. Not merely remembered as acting "once upon a time" or in some other mythic moment,[37] the God of Moses and Jesus intervened in specific times and places, liberating the Hebrews from Pharaoh and Jesus from death.

We have already noted that one of the most frequently cited characteristics of sound events like music are their transitory nature. Sound events are time-bound, history-bound events. Because of this existential quality music is able to image a God who, in the Judaeo-Christian tradition, intervenes in time and reveals Self in human history. Furthermore, this time bound art has the ability to engage the community in the present reality of worship and signal that union with God is an existential possibility, here and now.

The Judaeo-Christian God as an Elusive Presence. Whereas the God of Judaeo-Christian revelation is perceived as One who intervenes in history, it is also clear that this is an elusive presence. The God of Abraham and Jesus is One who is both present and hidden.[38] The paradox of Judaeo-Christian revelation is that the Divine Self is both recognizable while remaining the unnameable "I am who I am" (Ex 3:14). Even Christianity, which claims for itself the incarnate revelation of God in Jesus Christ, must reckon with a savior who came once in time and who will come again at the end of time. In the interim, however, while we long for and sometimes succeed in experiencing "real presence," we also struggle with God's "real absence."[39]

The paradox of all sound phenomena including music is that sound is perceivable but elusive, recognizable but uncontainable.

The apparently insubstantial nature of music is one of the reasons why it has symbolized the mysterious and wholly other since the dawn of creation. Music, as a nondiscursive symbol, as we have noted, is especially distinguished by its ambivalence of content. This elusiveness in form and content is part of the reason why music is so often used for communicating with the spirit world. In the Judaeo-Christian tradition music is an effective means for communicating with a God who is both present and hidden. Furthermore, music offers itself as a powerful symbol for the divine Self who is recognizable while remaining the unnameable. Music thus enables us to encounter and know God without presuming to capture or contain the divine Self.

The Judaeo-Christian God as Dynamic. Besides being a God who is remembered as having intervened in human history, the God of Jews and Christians is also perceived as a dynamic and responsive God. This characteristic not only emphasizes God's historical intervention but further expresses the belief that God has been and continues to be engaged in the individual and corporate lives of humankind. The "call-response" dynamic of the Scriptures presents a God who continuously initiates encounters and, with astounding regularity, calls upon unsuspecting prophets (Jer 1:4-8) and unwilling disciples (Jn 1:46-49). Moreover, it is the promised continuation of this divine dialogue that gives these religions life.

Sound in general and music in specific have the ability not only to announce presence but also to engage another in dialogue and communion. Because of sound's ability to resonate inside two individuals at the same time, it has the capacity to strike a common chord and elicit sympathetic vibrations from those who hear. It is dynamic in its ability to enter the world of the other and elicit a response. Thus music effectively reflects the dialogic impulse of God in the Judaeo-Christian tradition who continuously initiates dialogue with believers. This characteristic emphasizes not only God's historical intervention or personal nature but further embodies the belief that God has been and continues to be engaged in the individual and corporate life of humankind.

The Judaeo-Christian God as Relational. Closely related to the dynamic character of the Judaeo-Christian God is the relational basis of this revelation. The God of Jews and Christians not only reveals Self in time—in a dynamic way that calls forth an individual response from believers—but is a God who also calls us into relationship with Godself and each other. The appropriate response to this revelation is not simply personal belief and activity, but the forging of a common identity and way of life as a people (Ex 6:6), as a community (Acts 2:42). Ultimately, the God of Judaeo-Christian revelation is one who calls forth a network of relationships, sealed in a covenant.

As we have noted, sound events like music are fundamentally unitive: uniting singer with the song, listener with the song, singer with the listener, the listener with other listeners, and even in a new way the listener with herself or himself. To be in the presence of a sound event is to be engaged in that sound event and to be engaged with those who produce the sound, as well as with the others who hear it. Sound events such as music, therefore, are strong metaphors for the God who calls us and for the network of relationships demanded by such a call.

The Judaeo-Christian God as Personal. Not only is the God of Judaeo-Christian revelation recognized as a power intervening in history and calling us into relationship, but more so is this God imaged as a person who intervenes on behalf of a beloved. Time and time again the Scriptures present to us a God imaged as mother (Is 66:13), lover (Wis 2:8), friend (Ti 3:4), and father (Lk 11:2). Not an impersonal natural power or some arbitrary force of fate, this is a personal God who loves.

Sound encounters, as noted above, are not simply experiences of something other, but of *an*other. Sound encounters are keyed to personal encounters. They occur in the realm of acoustic space which is translated by the human imagination as an arena of personal presence. Thus the sound event by its very nature supports the revelation of a God who is perceived as a person. Music, in particular, is an infallible indicator of human presence since music, properly speaking, is a human creation that does not otherwise occur in nature.[40] Consequently music serves as a special sound metaphor for the unnameable God who chooses to reveal Self in personal terms.

Music as Revelatory in the Liturgical Event

We have indicated how sound, by its very nature, serves the revelation of God in the Judaeo-Christian tradition. Its temporality, seemingly insubstantial nature, dynamism, unitive properties, and evocation of the personal enable it to serve as a unique medium for communicating the presence of God. Sound phenomena are thus able to suggest presence without confinement, elicit wonder without distance, and enable union in a particular and unparalleled way.

Music as the most refined of all sound phenomena—especially as it unites to ritual—does even more in serving the revelation of the Judaeo-Christian God. We have noted above how music easily and consistently weds itself to the ritual moment. True in so many other religions, this is well attested throughout the history of Christianity. It is also true that in Christianity the liturgy is considered the church's first theology and the primary expression of the church's belief.[41] This concept was reaffirmed by the *Constitution on the Sacred Liturgy* which called the church's worship, especially the eucharist, the fount and summit of the church's life (n. 10). Music wed to ritual so conceived thus places music's revelatory power at the very center of belief.

If sound, by its very nature, resonates with essential characteristics of the God of Judaeo-Christianity, and if liturgy, more than any other event, is the locus for encounter with and revelation of such a God, then it is eminently understandable why music, as the most refined of sound phenomena, weds itself so intimately to Christian liturgy. The combination of the two enables the possibility of encounter and revelation as no other combination of human artifacts and events.

The unparalleled power resulting from the wedding of lyricism and rite becomes even clearer when one reckons with the word-centered nature of Judaeo-Christian revelation and liturgy. The God of Abraham and of Jesus is not only perceived as a personal God, but a God who speaks and whose word is law and promise. Ultimately God's word is at the core of Judaeo-Christian revelation and is central to the worship in this tradition.

Like the word, music is a sound event. Unlike the word, however, music is a presentational and not a discursive symbol. Music is not capable of a fixed meaning and is celebrated for its "ambivalence of content." Consequently there is no inherent clash or contradiction of meanings when presentational symbol weds to discursive symbol, that is, when music weds to texts. Rather, there is the possibility for new levels of meaning as the music heightens and interprets the text.

This natural alliance between text and tune is a further reason why one can speak of the integral relationship between music and Christian liturgy for, like no other art form, music has a special capacity to heighten and serve the word which occupies a central place in worship. Such an awareness was reflected in the *Constitution on the Sacred Liturgy* which, when noting the integral relationship between music and liturgy, pointed in particular to the binding of sacred song and text as the main reason for this integrality (n. 112).

In summary, therefore, music can be considered as a necessary or integral element in the liturgy because it has the capacity to reveal central images of God and the community as well as to realize the implications of those images at the very heart of the church's liturgy. Thus music has rightly been called "a sounding image of the Wisdom of God."[42] Furthermore, music has an unparalleled capacity to wed itself to that central element of the church's worship, the word. As it bonds with the word, music fulfills its proper ministerial function. Thus, as we noted earlier, Martin Luther could claim that "next to the Word of God, music deserves the highest praise."[43]

The Sacramental Nature of Christian Ritual Music

Part of the confusion about how or why music is integral to Christian worship may, in part, be a result of the language of integrality. Although "integral" is a useful term, there is yet much ambiguity about the exact meaning of the phrase "music forms an integral part of the solemn liturgy." The *Constitution on the Sacred Liturgy* offers "necessary" [*necessariam*] as a synonym to "integral" [*integralem*]. This is probably an unfortunate interpolation into the document, because it gives the impression that music is indispensable in Christian worship. Many people's experience and significant scholarly opinion, however, disagree with that stance.[44] Rather than speaking of the integral nature of Christian ritual music, or its "holiness,"[45] it seems more appropriate to employ more traditional language, and speak about the sacramental nature of Christian ritual music.

Although the church limited the designation "sacrament" to seven particular rituals, under the influence of theologians such as Peter Lombard (+ 1160), originally the term sacrament was not so narrowly defined. Prior to developments in the twelfth and thirteenth centuries, sacrament was a rather elusive concept, easily predicated of a wide range of ecclesial arts and artifacts. Augustine, for example, listed over three hundred actions and/or objects as "sacraments."[46] By the high Middle Ages, however, the term sacrament was being restricted to those seven rites of the church thought to convey sanctifying grace *ex opere operato*. All other rites, not thought to convey sanctifying grace, were called "sacramentals"—a term coined by Peter Lombard.[47]

In some respects the current situation in sacramental theology is akin to that which prevailed before the work of Lombard when the church did not limit itself to a vocabulary of seven sacraments. Today scholars such as Otto Semmelroth, Edward Schillebeeckx, and Karl Rahner have helped to expand our sacramental horizons. They and others have assisted us in understanding that Christ is the primordial sacrament, and that the church is the abiding presence of that primordial sacrament in the world, and remains the source of all other sacraments. Such formulations are now part of mainstream Roman Catholic thought, embedded in the documents of the Second Vatican Council which teaches that the church is the sacrament of Christ who, in turn, is the source of every other sacrament.[48]

It is in this broadening theological context that it is possible and appropriate to assert the sacramental character of Christian ritual music. Schillebeeckx, for example, asserts that sacraments are

> ... ecclesial acts of worship, in which the church in communion of grace with its heavenly head (i.e. together with Christ), pleads with the Father for the bestowal of grace on the recipient of the sacrament, and in which at the same time the church itself, as saving community in holy union with Christ, performs a saving act.[49]

As noted previously, music not only has the ability to wed itself to our ritual—to ecclesial acts of worship—but in some situations (i.e., our category "music alone") becomes itself the ecclesial act of worship. This is but the clearest example of Christian ritual music as sacrament, as ecclesial act of worship in which the community is "graced" by the presence of Christ[50] and in which the church, in union with Christ, performs a saving act.

According to Rahner, sacrament in the strict sense occurs

> ... when the church in her official, organized, public capacity precisely as the source of redemptive grace meets the individual in the actual ultimate accomplishment of her nature ... [which] bring[s] into activity the very essence of the church herself.[51]

What more powerful means for the church in its "public capacity" to meet the individual than in ritual song? As previously noted, music by its very nature is a unitive event, uniting the singer with the song, and singers with each other. In Christian ritual song the unitive event weds assembly with the source and the content of the song, who is Christ.[52] The song of the assembly is so rich that, according to the *Constitution on the Sacred Liturgy*, it is an event of the presence of Christ.[53] What fuller assertion could there be of the sacramental nature of Christian ritual music, especially the song of the assembly?

To assert the sacramentality of Christian ritual music is not to allege its superiority over other liturgical art forms, nor even to separate it from the other arts. Contrarily, to claim the sacramentality of Christian ritual music is to broaden the sacramental embrace beyond that allowed by the scholastic mind, so that it precisely might include the other liturgical arts. Ultimately, however, sacramental language should be employed for Christian ritual music because, more than any other language available to us, it effectively underscores and communicates music's power in worship.

The term sacrament does not occur in the New Testament. Rather, *sacramentum* is the Latin translation for the New Testament term *musterion* or secret. St. Paul teaches that *musterion* is not simply an impenetrable divine secret, but a divine secret in the process of being revealed (1 Cor 2:10ff.). Music at the service of Christian ritual is one of the agents of that revelation. Not only does music assist in this revelatory process, but it contributes something to the revelation of God and the engagement of the community that no other human artifacts or art form achieves. Thus can we assert music's integral or sacramental role in Christian worship, and note in a new way its unique contribution to the liturgical event.

Notes

1. "Sacred music, as an integral part of the solemn liturgy, participates in its general object, which is the glory of God and the sanctification and edification of the faithful." *Tra le sollecitudini* (1903) n. 1 as cited in R. Kevin Seasoltz, *The New Liturgy* (New York: Herder, 1966) 4.

2. *Constitution on the Sacred Liturgy* n. 112, as cited in *DOL* n. 112.

3. For a definition of this term, see my "Liturgical Music," *The New Dictionary of Sacramental Worship*, ed. Peter Fink (Collegeville: The Liturgical Press, 1990) 854-855.

4. For an introduction to this vast literature, see Kevin Irwin, *Liturgical Theology: A Primer*, American Essays in Liturgy (Collegeville: The Liturgical Press, 1991).

5. For an introduction to this literature, see above pp. 10-11.

6. William Morris, ed., *The American Heritage Dictionary of the English Language* (Boston: Houghton Mifflin Company, 1976), s.v. "sound."

7. Davies, *The Psychology of Music* 26-27.

8. Ibid. 26.

9. "The crucial quality about music, which distinguishes it from most of the visual arts, is a temporal one." Ibid. 47.

10. Hans Jonas, "The Nobility of Sight: A Study in the Phenomenology of the Senses," *Philosophy and Phenomenological Research* 14 (1954) 513.

11. Susanne Langer, *Feeling and Form* (New York: Charles Scribner's Sons, 1953) 110.

12. Susanne Langer, *Philosophy in a New Key: A Study in the Symbolism of Reason, Rite and Art*, 3rd ed. (Cambridge: Harvard University Press, 1976) 243.

13. Much of what follows is taken from the discussion of "The Musical Present" in Davies, *The Psychology of Music* 48-51.

14. Ibid. 49.

15. For an introduction to this facet of Plato's thought, see Eric Havelock, *Preface to Plato: A History of the Greek Mind* (Cambridge: Belknap Press of Harvard University, 1963).

16. See Walter Ong, *The Presence of the Word* (New Haven: Yale University Press, 1967) 123-125.

17. Ibid. 163.

18. Edmund Carpenter and Marshall McLuhan, "Acoustic Space," *Explorations in Communication*, ed. Edmund Carpenter and Marshall McLuhan (Boston: Beacon Press, 1960) 67.

19. Ong, *The Presence of the Word* 164.

20. Walter Ong, "'I see what you say': Sense Analogues for Intellect," *Interfaces of the Word* (Ithaca and London: Cornell University Press, 1977) 140-141.

21. Margin Buber, *I and Thou*, trans. and introduced by Walter Kaufmann (New York: Charles Scribner's Sons, 1970).

22. Ibid. 54-55; emphasis mine.

23. Martin Buber, *Between Man and Man*, trans. Ronald Gregor Smith (New York: Macmillan Publishing Co., 1965), especially "Dialogue" 1-39.

24. See Huijbers, *The Performing Audience,* 127-129; for a more complete discussion of these types, see Edward Foley and Mary McGann, *Music and the Eucharistic Prayer*, American Essays in Liturgy (Collegeville: The Liturgical Press, 1988) 11-15.

25. If, however, the procession is not an integral part of this ritual, and the birthday song is intoned without any accompanying action, then it would be categorized as *music united to a text*.

26. Raimundo Panikkar, "Man as a Ritual Being," *Chicago Studies* 16:1 (1977) 10.

27. "Language, in the strict sense, is discursive; it has permanent units of meaning which are combinable into larger units . . . It differs from wordless symbolism, which is non-discursive and untranslatable, does not allow of definitions within its own system, and cannot directly convey generalities. The meanings given through language are successively understood and gathered into a whole by the process called discourse; the meanings of all other symbolic elements that compose a larger, articulate symbol are understood only through the meaning of the whole, through their relations within the total structure. Their very functioning as symbols depends on the fact that they are involved in a simultaneous, integral presentation. Langer, *Philosophy in a New Key* 96-97.

28. Panikkar, "Man as a Ritual Being" 8-9.

29. Paul Tillich, *Theology of Culture*, ed. Robert Kimball (New York: Oxford University Press, 1975) 57.

30. Langer, *Philosophy in a New Key* 101.

31. For a survey of the philosophical discussions of music as a symbol up until the mid-twentieth century, see Gordon Epperson, *The Musical Symbol: A Study of the Philosophic Theory of Music* (Ames: Iowa State University Press, 1967).

32. See my *Music in Ritual: A Pre-Theological Investigation* 9-13; also, the discussion in Jean-Jacques Nattiez, *Music and Discourse: Toward a Semiology of Music,* trans. Carolyn Abbate (Princeton, NJ: Princeton University Press, 1990) 107-129.

33. van der Leeuw, *Sacred and Profane Beauty: The Holy in Art* 215.

34. Bruno Nettl, *Music in Primitive Culture* (Cambridge, MA: Harvard University Press, 1965) 6.

35. "The legends and myths of nearly all pagan peoples have sought to explain the elaborate use of music in their worship by indicating that the art of music was a gift of the gods to men." Quasten, *Music and Worship in Pagan and Christian Antiquity* 1.

36. "Christian Ritual Music" is the term employed in *The Music of Christian Ritual: Universa Laus Guidelines 1980* to describe "the vocal and instrumental practices integral to Christian Liturgy," n. 1.3 as cited in *The Bulletin of Universa Laus* 30 (1980) 5. In order to establish continuity more clearly between the phenomenon of ritual music and that of Christian ritual music, the latter term will be employed for the duration of this article instead of its previously employed synonym, "liturgical music."

37. Mircea Eliade, *The Sacred and the Profane*, trans. Willard R. Trask (New York: Harper & Row, 1961) 110-111.

38. Terrien, *The Elusive Presence* 470.

39. Donald Grey, "A Real Absence: A Note on the Eucharist," *Living Bread, Saving Cup*, ed. R. Kevin Seasoltz (Collegeville: The Liturgical Press, 1982) 190-196.

40. Victor Zuckerkandl, *Man the Musician: Sound and Symbol*, 2 vols., trans. Norbert Guterman, Bollingen Series 44-2 (Princeton: Princeton University Press, 1973) 2:15.

41. The *locus classicus* of this notion is the maxim of Prosper of Aquitaine, *"legem credendi lex statuat suplicandi"* (PL 51:209); for a further discussion of this concept see Paul De Clerck, "'Lex Orandi, Lex Credendi,' Sens originel et avatars historiques d'un adage équivoque," *Questions liturgiques* 59 (1978) 193-212.

42. Söhngen, "Music and Theology: A Systematic Approach" 14.

43. See above, p. 104, n. 1.

44. "In Christian liturgy, music is not indispensable, but its contribution is irreplaceable." *The Music of Christian Ritual: Universa Laus Guidelines* 1980, Conviction 21, as cited in *The Bulletin of Universa Laus* 30 (1980) 14.

45. In *Tra le sollecitudini* Pius X delineated three criteria for "sacred music," the first of which was that it must be holy (n. 2). Although the *Constitution on the Sacred Liturgy* reinterpreted holiness in terms of the function of the music in the ritual and not simply the music in and of itself, it continues to use the term: "sacred music will be the more holy the more closely it is joined to the liturgical rite" (n. 112).

46. For a discussion of the flexible meaning of sacrament in Augustine, and a relatively exhaustive listing of references, see C. Coutourier, "'Sacramentum' et 'Mysterium' dans l'oeuvre de Saint Augustine," *Etudes augustiniennes* (Paris: Aubier, 1953) 161-301.

47. *Sententiae* 4.6.8 (PL 192:855).

48. See the *Dogmatic Constitution on the Church* nn. 1, 9, and 48; also the *General Catechetical Directory* n. 55.

49. Edward Schillebeeckx, *Christ the Sacrament of the Encounter with God* (New York: Sheed and Ward, 1963) 66.

50. The *Constitution on the Sacred Liturgy* unequivocally teaches that Christ is present when the church sings (n. 7).

51. Karl Rahner, *The Church and the Sacraments*, Quaestiones Disputatae 9, trans. W.J. O'Hara (Freiburg im Br.: Herder, 1963) 22.

52. Clement of Alexandria, *Protreptikos* I.6.5.

53. See n. 7.

6

From *Music in Catholic Worship* to the "Milwaukee Document"

Introduction

THE INTRODUCTION TO *LITURGICAL MUSIC TODAY* CONTAINS THE FOLLOWING assessment of *Music in Catholic Worship*:

> Ten years ago the Bishops' Committee on the Liturgy published *Music in Catholic Worship*, itself the revision of an earlier statement. That document has proven to be very useful in setting out the principles for Church music in the reformed liturgy. It has served well over these years. Since the Roman liturgical books were still in the process of revision ten years ago, the Committee recognizes that there are subjects that *Music in Catholic Worship* addressed only briefly or not at all ... Moreover, the passage of time has raised a number of unforeseen issues in need of clarification and questions revealing new possibilities for liturgical music. We take this opportunity to note these developments. (nn. 2-3)

In many respects this assessment of MCW is as valid today as it was in 1982. MCW continues to serve as a most useful statement of key principles for church music in the reformed liturgy. Its influence was in no way eclipsed by the publication of LMT which serves more as an appendix than as the hoped for companion[1] to MCW. Ironically, the uneven quality of LMT has rendered its predecessor more influential than ever.

It is also true, however, that in the years since its publication, new issues have arisen which are not adequately addressed by

MCW nor by LMT. It was, in part, because of such developments that *The Milwaukee Symposia for Church Composers: A Ten-Year Report* (MSCC) was written. In order to contextualize the latter, it is useful to revisit MCW (and, to a lesser degree, LMT). Such a revisiting will mean reaffirming MCW's solid approach and content, underscoring many of the valuable principles contained therein, demonstrating where lacunae exist and noting those few places where the document has proven to be misdirected. More specifically, I would like to offer a critical reappraisal of what I believe to be the core of MCW, i.e., section III on the musical, liturgical, and pastoral judgments. This will entail offering specific affirmations of what the document asserts as central or essential to these judgments, suggesting what is implied in the document and needs to be made more explicit, raising specific problems that the document does not address, noting errors in the document, and suggesting how MSCC has attempted to respond.

The Musical Judgment

In an oft quoted passage, MCW explains the nature of the musical judgment by asking "Is the music technically, aesthetically and expressively good?" It continues:

> This judgment is basic and primary and should be made by competent musicians. Only artistically sound music will be effective in the long run. To admit the cheap, the trite, the musical cliché often found in popular songs for the purpose of "instant liturgy" is to cheapen the liturgy, to expose it to ridicule and to invite failure. (n. 26)

Essential here is the age-old affirmation that quality music begets quality worship. This fundamental principle is balanced by a welcomed clarification between style and value, and MCW happily admits that these are two distinctive judgments (n. 28), noting that value judgments must be made within and not across styles.

Problem One

Although affirming the need for quality musical composition and distinguishing between value and style are important parts of the document, their formulation in MCW admits of a series of problems. The first is a clear impression that musical judgments should be made within the framework of those nineteenth-century

FROM *MUSIC IN CATHOLIC WORSHIP* 129

European conservatory standards which still pervade many if not most schools of composition in this country. This impression is a cumulative response to: (1) the document's caution about popular music which, MCW asserts, has a tendency to employ "musical clichés"; (2) the call for decisions to be made by "competent" musicians; and (3) the call for "artistically sound" music. This language suggests that popular music is prone to be poor music and conversely that the opposite kind of music—i.e., music for the elite or concert hall music—is better. It further suggests that since only "competent musicians" are really capable of distinguishing between good and bad music, and since most people are not competent musicians, therefore, most people are incapable of rendering any credible musical judgment about our worship music.

As a corrective, it is important to recognize that untrained musicians—ordinary people—very definitely have something to say about the quality of our worship music. Although the degreed musician might be able to apply technical names to different sounds or explain how a piece is constructed, it does not follow, therefore, that only degreed musicians can decide if a piece is good or not. What might be considered a *"Volk"* standard must be part of the equation in making compositional decisions about music's value.

Thus MSCC notes:

> One step toward integrating the various facets of the musical-liturgical-pastoral judgment is an integration of the various perspectives and peoples involved. For example, MCW notes that judgments about the technical, aesthetic and expressive quality of a musical work should be made by a competent musician.[2] Professional musicians bring a wealth of information and experience to the task of judging the quality of a musical work. Yet, people who are not trained musicians also have much to say about the quality of worship music.[3] On the other hand, while detailing the nature of the pastoral judgment, MCW notes that while a musician may judge that a certain work is good music, this judgment says nothing about whether or how this music is to be used in worship.[4] Some have drawn the questionable conclusion from this statement that the pastoral judgment can be made apart from the musical one, and by people other than the musician. Yet, just as people who are not trained musicians have something to contribute when assessing the quality of worship music, so do musical professionals have something to say about the pasto-

ral selection and use of such music. The integration of various people and perspectives in all facets of the musical-liturgical-pastoral judgment are required if the integrity of that judgment is to be respected and promoted. (n. 83)

Problem Two

A second related problem in MCW's formulation of the musical judgment is its ethnocentrism. Implicit distinctions between "artistically sound" and "popular" music suggest a northern European perspective, generally adopted in the United States, in which art music and popular or folk music have developed separately. Many cultures, however, are incapable of understanding this distinction. The assertion that musical judgments can only be made by competent musicians becomes particularly unacceptable when we move outside western culture. In many traditional societies where music is bound to social custom and tribal ritual, it is not the degreed or specially trained musicians who ultimately judge the quality of music. It is the people. Writing about the music of Africa, for example, John Miller Chernoff notes:

> The essential criteria for distinguishing excellence in African music are . . . as much ethical as aesthetic. Yet African music does not become the subject of abstract and systematic discussions about morality and ethics, and people do not become analytical about the fundamental social themes displayed in their music: the point is to participate in the appropriate way. If the music is good, people listen, dance, and enjoy themselves. If it is bad, they will try to correct it in whatever way they can, perhaps by making fun of a vain dancer or anyone present with a bad attitude, perhaps by offering suggestions or encouragement to the musicians, perhaps by buying some beer, or perhaps, if their mood is hopeless, by being sensible enough to leave the place . . . Everything one does becomes an act of "criticism": people express their opinions by participating.[5]

Why should it be any different for us, especially if we avoid implicit distinctions between "artistically sound" and popular music, between art and folk music—distinctions which many ethnomusicologists schooled in non-western music seriously question. As John Blacking clearly asserts: "All music is folk music."[6] To continue explicitly or implicitly such distinctions, however, is not only to disallow ordinary people from participating in making musical judgments, it is also to assert that our cultural perspective is superior. As a corrective, I would suggest that a thorough musical judgment not only recognizes that the *Volk*-standard must be part of the equation in making compositional decisions about music's value, but also admits that such standards differ from people to people and from culture to culture. Let us be explicit about our rejection of ethnocentrism in rendering musical judgments. It is only by doing so that we will be able to cherish the "rich diversity of the cultural heritage of the many peoples of our country" of which LMT so eloquently speaks (n. 54).

MSCC addresses these issues in the section entitled "Cross-Cultural Music Making" (nn. 56-63). Paragraph 60 is particularly important in this regard:

> From a musical perspective, accepting the challenge of cross-cultural worship requires addressing the ethnocentrism that has marked Western Christian music for the last millennium. While in times past there may have been good reasons for upholding Gregorian Chant and the music of Palestrina as the best models of Christian ritual music, the continuation of such assertions carries the cultural message that medieval and Renaissance music of Western Europe is somehow intrinsically better than music of other eras or other cultures. The development of common practice procedures in tonal music that eventually crystallized into compositional rules in the West further uphold the superiority of the style of composition flourishing in Northern Europe from the 17th to the 19th centuries. This Bach-Beethoven-Brahms paradigm is consistently employed as the standard by which all other composition—including worship music—has been judged. If one decides to compose in a particular style—such as that of Bach—then one must follow the compositional rules that govern that style. It is unacceptable, however, to impose arbitrarily the compositional canons of one time or place upon that of another.[7] A cross-cultural perspective will curtail our bias for music of a specific age and culture. This is not to suggest that the treasure of sacred music lauded by CSL[8] is to be rejected. Many pieces from this treasury are most useful in contemporary worship but they have no intrinsic musical superiority. Rather, they—like all our ritual music—must be judged on their ability to serve the rite and enable the people's prayer through their full, conscious and active participation.

Problem Three

A final related problem is what I perceive to be MCW's bias for evaluating music in terms of the page instead of the performance. Our western classical bias is that we can and must judge a composition according to what is in the score and, when appropriate, offer a separate judgment about the quality of the musicians and the musical performance. The difficulty with such an evaluation, as underscored in the previous quote from Chernoff, is that it does not respect the nature of the musical event and the compositional needs of such an event. Specifically, I would suggest that some styles of music cannot simply be musically evaluated by means of the musical score. Much gospel music, for example, is constructed to be improvised. Harmonic, rhythmic, and even structural variations are at the core of this type of music whereas they are not, for example, part of a motet by Palestrina or an anthem by Lovelace. Judging a song like "Jesus in the Morning"[9] simply by analyzing what appears on the page, or by playing the given accompaniment, is totally inadequate. Rather, such music must be judged not only by its explicit compositional quality but also by it improvisational possibilities. It is only from this perspective that the mantras of Jacques Berthier, the "Litany of the Saints" by Robert Hutmacher, and similar aleatoric or improvisationally conceived works must be judged.

MSCC begins to address this issue in the opening paragraph of the section on "Models of Musical Leadership" when it notes: "Christian ritual music is an event and not simply music on a page.[10] It is the whole of the event that needs to be prepared and evaluated in terms of its service of the liturgy" (n. 64).

The Liturgical Judgment

Turning to the liturgical judgment, MCW differentiates between (A) structural requirements, (B) textual requirements, and (C) ministerial requirements or what the document calls role differentiation.

A. Structural Requirements

Outlining the nature of the structural requirements, MCW notes:

> The choice of sung parts, the balance between them and the style of the musical setting used should reflect the relative

importance of the parts of the Mass (or other service) and the nature of each part. Thus elaborate settings of the entrance song, "Lord have mercy" and "Glory to God" may make the proclamation of the word seem unimportant; and [an] overly elaborate offertory song [sic] with a spoken "Holy, Holy, Holy Lord" may make the eucharistic prayer seem less important. (n. 31)

Basic to this structural component of the liturgical judgment is the requirement of correspondence in style and performance length between various liturgical elements and their liturgical nature and importance as outlined in the *General Instruction of the Roman Missal*. This section of MCW also implies that such judgments require not only consideration of individual parts, like the "Lord, have mercy," but of entire liturgical units, like the entrance rite. This presumption becomes explicit in LMT (n. 15).

Problem One

Although MCW begins to suggest the musical consideration of liturgical units, this concept is yet underdeveloped. MCW, for example, does not explicitly or implicitly suggest that there should be musical integrity between the various individual elements that comprise a liturgical unit. For example, there is no presumption that in the introductory rites there would be complementarity in style, tonality, or key between the entrance song, *Kyrie*, and *Gloria*, but only that there be correspondence in style and performance length between the individual part and its musical setting. Without a macro-structural approach, however, our worship music will continue to introduce a series of beginnings and endings within a single liturgical unit and perpetuate the constant fragmentation that besets so much of our worship. This is one of the few places where LMT actually demonstrates an advance over MCW, noting:

> ... it needs to be recognized that a certain musical integrity within a liturgical prayer or rite can be achieved only by unity in the musical composition. Thus, it is recommended that for the acclamations in the eucharistic prayer one musical style be employed. (n. 15)

Both documents need to go further and expect musical integrity (e.g., compositional style, tonality, key, meter, etc.) among the various elements within each liturgical unit. This requirement would make demands on the musical practitioner to be more careful about the choice of music and put demands on composers as well to stop producing isolated pieces and, instead, become serious about tackling the musical composition of liturgical units.

MSCC devotes an entire section to "Liturgical and Musical Structures" (nn. 37-44). On this particular issue paragraph 43 is instructive:

> Integrity and unity in the rite suggest that the musical contour support the larger ritual units. When various pieces of music that are incompatible in key, in mode or in compositional style are employed within the same liturgical unit, fragmentation may occur. Such a juxtaposition of differing musical modes—especially within a single liturgical unit like an entrance rite—communicates, if subconsciously, to the assembly that there is no liturgical unit but, instead, a string of unrelated elements. The ideal is a unified and balanced use of the various musical elements within the various liturgical units. For example, LMT recommends the employment of acclamations of a single unified style throughout the eucharistic prayer.

Problem Two

A second problem with this section of MCW is that it ignores instrumental music and gives the faulty impression that only music with a text can truly serve the liturgy. An earlier part of the document does infer that beyond any text music adds a special dimension to the worship,[11] and a latter section of the document does note that instrumental music is appropriate at specific (though clearly secondary) moments in the liturgy.[12] LMT offers a mixed message on this topic, on the one hand noting the ministerial function of instrumental music (n. 58) while limiting an earlier key discussion to the place, function, and form of "song" (nn. 9-11).

What is needed is a stronger recognition that instrumental as well as vocal music can and must serve central ritual units of our worship according to the above delineated criteria. A single flute at the entrance procession on Ash Wednesday, a handbell peal for the gospel procession during Easter, J.S. Bach's *Alle Menschen müssen sterben* as the responsorial during a funeral Mass: although not necessarily the norm in our culture, these exemplify the legitimate place for music alone at the center of our worship. Such an awareness will enable us to appreciate more fully other cultures in which untexted instrumental music plays a central ritual role.[13]

Whereas MSCC does speak of instrumental music on a number of occasions,[14] it does not specifically address this issue.

B. Textual Requirements

Turning to a discussion of textual requirements, MCW poses the following questions:

> Does the music express and interpret the text correctly and made it more meaningful? Is the form of the text respected? In making these judgments the principal classes of texts must be kept in mind: proclamations, acclamations, psalms and hymns, and prayers. Each has a specific function which must be served by the music chosen for a text. In most instances there is an official text approved by the episcopal conference. "Vernacular texts set to music composed in earlier periods," however, "may be used in liturgical texts." As noted elsewhere, criteria have been provided for the texts which may replace the processional chants of Mass. In these cases and in the choice of all supplementary music, the texts "must always be in conformity with Catholic doctrine; indeed they should be drawn chiefly from holy scripture and from liturgical sources." (n. 32)

Essential to this section is the presumption that music must serve the text, elaborating, unfolding, and nuancing the words. Also fundamental here is the requirement of integrity between the form of the text and the form of the music. Finally, the document is clear about the need for orthodoxy in our liturgical texts. Two further things seem to be implied in this section. The first is the recognition of a need for integrity between the style of the liturgical text and the style of the music employed for such a setting. Thus acclamations should be acclamatory and gospel processions should be processional. Second, there is the presumption of a well-crafted wedding between text and tune, a wedding that respects the sense lines, meter, and accents or tonality of the language.

Problem One

One major lacuna in this section is any recognition of the need for lyricism or poetry in our texts. Apart from orthodoxy, the question of a text's lyrical and metaphoric richness cannot be overlooked. Otherwise we increase the risk of reducing liturgical song to catechetics or apologetics instead of a true entry point into the mystery. As a corrective we might consider applying the characteristics of quality and appropriateness as outlined in *Environment and Art in Catholic Worship* (nn. 20-22) to our musical texts. It is especially the latter, requiring that a work of art "be capable of bearing the weight, awe, reverence and wonder which the liturgical action expresses" that could help clarify the poetic demands of our liturgical texts.

MSCC devotes an entire section to "Textual Considerations" (nn. 45-55). It specifically addresses the issue of the poetic demands of liturgical texts in paragraph 47, when it notes:

> Recovering the basic lyricism of Christian worship means that the texts themselves must possess a certain lyricism so that they are more effective, whether proclaimed or set to music. After almost 30 years of English liturgy we are growing more conscious of the lyrical-musical requirements of our worship texts. In the early stages of vernacular liturgy concerns about intelligibility and the orthodoxy of texts were the priority. The latter concern was reflected in CSL, which noted that texts to be sung "must always be consistent with Catholic teaching; indeed they should be drawn chiefly from holy Scripture and from liturgical sources."[15] While important, concerns about orthodoxy and accessibility are only part of the necessary criteria for shaping a vernacular liturgy. In addition, attention to the poetic quality of a text, its singability and symbolic richness are also essential. The texts of our worship are not only official reflections of belief, but modes of liturgical formation. The texts we proclaim and sing are words by which we live. Such texts for proclamation and song demand not only orthodoxy, but character and substance so that they can continue to enrich lives beyond their first sounding or last hearing.

Problem Two

A second major lacuna in this section and in the whole of LMT is any discussion of inclusive language. This is actually a series of issues ranging from the use of gender specific God-language to the reediting of traditional music in which sexisms are wedded to some of our most treasured sacred verses. Although there are few clearings in this linguistic thicket, we must at least raise the issue and attempt to widen the clearing.

MSCC does just that in paragraph 54 when it remarks:

> Justice demands not only the avoidance of gender exclusive language,[16] but also of language that further marginalizes those with physical or mental disabilities, the elderly, or those who are socially stigmatized. As noted by *Fulfilled in your Hearing*, "even in parishes that are more or less uniform in ethnic, social or economic background, there is great diversity: men and women, old and young, the successes and the failures, the joyful and the bereaved, the fervent and the halfhearted, the strong and the weak."[17] While every text will not speak to each of these groups with the same intensity or effectiveness, those responsible for producing liturgical texts must strive to ensure that such texts do not alienate worshippers.

C. Ministerial Requirements (Role Differentiation)

Problem One

In regard to the various musical roles within worship, MCW offers a mixed message on the role of the congregation vis-à-vis the choir. Initially the document implies that the congregation holds a primary musical role by listing the congregation before the cantor, choir, or instrumentalists when discussing the various roles.[18] Later on, however, MCW notes that "a well-trained choir adds beauty and solemnity to the liturgy and also [sic] assists and encourages the singing of the congregation" (n. 36). The structure of that sentence and especially the use of the word "also" suggests that the choir's first role is not to support the song of the congregation but to do something else. I find this to be an inappropriate emphasis and would suggest that the section be readjusted to affirm the primacy of congregational song and the redirection of every musical ministry to support that enterprise.

LMT offers a few paragraphs on various musical ministers.[19] In general, these paragraphs implicitly recognize the primacy of the assembly but do not address the relationship between the congregation and the choir raised above. They do, however, offer a distinction between the cantor and the psalmist which I find most unhelpful and historically questionable.[20] The distinction should be eliminated.

MSCC underscores the importance of the assembly in n. 9, which is an articulation of certain foundational principles for the entirety of the document. Principle n. 3 is: "the assembly is primary,[21] and has a central role in sung worship." That principle is illustrated throughout the document which is anchored in the assembly.[22]

The relationship between the assembly and the choir is clarified in n. 72 of that document, which speaks not only of the choir but of all musical leadership in worship:

> Those who assume musical leadership in worship need to balance their skills with an awareness that their musicianship is always at the service of the assembly. There is no doubt that Christian liturgy benefits from the presence of skilled musicians even as it calls forth from them a new and necessary discipline. This discipline, seldom taught in our universities or conservatories, puts musicianship in an auxiliary role, handmaid to the liturgy. As noted in LMT, church musicians are called to be disciples first and then ministers.[23] Our society may provide a variety of models for musicians, but many are devised for entertainment and are not appropriate for the liturgy. The nature of the liturgy requires a unique style of musical leadership: one that is, at its core, both professional and pastoral.

Problem Two

More problematic is the total disregard in this section of any consideration of performance styles appropriate to pastoral musicians. As I have argued elsewhere,[24] the single most powerful musical force for shaping the worship and belief of our assemblies is the style of musical performance employed in our worship. One can critique the quality of contemporary composition, the arrangements of these compositions, or their presentation by publishers. These are no more important, however, than the quality of the musical leadership and the style of the musical performance that translates the work of the composer from manuscript to liturgical event. This is critical for, in my estimation, how people lead the music has as much or more influence on congregational participation than what music is sung. My fear, however, is that both are struggling under the influence of an entertainment model of worship which could have devastating long range effects on our common prayer.

As a corrective to this lacuna in MCW we need to address the requirements of a pastoral standard of musical performance within the liturgy. In this regard the reflections of Eric Routley could be a useful starting point. He comments:

> The communication achieved by any work of art always has a content of transfiguration or thrill; we gasp, sigh or exclaim "how beautiful that is!" If that is all we do the artist's purpose is not necessarily fulfilled; and, conversely, if that is all the artist hopes to get from us, he is not doing his duty as an artist ... Just as Jesus would not let people hold onto moments of thrill and transfiguration (Mark 9:5-8; John 6:22-27), so artists who design their work so that thrill or sensation is its chief purpose are defective artists. This is especially obvious in church music, for its purpose is to assist the believer in his journey towards God, not to attach him to the sensations of this world.[25]

The pastoral standard we need to cultivate in our worship music means secure musicianship wedded to a willingness to submit to the ritual; it means enough artistry to allow the voice of the assembly to be the center of attention; and it means enough musical acumen to enable the singing not the song, the music making not the music itself to lead believers into the mystery.

MSCC addresses issues of musical leadership throughout the document. A specific section entitled "Models of Musical Leadership" is found in nn. 64-72. Particularly helpful, in light of the above critique, is n. 66:

> The effect of musically unskilled leadership is often easy to identify. Musical uncertainty in a vocalist or instrumentalist evokes similar insecurity and uncertainty in the assembly. Halting musical leadership can effectively destroy the song of the community. Musical competency is essential in order to avoid this dilemma. Sometimes more difficult is gauging the potential ill effects of over-performance on the part of the musical leadership in worship. In some respects this is a result of the pervasive influence of television in U.S. culture and the promotion of the entertainment model as the primary mode of public discourse in our society.[26] We are used to performers who dazzle us with their talent. There is sometimes the expectation on the part of the assembly that worship will provide the same experiences. Musical leadership cast in the entertainment mode transforms an assembly into an audience and believers into liturgical consumers. Music ministers need to examine their assumed model of musical leadership, to en-

sure that they habitually draw the assembly into the center of worship.

The Pastoral Judgment

Finally we turn to a consideration of the pastoral judgment. This section is, on the one hand, one of the great achievements of MCW, and on the other hand the most frustrating three paragraphs of the entire document. The core of this section, as I read it, comes in the form of a question. The document asks: "Does music in the celebration enable these people to express their faith, in this place, in this age, in this culture?" (n. 39) The great value of this statement, of course, is the affirmation of the real needs of real people in concrete times, cultures, and contexts. What music helps them pray?

Problem One

The central problem with this section, however, is that it can appear to undo completely the musical judgment. As MCW itself later remarks, "A musician may judge that a certain composition or style of composition is good music but his musical judgment really says nothing about whether and how this music is to be used in this celebration" (n. 41). My presumption as I read these paragraphs is that, ultimately, the pastoral decision is the most important and although the musical judgment is theoretically important, it can be discounted or ignored in the face of pastoral concerns. One of the reasons that I believe this apparent opposition between the musical and the pastoral judgment exists in MCW is because, as previously noted, this document excludes ordinary people from participating in the musical judgment. Ironically, the professional musician similarly seems to be excluded or at least made peripheral to the pastoral judgment. As a corrective, I would suggest that MCW needs to be recast so that, as suggested earlier, musical judgments are achieved through a dialogue between the musician and the congregation, a dialogue between popular taste and musical insight. If the preferences of the people can have some bearing on musical decisions, then in turn it seems that the insights of the professionally trained musician could have more bearing on the pastoral judgment.

MSCC (n. 82) addresses the apparent tension between the musical, liturgical, and pastoral judgment by stressing that these, in fact, are three facets of a single judgment and cannot be made sequentially or in opposition to each other:

> One difficulty is the tendency to treat the musical-liturgical-pastoral judgment as three separate judgments. MCW introduces the sections on this topic by noting that "a threefold judgment must be made: musical, liturgical and pastoral."[27] Yet the ensuing sections of MCW contribute to a fragmentation of this single, multi-faceted judgment by treating the musical, liturgical and pastoral aspects separately, without a discussion of their integration.[28] This presentation has given the impression that there is a chronological progression to these judgments, with priority given to the final (pastoral) judgment. Thus the various judgments—especially the musical and the pastoral—are sometimes perceived to be in opposition to each other. To avoid such conflicts and to respect more completely the formulation found in MCW, it is necessary to admit of a single, multi-faceted judgment for evaluating musical elements in worship. A model for this can be found in *Environment and Art in Catholic Worship* whose standards of quality and appropriateness are distinctive yet complementary.[29] Acknowledging the need for an integrated judgment requires a balancing of the various facets of this single judgment, and not the opposition of one element to another. The process of the judgment, therefore, is not chronological but dynamic and interactive.

Problem Two

This apparent dichotomy between the musical and pastoral judgments in MCW might further be dissolved through correction of another weakness in this section of the document. The prism provided by Robert Bellah et al. in *Habits of the Heart* renders the collective individualism of the previously cited core sentence of this section somewhat disturbing. "Does music in the celebration enable these people to express their faith in this place, in this age, in this culture?" Where is the acknowledgement that liturgy is not owned or even defined by any single community but an act of Christ? Where is the acknowledgment that each liturgical act calls forth the faith of an individual wedded to the faith of the church? Where is the acknowledgement that besides worship attending to this place, this age, and this culture, it must also be open to the worship of other people from other places and cultures: those who have gone before and those who will come after.

Here LMT offers an uncharacteristic corrective to MCW, noting that:

> The music selected must express the prayer of those who celebrate, while at the same time guarding against the imposition of private meanings of public rites. Individual preference is not, of itself, a sufficient principle for the choice of music in the liturgy. (n. 12)

Emphasizing the true catholic nature of our worship guards against creeping individualism. It also offers a certain integrity to the musical judgments: for if we recognize that even local worship must reach beyond itself to the wider church, then we find ourselves forced beyond personal taste to regional or even national standards of composition, to renewed appreciation of the music that nurtured our forebears in faith, and a new openness to the cultural expressions emerging for the church of the next generation.

MSCC stresses the collective nature of the liturgical enterprise with its continuous emphasis on the assembly, as previously noted. It also offers this caution: "In the United States there is a tendency to overemphasize the individual, to the detriment of our collective consciousness. Redemption in the Judaeo-Christian tradition is a collective, not a private reality" (n. 53).

Conclusion

It should be clear from what preceded that MSCC does not supplant MCW as an instrument of reform for the post-conciliar liturgy. The most obvious reason for such is that the latter is an official document of the U.S. hierarchy,[30] whereas the former is simply a statement of various composers, musicians, and theologians. Apart from canonical considerations, however, it should also be clear that MSCC presumes the background of MCW, affirms most of what is articulated in that document, and is able to provide further development—to a large extent—because of the strong foundation of MCW. In many respects MSCC can be understood as a natural, organic development from MCW which, in turn, will itself yield to other developments. So will the reform continue to unfold, as we explore the integration of liturgy and music envisioned by the Second Vatican Council.[31]

Notes

1. "This statement . . . should be read as a companion to *Music in Catholic Worship* and *Environment and Art in Catholic Worship*." LMT n. 3.
2. MCW n. 26.
3. The assertion that musical judgments can only be made by specialized musicians becomes particularly difficult to support when one moves into other cultures; see, for example, John Miller Chernoff, *African Rhythm and African Sensibility: Aesthetics and Social Action in African Musical Idioms* (Chicago and London: University of Chicago Press, 1979), especially 153ff.
4. MCW n. 41.
5. Chernoff, *African Rhythm and African Sensibility* 153.
6. He continues: "Distinctions between the surface complexity of different musical styles and techniques do not tell us anything useful about the expressive purposes and power of music, or about the intellectual organization involved in its creation. Music is too deeply concerned with human feelings and experiences in society, and its patterns are too often generated by surprising outburst of unconscious cerebration for it to be subject to arbitrary rules, like the rules of games. Many if not all of music's essential processes may be found in the constitution of the human body and in patterns of interaction of human bodies in society. Thus all music is structurally as well as functionally folk music. The makers of "art" music are not innately more sensitive or cleverer than "folk" musicians: the structures of their music simply express . . . the numerically larger systems of interaction of folk in their societies, the consequences of a more extensive division of labor, and an accumulated technological tradition." John Blacking, *How Musical Is Man* (Seattle and London: University of Washington Press, 1974) x-xi.
7. "Ethnomusicologists are great egalitarians. They avoid value-judgments that would rank the music of Society A over that of Society B. They prefer to report a society's own ratings of its musicians than to impose judgements from the outside." Helen Myers, "Ethnomusicology," *The New Oxford Companion to Music*, ed. Denis Arnold, 2 vols. (Oxford: Oxford University Press, 1988 [1983]) 1:646.
8. CSL n. 114.
9. In *Lead Me, Guide Me* (Chicago: GIA Publications, 1987) n. 131.
10. Contemporary musicologists, such as Frederick Mauk, are beginning to recognize this lacuna in the study of western musical traditions which tend to "focus upon music paper [notation] and other documents rather than upon sound [performance]." Frederick Mauk, "Resurrection and Insurrection," *Journal of Aesthetics and Art Criticism* 45:2 (1986) 1. Another sign of concern about the musical event is the strong interest among musicologists in this century on performance practices.

11. "In addition to expressing texts, music can also unveil a dimension of meaning and feeling, a communication of ideas and intuitions which words alone cannot yield." MCW nn. 8-11.

12. (1) prelude, (2) soft background to a spoken psalm, (3) the preparation of the gifts in place of singing, (4) during portions of the communion rite, and (5) the recessional. MCW n. 37.

13. For example, drumming in Ghana. See J.H. Kwabena Nketia, *Drumming in Akan Communities of Ghana* (London: University of Ghana and Thomas Nelson and Sons, 1963) passim.

14. For example, nn. 21, 27, 45, 66, 67, 70, and 77.

15. CSL n. 121; reiterated in MCW n. 32.

16. See NCCB document "Criteria for the Evaluation of Inclusive Language Translations of Scriptural Texts proposed for Liturgical Use" (1990).

17. p. 5.

18. n. 33, and nn. 34-37.

19. nn. 63-70.

20. "The cantor's role is distinct from that of the psalmist, whose ministry is the singing of the verses of the responsorial psalm and communion psalm. Frequently the two roles will be combined in one person." LMT n. 69. Another historically inaccurate definition in LMT is the antiphonal style of psalm-singing in n. 37.

21. *Environment and Art in Catholic Worship* nn. 28 and 41.

22. The word itself reoccurs 60 times throughout the document: e.g., nn. 11, 16, 18, 21, 22, 25, 26, 27, 35, 43, 62, 64, 65, 66, 67, 71, 72, 74, 77, 80, and the "Afterword."

23. LMT n. 64.

24. Mary McGann and Edward Foley, "Why Do Congregations Sing?" *Proceedings of the North American Academy of Liturgy* 3 (1990) 87-97.

25. Eric Routley, *Church Music and the Christian Faith* (Carol Stream, IL: Agape, 1978) 85-86.

26. Neil Postman, *Amusing Ourselves to Death: Public Discourse in the Age of Show Business* (New York: Penguin Books, 1985) passim.

27. MCW n. 25.

28. LMT also gives the impression that these are three separate judgments, for example, "Particular decisions about choice and placement of wedding music should grow out of the three judgments proposed in MCW" n. 29.

29. *Environment and Art in Catholic Worship* nn. 19-23.

30. On the canonical import of such a document, see John Huels, *Liturgical Law: An Introduction*, American Essays in Liturgy (Washington, DC: The Pastoral Press, 1987), especially 8-17.

31. CSL n. 112.

7

Musical Forms, Referential Meaning, and Belief[1]

Introduction

IN A TELLING ARRANGEMENT OF MATERIALS, THE U.S. BISHOPS' DOCUMENT *Music in Catholic Worship* does not begin with any specific discussion of music but rather with an opening section entitled "The Theology of Celebration." In the first paragraph of that section MCW admits to what might be considered a two-fold dynamic in worship: in worship believers "express their faith . . . and, by expressing it, renew and deepen it" (n. 1). This insight is related to a pivotal paragraph in the *Constitution on the Sacred Liturgy* which calls the liturgy the "summit toward which the activity of the Church is directed . . . [and] the fount from which all the Church's power flows" (n. 10).

In some ways this is not a new concept in Christian theology, which for centuries has acknowledged that worship and sacraments are both expressive and creative or, in scholastic terms, both "signify" and "cause."[2] What is new, however, is the implicit suggestion in MCW that worship and sacraments have their effect or produce their cause through their very ability to signify (*causant significando*). Whereas scholastic theologians like Thomas Aquinas (+ 1274) held for instrumental, efficient causality in which God alone is the primary "efficient" agent and the sacramental rite is only a secondary or "instrumental" agent,[3] a growing number of twentieth-century theologians hold for what has been called sacramental or symbolic causality. This is an attempt to forge a stronger link between sign and cause, between the expressive and creative dynamic of worship and sacraments noted in the first paragraph of MCW. From this perspective the worship symbol or sacramental symbol is not only thought to be caused by grace but is itself also a cause of grace.

Sacramental-Symbolic Causality

Karl Rahner has been a particular advocate of this concept of sacramental-symbolic causality. Rahner's advocacy of sacramental-symbolic causality is rooted in his theological anthropology which holds that all being is fundamentally symbolic.[4] For Rahner "the symbol is primarily the self-realization of a being in the other, which is constitutive of its essence."[5] This symbolic attentiveness is so strong for Rahner that for him "the whole of theology is incomprehensible if it is not seen essentially as a theology of symbols."[6] Although Rahner's approach is not beyond critique,[7] he has been a most persuasive proponent for the symbolic nature of being, of theology, and therefore of worship which can be considered our first theology.[8]

Rahner's emphasis on the symbolic nature of being—a view shared by a growing number of theologians—finds resonance outside theology in the writings of philosophers, anthropologists, linguists, and a host of others. At the outset of this century there even emerged a new science primarily concerned with systems of signs or symbols known as semiology.[9] It is through the continuing dialogue with philosophers like Ernst Cassirer,[10] anthropologists such as Clifford Geertz,[11] and semiologists like Charles Peirce[12] as well as theologians such as Rahner that we are beginning to appreciate Christian life, and the theology reflecting upon that life, as essentially symbolic ventures. From this perspective it is appropriate, as well, to consider the worship which celebrates that life as fundamentally symbolic.

It is in this context that one can appreciate anew the sequence of thought in the opening section from MCW on "The Theology of Celebration." After the first paragraph addressing the twofold dynamic of worship (i.e., its expressive and creative power), the document launches into a discussion of signs and symbols. It is this discussion which is essential to the theology of celebration outlined in the document, and which serves as a critical key for interpreting the rest of the document.

More specifically, the symbolic framework for MCW leads one to ask: if it is valid to assume the symbolic nature of all being and, by consequence, the symbolic foundation of all theology which is a reflection on our being in God; and if it is valid to assert the symbolic nature of the worship which celebrates the core of our being and is itself our first theology; and if it is appropriate to suggest that in human discourse symbols effect or give rise to thought[13] or, in theological terms, not only mediate faith (i.e., are the instrumental cause of faith), but actually effect or give rise to faith[14] (i.e., are the sacramental/symbolic cause); then is it not valid to conclude that the constituent forms of our worship symbols which enable them to cause by signifying, their surface structures which are essential to their capacity for connoting meaning, that the very configuration, shape, and form of our worship symbols are intimately wed to the way in which God's self-communication is mediated, and to the nature of the faith called forth in worship?

Is this not why we are so concerned about the words employed in our worship? Language, one of our most important symbol systems, is not neutral but integrally linked to the images of God and church that it evokes (and, therefore, to the self-communication of that God and the shaping of the church through such images). Is this not why we are so concerned about the physical design of our worship spaces? Spatial configuration and the deployment within such a configuration is another potent symbol system in the liturgy, which also is intimately wed to the images of God and church that it evokes (and, therefore, to the self-communication of that God and the shaping of the church through such images). Similarly should we be concerned about the music we employ in our worship, in all of its aspects? For this, too, is a powerful symbol system[15] which expresses and creates our faith, images of God and church.

Whereas much discussion of worship music often focuses on the signification of the texts, too little attention is given to the non-textual elements of the music symbol. Much of this is due to the more illusive nature of these "non-discursive" or "presentational" elements. It is Susanne Langer who offers the most cogent discussions of discursive and presentational symbols.[16] Language, according to Langer, is discursive in the strict sense, since it is capable of more permanent units of meaning[17] which can be combined into larger units. On the other hand, presentational symbols like an organ suite or chaconne for violin, are wordless, nondiscursive, and untranslatable. They are less capable of discreet units of meaning, cannot directly convey generalities, and are less capable of allowing clear definitions within their own system.[18]

> The meanings given through language are successively understood, and gathered into a whole by the process called discourse; the meanings of all other symbolic elements that compose a larger, articulate symbol are understood only through the meaning of the whole, through their relations with the total structure. This very functioning as symbols depends on the fact that they are involved in a simultaneous, integral presentation. This kind of semantic may be called "presentational symbolism" to characterize its essential distinction from discursive symbolism or "language" proper.[19]

Although some have pressed for a more linguistic understanding of music than Langer would seem to allow,[20] her formulation continues to be effective in alerting us to the challenge of discovering or positing meaning of the musical symbol.

Structures and Referential Meaning

Whereas Langer's presentational caution may seem especially pointed when considering musical elements like melody or rhythm, it may be less important when exploring the structures or configurations of musical forms[21] operative in worship music, in an attempt to discover what significance, if any, such forms might have upon God's self-communication and the nature of the faith called forth through such forms. It may be that the structure or configuration of musical forms, either in worship music or in other types of music, can more easily be considered in terms other than purely presentational-symbolic ones. Specifically, it may be possible to draw parallels between the musical structure or organization of a piece of worship music (or, better, a genre of worship music) and the ecclesial structure or image expressed and created by such music.

This hypothesis is based upon the presupposition that music is capable not only of meaning in and of itself (i.e., is self-referential), but is also capable of referring in some way to the extramusical world of concepts, actions, emotional states, and characters (i.e., is extra-referential).[22] A large number of theorists and practitioners hold that music is incapable of referring to anything outside of itself.[23] Langer herself would lean in this direction. Such a perspective is succinctly summarized by the American composer Edgard Varèse (+ 1965), who wrote "I believe my music is not able to express anything other than itself."[24]

There are, on the other hand, a growing number of thinkers who hold that music has two referential options and that one of the semiological peculiarities of music is precisely due to the existence of these two domains: intrinsic and extra-musical referring.[25] Thus, while attempting to respect the insights of philosophers like Langer who underscore the ambiguity of the musical symbol and dissuade us from postulating that, for example, certain sounds can be linked with certain emotions,[26] some believe it is possible to demonstrate that music, like other non-discursive art forms, is capable of extra-musical referring. Outside the realm of worship music, similar proposals have already been made by specialists in ethnoart and ethnomusicology. For example, in his 1961 study focusing on the visual arts entitled "Art Styles as Cultural Cognitive Maps," J.L. Fischer suggests that:

> in expressive aspects of culture, such as visual and other arts, a very important determinant of the art form is social fantasy, that is, the artist's fantasies about social situations which will give [the artist] security or pleasure... Regardless of the overt content of visual art... there is always or nearly always at the same time the expression of some fantasied social situation which will bear a definite relation to the real and desired social situations of the artists and [the artist's] society.[27]

To illustrate his point, Fischer postulates two ideal types of societies with respect to the development of social hierarchy: (1) the authoritarian type in which social hierarchy is positively valued; and (2) the egalitarian type in which hierarchy as a principle of organization is rejected. From these ideal types Fischer moves to statistical testing, from which he deduces a number of hypothetical polar contrasts in art styles:[28]

1. Design repetitive of a number of rather simple elements should characterize the egalitarian societies; design integrating a number of unlike elements should be characteristic of the hierarchical societies.

2. Design with a large amount of empty or irrelevant space should characterize the egalitarian societies; design with little irrelevant (empty) space should characterize the hierarchical societies.

3. Symmetrical design (a special case of repetition) should characterize the egalitarian societies; asymmetrical design should characterize the hierarchical societies.

4. Figures without enclosures should characterize the egalitarian societies; enclosed figures should characterize the hierarchical societies.

Although not providing the statistical analysis of Fischer, Enrique Dussel offers related reflections on the relationship between art and social class, contending that "expression in objects (words, images, sculpture, buildings, etc.) manifests, justifies, or criticizes the given structure of a society."[29] Though such reflections and studies are not without their difficulties,[30] they provide an intriguing and potentially useful means for understanding the relationship of the arts to the societies (civic and ecclesial) that produce them.

From a musical perspective, similar insights on the relationship between musical form and social structure are provided by Alan Lomax in his 1962 study on "Song Structure and Social Structure."[31] Employing a system for rating song performance according to a series of qualitative judgments called "cantometrics," Lomax hypothesizes that "musical structure mirrors social structure or that, perhaps, both structures are a reflection of deeper patterning motives of which we are only dimly aware."[32] Although others have made related assertions previous to Lomax,[33] it was Lomax who provided a pivotal formulation of this insight and provided a tool (i.e., cantometrics) for assessing to what extent there might be a relationship between musical structures and social structures. Researchers after Lomax have further explored his hypothesis and affirmed that, from qualitative and quantitative research, it is possible to demonstrate that a link does exist between song or "sound" structure and social structure.[34] What is less clear, from the viewpoint of such researchers, is whether sound structure or song style is a causative reflection of social institutions or an emblem of social identity.[35]

It is noteworthy that in these studies extra-referential meaning was proposed at the level of social structures and not about some other aspect of societal life. Why this is true is probably debatable, but one could surmise that, at least in part, it is related to the significant social function which music fulfills in many societies.[36] Similarly I would suggest that music fulfills a significant "social" function within worship and, therefore, should be treated as a source of extra-referential meaning, especially from this "social" perspective. More specifically, since at a very basic level liturgy can rightly be considered "an act of ecclesial performative meaning,"[37] it is appropriate to consider extra-referential meaning of music in worship at an ecclesial level. This is parallel to Lomax's imputing meaning in terms of social structures, but now from social structures considered theologically, i.e., ecclesially.

Our previous assertions about symbolic causality suggest that there may be more surety in our treatment of the relationship between song structure and ecclesial structure as to the latter's causative or emblematic nature than that of some of the social scientists cited above. Whereas some ethnomusicologists are unsure whether sound structure or song style is a causative reflection of social institutions or an emblem of social identity, the frame of symbolic causality suggests that it must be both. Sound structure is a symbolic reality which does reflect the social reality in which it functions, but it also serves to rehearse, perpetuate, and even create that reality as well. Although sound structure may not be the first cause of the social structure, it can and does serve not only to perpetuate but to recreate the social structure through its signifying power. It is from this perspective that we will examine contemporary liturgical-musical forms.

Forms, Contemporary Roman Catholic Liturgical Music, and Meaning

The need to focus this discussion, in an exploration of the implicit ecclesial referents (as both causative and emblematic) in the forms of worship music, suggests that these reflections be limited historically, denominationally, and geographically. Thus the remainder of this essay will concern itself with musical forms in contemporary Roman Catholic worship in the U.S. This is still an enormous field for reflection. Virtually every musical form known to western music occurs in some Roman Catholic liturgy in the U.S. today. The introductory nature of this essay does not allow for a consideration of all of these forms. Nor does it allow us to consider a variety of forms from multiple perspectives, e.g., from the viewpoint of the composer, from the viewpoint of the composition on a page, or from the viewpoint of the musical performance.[38] In an attempt to focus this discussion even further, we will take our cue from Lomax's study of song structure and social structure, and consider only sung musical forms (both accompanied and unaccompanied), and these only in terms of their musical performance.[39]

Even here, however, we need to specify further. It is possible, for example, to look at sung musical forms in terms of their performance from the viewpoint of a non-participating observer of the music,[40] from the viewpoint of the assembly, or from the viewpoint of the musician(s) responsible for leading the music. Since these reflections are not based upon any systematic field work or participant observation of a specific worshiping community, and since Roman Catholic liturgical documents in the U.S. speak about the "primacy of the assembly,"[41] it seems appropriate to frame this discussion of the performance of sung liturgical-musical forms from the viewpoint of the assembly.

A final filter that will be employed during these reflections is Margaret Mary Kelleher's useful distinction between public meaning, personal meaning, and official meaning. She elaborates:

> In its liturgical praxis an assembly mediates a public horizon, a world of meaning which provides a context for the assembly's worship. This public world of meaning must be distinguished from the meanings that are personally appropriated by members of the assembly as well as from the meanings identified in official texts or commentaries on a rite, since individuals may not appropriate all that is publicly mediated and liturgical praxis may mediate meanings that are not included in the official rite. Although public and private meanings must be distinguished, public horizons play a significant role in the ongoing mediation of both individual and collective subjects.[42]

It is especially the public meaning that concerns us here and, therefore, our consideration of musical-liturgical forms sung by the assembly will focus on this public meaning, and secondarily on official meaning.[43]

Does the Assembly Sing?

Whereas there are innumerable ways to structure the musical performance of liturgical song, one of the most basic, binary questions that can be asked about the structure of a musical performance from the viewpoint of the assembly is whether or not the assembly is actively engaged in the singing. Apart from the nature of the text, the structure of the melody, or the quality of the composition, whether or not the congregation sings the music is key in assessing something of the music's symbolic causality. For example, in contemporary Roman Catholic worship in the U.S., the active participation of the assembly in the worship music is strongly valued and is a common standard by which the pastoral effectiveness of public worship is judged.[44] This belief is related to an interpretation of official church teaching which holds that music is integral to worship[45] and, therefore, suggests that assemblies that sing are fulfilling an integral role in the rite. Thus, from the viewpoint of official as well as public meaning, the musical engagement of the congregation in the worship song symbolizes that the assembly is important enough to be an actor in the ritual. Furthermore, the assembly's active engagement in the song expresses and creates an awareness—at least at the level of public meaning—of their integrality to the rite.[46]

Does Only the Assembly Sing?

Besides discovering whether or not the assembly is actively engaged in a piece of liturgical music, an appropriate assessment of the musical symbol as an ecclesial referent requires discovering how much of the singing is accomplished by the assembly. One extreme possibility is that *only* the assembly is singing. The fact that the assembly alone might sing a ritual song symbolizes not only its importance and integrality with the rite, but also suggests a certain self-sufficiency insofar as the assembly appears capable of performing this ritual action by itself. This assessment would be underscored if only the assembly sang, and did so a cappella.[47] From a ministerial perspective, the assembly in such a situation is not only fulfilling a important ministry in the worship, but is providing this ministry (at least in part) for and to itself. Since worship is not only a theoretical ecclesial act, but an event that expresses and creates ecclesial meaning,[48] the sole-singing assembly defines itself at the level of public meaning as the subject of the liturgical action[49] and therefore as a particular expression of the worshiping church itself.

Does Only Another Musical Minister(s) Sing?

The opposite extreme of worship song performed only by the assembly is the musical-liturgical moment in which only a soloist, the choir, or some other combination of musical-liturgical forces separate from the assembly sings. In this situation, as in the previous one, one could first suggest that those who are doing the singing are important since they are engaged in an art form that the church considers integral to the rite. From the viewpoint of the assembly, however, its exclusion from the song that is performed only by other ministers communicates at the level of public meaning that the assembly is not only less important than the music ministers who assume an integral role providing music for the rite, but that the assembly itself is not integral or necessary to the musical ritual. Ecclesiologically, the assembly is not disclosed or rehearsed as the subject of the liturgical action, nor as integral to the definition of church reflected in the musical-liturgical event.[50]

The Integration Variable

We must take many variables into consideration when assessing the significance of the assembly's singing or non-singing. One of these is the relationship between this singing or non-singing and the relative importance of the musical-liturgical moment. All elements in a liturgy are not of equal import. Various liturgical books and instructions on the Roman Rite, for example, note that some elements are primary and others are secondary.[51] Aside from these official instructions or commentaries (official meaning), the worshiping community itself develops certain perceptions about the relative importance of various liturgical moments (private meaning)—perceptions which are often at odds with official documents,[52] and which might even be at odds, or quite different, from the public meaning of the rite. Part of assessing the significance of an assembly's song in the shaping of its ecclesial identity, therefore, depends not only upon whether or not the assembly sings, but also upon whether or not its song is wed to those worship elements which its members perceive to be significant. Furthermore, it would be important to discover the relationship between the assembly's perception of the relative import of various elements in the rite and the viewpoint of the official books on this matter (i.e., the fusion of private and official meaning). For example, if the assembly at the mythical St. Hierarchia perceives the "Holy" to be a relatively insignificant moment in the eucharistic liturgy, then the assembly's identity is not ostensibly diminished when the "Holy" is sung by the choir alone. Since the "Holy" is considered an essential element of the rite by the official liturgical books, however, and is ordinarily sung by the assembly,[53] then from the viewpoint of the official meaning of the rite as well as from the public meaning of the rite—despite what members of the assembly might believe personally—the community's self identity is diminished, or at least secondary to that of the musical specialists. Finally, if the assembly at St. Hierarchia perceives the "Holy" to be an important moment, one could suggest that the community's self identity is even further diminished: now at the level of official, public, *and* personal meaning.

The Frequency Variable

Another important variable in assessing the significance of whether or not the assembly sings or does not sing, or the possible significance of their singing primary or secondary elements in the rite, is discovering to what extent these occur as a pattern, or as isolated incidents. For example, in the hypothetical congregation of St. Democratia which *always* sings everything as an assembly and does so a cappella, without any distinctive singing—in whole or in part—by ministers other than the assembly, the congregation (at least in its song) is publicly defining itself and its worship only in egalitarian terms, without any ministerial or hierarchical distinctions. If we postulate an opposite kind of worship community at St. Hierarchia, in which the congregation never sings and the worship music is only performed by ministers other than the congregation, we could suggest that the public self-definition expressed and created by this worship song is that of a bifurcated church in which specialists actively minister to the assembly, while the assembly actively ministers to no one. The reality regarding the frequency of assembly song in most of our churches is clearly somewhere in between these two extremes. Having a grasp of this variable is crucial in attempting to assess how the performance structure of our worship music is symbolically causative in regards to a community's ecclesial identity.

The Quality Variable

Another variable that needs to be taken into consideration when assessing the significance of an assembly's song in the shaping of its ecclesial identity is the illusive but nonetheless real issue of the quality of the musical performance. More specifically, any significant disparity in the quality of musical performance by the assembly as contrasted with the musical performance by other music ministers contributes to the shaping of the ecclesial identity of both. For example, imagine these two extreme musical-liturgical events. One is a hymn sung during the liturgy by the assembly alone, accompanied by an organist who makes no changes in registration throughout the hymn, repeats the same, four-part accompaniment stanza after stanza, and does so in a relatively uninspired manner, devoid of any variations in tempo, dynamics, or interpretation. Contrast this with a choir anthem, accompanied by organ, oboe, and flute, with numerous changes in organ manuals and registration throughout, punctuated by breathtaking unaccompanied choral moments, rife with rubatos, decrescendos, and imaginative music making. Now, imagine these two liturgical-musical moments side-by-side: the flat, unadorned congregational hymn followed by the animated, well-honed choral anthem. The mustering of musical imagination and skill that characterize the latter is a powerful, self-defining aspect of not only the music, but also the choir that sings the music. Even if there were parity between assembly and choir in terms of the amount of music each sang, the structure of the music each sang, and the integration to the rite of the music that each sang, the disparity in terms of musical quality would yet rehearse the choir at the level of public meaning not only as capable of more artistry, but also as worthy of more artistic investment.

A Survey of Forms

Aware that numerous variables significantly impact upon the assembly's song,[54] it is my hypothesis that, apart from these variables, the very form and musical structure of that song can be considered to have ecclesial referents, and contribute to the expression and creation of an assembly's ecclesial identity—at least at the level of public meaning. Although implicit reference has been made, in passing, to some types of forms, it might be useful to present, in a more explicit manner, a survey of a few basic musical-liturgical forms that occur in contemporary Roman Catholic worship, and provide some comment upon how they might operate as ecclesial referents.

Litany

A litany is a series of petitions, intoned by a leader, each of which is followed by a congregational response. Ordinarily the petitions are relatively brief, have a changing text, and are sung to the same musical formula. The response is ordinarily also brief, for the most part unchanging both musically and textually. One of the most well-known examples of a litany in the west is the Litany of All Saints:

Schematically, the opening thirteen lines of text and music could be presented as:[55]

AAAA	AAAA
AAAA^1	AAAA^1
AAAA	AAAA
BBBB	BBBB
BBBB^1	BBBB^1
EEEE	FFFF
EEEE^1	FFFF
EEEE^2	FFFF
EEEE^3	FFFF
EEEE^4	FFFF^1
EEEE^5	FFFF^1
EEEE^6	FFFF^1
EEEE^7	FFFF^1

From the viewpoint of the assembly's experience of the musical form, the form symbolizes neither "assembly alone" nor "other minister alone" but "assembly and other together." It does so, from a formal perspective, with a definite degree of parity: the length and musical complexity of the leader's part is matched in length and musical complexity by the assembly. There is also, however, ministerial differentiation in this form since the text of the leader changes whereas the text of the assembly is more apt to be constant. The ecclesiological image imbedded in this form could be thought to exhibit a number of characteristics: (1) leadership has a role; (2) leadership cannot complete its task without the response of the assembly; (3) the assembly has a consistent, even insistent role in the event; (4) there is significant parity between the two roles; (5) the assembly sings texts and music that the leadership never sings; and (6) leadership's role is to initiate as well as to provide textual variations not shared by the assembly.

Responsory[56]

A responsory, like the litany, also calls for a level of alternation of music between a leader and the congregation. These are sometimes identified as verse and refrain. Though similar to the litany, the responsory is ordinarily distinguished from the latter in three ways. First, the verses intoned by the leader as well as the assembly responses are usually longer than those of a litany. Second, the music for the leader(s) may change from verse to verse or, if based on a formula (such as a psalm tone), shows much more variation from verse to verse. Third, there is not always parity between the length of the texts for verse and refrain, nor for the musical settings of these texts in terms of their complexity.

A responsory in the current repertoire that demonstrates some of these differences with the litany form is Christopher Willcock's setting of Psalm 91:

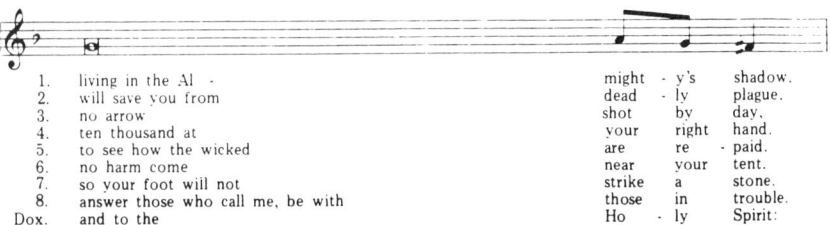

1.	living in the Al -	might - y's	shadow.
2.	will save you from	dead - ly	plague.
3.	no arrow	shot by	day,
4.	ten thousand at	your right	hand.
5.	to see how the wicked	are re -	paid.
6.	no harm come	near your	tent.
7.	so your foot will not	strike a	stone.
8.	answer those who call me, be with	those in	trouble.
Dox.	and to the	Ho - ly	Spirit:

Schematically, the text and music of this psalm could be outlined as:

        AAAA   AAAA
        BBBBBBBB   AAAA
        BBBBBBBB^1 AAAA
        BBBBBBBB^2 AAAA
        BBBBBBBB^3 AAAA
        BBBBBBBB^4 AAAA
        BBBBBBBB^5 AAAA
        BBBBBBBB^6 AAAA
        BBBBBBBB^7 AAAA

From the viewpoint of the assembly's experience of the musical form, the responsory like the litany says neither "assembly alone" nor "other minister alone" but "assembly and other together." It does so, however, with less parity between the musical and textual roles for leader and assembly: the length and musical complexity of the leader's part is greater than that required of the assembly. There is, by consequence, greater ministerial differentiation in this form than in the litany. The ecclesiological image imbedded in this form could be thought to exhibit a number of characteristics: (1) leadership has a role; (2) leadership cannot complete its task without the response of the assembly; (3) the assembly has a consistent role in the musical event; (4) there is some noticeable difference between the textual variation and musical complexity of the leader's part in relationship to the assembly's part, suggesting a clear difference in abilities and gifts between the two; (5) the assembly sings nothing that has not first been sung by the leadership; and (6) leadership in this form has an initiating function and, further, provides textual and musical counterpoint to (not just variation on) the assembly's part requiring a different level of skill and achieving a different kind of musical artistry.

Alternatim

In the strict sense, alternatim is the musical performance of a liturgical text by two (sometimes more) individuals or groups in alternation, each singing a single verse or short section of the text in turn.[57] Alternatim became a basic form for the performance of psalmody in monastic celebrations of the liturgy of the hours in the medieval west. It is also the form underlying the performance of many versicles and responses, for example, the following for use at morning prayer:[58]

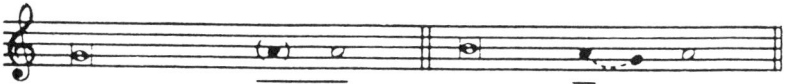

Cantor:
In you, O Lord, is the source of life.

All:
In your light we shall see light.

Cantor:
Send forth your light and your truth.

All:
Let these be our guide.

Cantor:
Fill us each morning with your constant love.

All:
That we may sing and be glad all our life.

Cantor:
Let us see your mighty acts.

All:
May your children see your glorious might.

Cantor:
Lord our God, may your blessing be upon us.

All:
And give us success in all we do.

Schematically this versicle-response could be presented as:

162 CHAPTER 7

AAAA	BBBB
AAAA^1	BBBB^1
AAAA^2	BBBB^2
AAAA^3	BBBB^3
AAAA^4	BBBB^4
AAAA^5	BBBB^5

From the viewpoint of the assembly's experience of the musical form, alternatim, like the previously considered forms, says "assembly and other together." It does so with even more parity between the musical and textual roles for leader and assembly than the litany: the length and textual-musical complexity of the leader's part is virtually identical to that of the assembly. There is, by consequence, greater ministerial complementarity in this form than in any other thus far considered. The ecclesiological image imbedded in this form has the following characteristics: (1) leadership has a role; (2) leadership cannot complete its task without the response of the assembly; (3) the assembly has a complementary, equally complex and equally important role in the musical event; (4) thus leadership, in this form, could be defined more in terms of its responsibility for initiation and collaboration than musical substitution or artistic supplementation.

Ostinato

Over the past few decades sung ostinato forms have made their way into the standard repertoire of many Roman Catholic communities in this country. Ostinato refers to the extended repetition of what is ordinarily a brief musical pattern in a composition or a section of a composition. Although an ostinato might be melodic, rhythmic, or harmonic, it is especially what might be considered a combination of the harmonic and melodic ostinato that has recently made its mark on Roman Catholic congregational song, particularly through the work of Jacques Berthier. One well-known example of a Berthier ostinato for congregation is *Ubi Caritas*.

Over and around this repeated eight measure ostinato, the composer presumes the addition of instrumental improvisations, choral harmonies, and solo texts.[59] Given the somewhat aleatoric nature of this music, the following schema is more illustrative than descriptive. Since instrumental improvisation is integral to the performance of this text, such will be indicated here.

1st repetition of ostinato:
Choir	AAAAAAAA
	AAAAAAAA
Assembly	AAAAAAAA
Choir	AAAAAAAA
	AAAAAAAA
Instruments	--------

2nd repetition of ostinato:
Choir	aaaaaaaa
	aaaaaaaa
Assembly	AAAAAAAA
Choir	aaaaaaaa
	aaaaaaaa
Instruments	--------

3rd repetition of ostinato:
Cantor	BBBB
Choir	aaaaaaaa
	aaaaaaaa
Assembly	AAAAAAAA
Choir	aaaaaaaa
	aaaaaaaa
Instruments	--------

4th repetition of ostinato:
Cantor	BBBB
Choir	aaaaaaaa
	aaaaaaaa
Assembly	AAAAAAAA
Choir	aaaaaaaa
	aaaaaaaa
Instruments	--------
etc.	

From the viewpoint of the assembly's experience of the musical form, such an ostinato form says "assembly and other together," but in a quite different way than litany, responsory, or alternatim. The latter achieve their varying degrees of musical complementarity through the interchange or alternation of discreet textual and musical units (phrases). There is a presumed linkage between such interchange or alternation, but there is little convergence. Where convergence does occur—for example, during the refrain of the responsory, when the leader (with possible choral and instrumental support) joins in on the assembly's part—the distinctive musical role of the assembly is shared by others. In the ostinato form, however, convergence does not simply mean doubling the assembly's part. Rather, it presumes supporting the assembly's part (e.g., the choir's role, as schematized above in the second repetition of the ostinato and following), as well as providing a counterpoint to and dialogue with their part (e.g., the cantor's and instrumentalist's role) without taking it over. Musically the ostinato is a way of saying "we" without assimilation: allowing the "you" and "I" to remain.[60]

The ecclesiological image imbedded in this form has the following characteristics: (1) the assembly has a foundational role; (2) the role of the leadership is unintelligible without the *cantus firmus* of the assembly; (3) other specialists (choir and instrumentalists) both support and play off of the assembly's part; (4) the differentiation of special skills and gifts (e.g., those required of the cantor) is only fully revealed in the moment of mutual convergence; (5) hierarchically, it appears that the assembly is of central importance here, and in some ways the musical leader.

Chorale

A final form considered here is the chorale. This is a specific type of congregational hymn born of the sixteenth-century Reformation. These were strophic, metrical, unison, vernacular hymns, and ordinarily unaccompanied tunes and texts. Many chorales are in barform [AAB]. One well-known chorale is the previously discussed *Ein feste Burg* by Martin Luther.[61] This hymn can be schematized as:

AAAA	(A mighty fortress . . .)
BBBB	(A sword and shield . . .)
AAAA^1	(He breaks the . . .)
BBBB^1	(And wins salvation . . .)

CCCC	(The old evil foe,)
DDDD	(Sworn to work us woe,)
EEEE	(With dread craft and might)
FFFF	(He arms himself to fight.)
BBBB²	(On earth he has . . .)

From the viewpoint of the assembly's experience of the musical form, the chorale communicates something very different than the previously discussed forms. More than any other form, the chorale says "we"! There is no assembly and other here, nor is there any leadership outside the assembly.[62] There is simply assembly. Ecclesiologically such music defines the assembly and only the assembly in the singing of the chorale as the subject of the liturgy. Given the self-rehearsing nature of the chorale, its limited musical range, rhythmic regularity, and grammatical simplicity,[63] one could further suggest that it is the whole of the assembly which is presumed to be the subject of the liturgy in the singing of this chorale. This is not music designed for specialists, ministers with special training or people with special gifts.

Summary

The basic contention of this essay is that the very shape and form of our worship symbols are intimately wed to the way in which God's self-communication is mediated, and to the nature of the faith called forth in worship. Positing the essentially symbolic nature of all life and, therefore, the symbolic nature of both first order and second order language in theology, theologians like Rahner provide us with the frame for suggesting that our worship symbols not only are caused by grace but themselves are a cause of grace. Thus we need attend to the surface structures and configurations of our worship symbols, and be concerned about the ways in which they mediate God's self-communication and the faith that they shape.

More specifically, it was argued that music, as one of the key symbolic languages of our worship, not only expresses faith but also helps create faith. This is true not only because of the texts sung in worship, but also because of the very structure of our worship music. In particular, the varying structures of our worship music carry implicit ecclesiological messages about the worshiping community. For example, at the level of public meaning, such forms communicate to what extent the assembly might be considered as the subject of the liturgical action. And in so communicating, these forms create that meaning as well. The exploration of a few standard forms operative in contemporary Roman Catholic worship music in the U.S. illustrated this point.

This investigation suggests that, whereas further exploration of the theological referents of our liturgical-musical forms is required, a few preliminary conclusions are yet possible at this time. These include: (1) the analysis of musical-liturgical forms is one valuable way for grasping the implicit theological referents of our worship music; (2) the richness of the paschal mystery celebrated in Christian worship suggests a multiplicity of forms, for just as no single "theme" or liturgical structure is capable of encompassing the fullness of this redemptive mystery, so no single musical form is capable of the same; (3) since Roman Catholic worship, at the official level, affirms the centrality of the assembly, so does that suggest a preponderance of musical-liturgical forms that place the assembly at the center of the liturgical performance; (4) certain musical forms, by their very nature, may be more appropriate to certain liturgical moments: for example, a community's joint proclamation of faith ("We believe") finds resonance in the "we structure" of a chorale, whereas the interactive, dialogic nature of a procession suggests a more interactive or responsorial type of music to accompany and interact with it; (5) different forms may be more appropriate to the ethos of different liturgical feasts or seasons: for example, the reflective even introspective nature of Lent might suggest an increased employment of ostinato forms with their meditative-like repetition, whereas missionary impulses of the Easter-Pentecost axis might suggest more acclamations or sturdy hymns.

MCW's insightful statement that in worship believers express their faith and, by expressing it, renew and deepen it remains a rich source for our theological and pastoral reflection. Even more, it provides pastoral impetus for realizing the promise and challenge of the *Constitution on the Sacred Liturgy*: that liturgy become both fount and summit of our life in faith together.

Notes

1. The basic hypothesis of this essay was first set forth in my "Meaning, Musical Forms and Faith," *Pastoral Music* 7 (June-July, 1983) 11-15.
2. For example, canon 6 from the seventh session of the Council of Trent (3 March 1547) condemns anyone who says that "the sacraments of

the New Law do not contain the grace which they signify (*non continere gratiam quam significant*), or that they do not confer that grace on those who place no obstacles in its way," *Canons and Decrees of the Council of Trent* 52 and 330.

3. Thomas Aquinas, *Summa Theologica* 3, q. 62, a. 1.

4. Karl Rahner, "The Theology of the Symbol," *Theological Investigations*, vol. 4 (Baltimore: Helicon, 1966) 221-252.

5. Michael Skelley, *The Liturgy of the World: Karl Rahner's Theology of Worship* (Collegeville: The Liturgical Press, 1991) 41.

6. Ibid.

7. See, for example, the insightful assessment and critique of Rahner's explanation of symbolic causality in David Power, *The Eucharistic Mystery* (New York: Crossroad, 1992) 271-274.

8. There is a long tradition, especially in the eastern Churches, for defining liturgy as *theologia prima*. This definition has gained much currency in post-conciliar reflections on worship. See, for example, Gerard Lukken's formulation in "The Unique Expression of Faith in the Liturgy," *Liturgical Expression of Faith*, Concilium 82, ed. Herman Schmidt and David Power, trans. David Smith (New York: Herder and Herder, 1973) 16. David Power prefers to speak of "first order language" and "second order language." For a survey of Power's thought on this and a further introduction to the concept of *theologia prima*, see Irwin, *Liturgical Theology: A Primer* 29-31 and passim.

9. For an introduction, see Pierre Guiraud, *Semiology*, trans. George Gross (London: Routledge & Kegan Paul, 1975).

10. See, for example, his *The Philosophy of Symbolic Forms*, 3 vols., trans Ralph Manheim (New Haven-London: Yale University Press, 1955).

11. See, for example, his "Religion as a Cultural System," in *The Interpretation of Cultures* (New York: Basic Books, 1973) 87-125.

12. His works are published posthumously in *Collected Papers*, 8 vols., ed. Charles Hartshorne, Paul Weiss, and Arthur Burks (Cambridge, MA: Harvard University Press, 1931-1958).

13. Paul Ricoeur, *The Symbolism of Evil*, trans. Emerson Buchanan (Boston: Beacon Press, 1967) 19.

14. That is, they both signify and effect the self-communication of God which calls forth our faith. Thus the 1972 version of MCW notes that "good celebrations foster and nourish faith. Poor celebrations weaken and destroy faith" (n. 6).

15. For an introduction to music as symbol, see Epperson, *The Musical Symbol*.

16. What follows is drawn from her *Philosophy in a New Key: A Study in the Symbolism of Reason, Rite and Art*, 3rd ed. (Cambridge, MA: Harvard University Press, 1976) 79-102.

17. As evidenced by the existence of dictionaries.

18. Thus although there are dictionaries of musical terms, there are no dictionaries of melodies, harmonies, and forms.

19. Langer, *Philosophy* 97.

20. An extreme example is Deryck Cooke who attempts to establish the terms of music's linguistic vocabulary in *The Language of Music* (Oxford: Oxford University Press, 1959).

21. In one sense the phrase "musical form" encompasses all elements of a musical composition, including its melody, rhythm, harmonies, etc. Thus "to change even a single pitch or rhythm . . . changes the shape of that composition, even if only in detail" (Don Randel, ed., *The New Harvard Dictionary of Music*, s.v. "form"). On the other hand, form is also employed more simply to mean "the structure and design of a composition" (Michael Kennedy, *The Concise Oxford Dictionary of Music*, 3rd ed. [New York: Oxford University Press, 1980], s.v. "form"). It is in this latter, more generic sense that we will use the term "musical form" in this essay.

22. Leonard Meyer, *Emotion and Meaning in Music* (Chicago and London: The University of Chicago Press, 1956) 1.

23. Meyer (p. 1) calls this group "absolutists" and describes them as people "who insist that musical meaning lies exclusively within the context of the work itself, in the perception of the relationships set forth within the musical work of art." Epperson, cited above, falls into this category, as demonstrated by his statement: "That music qua music is by definition nonreferential should by now be obvious." *The Musical Symbol* 181.

24. Edgard Varèse, *Ecrits* (Paris: Christian Bourgois, 1983) 41 as cited in Nattiez, *Music and Discourse* 108.

25. Or introversive semiosis and extroversive semiosis, as discussed by Nattiez, *Music and Discourse* 117.

26. This is precisely what Deryck Cooke attempts: the major third expresses pleasure (p. 51), the minor third is tragic (p. 64), etc.

27. J.L. Fischer, "Art Styles as Cultural Cognitive Maps," *American Anthropologist* 63 (1961) 79-80.

28. Ibid. 81-89.

29. Enrique Dussel, "Christian Art of the Oppressed in Latin America: Towards an Aesthetics of Liberation," *Symbol and Art in Worship*, Concilium 132 (1980) 43.

30. See, for example, the critique of Fischer's work in Harry Silver, "Ethnoart," *Annual Review of Anthropology* 8 (1979) 277.

31. Alan Lomax, "Song Structure and Social Structure," *Ethnology* 1 (1962) 425-451.

32. Ibid. 435. This insight is affirmed by Alan Merriam in his early study, *The Anthropology of Music*, in which he suggests that one of the ways to study music in its symbolic aspects "is through the ways in

which music reflects other cultural behavior, organization, and values" (p. 247).

33. For example, on gender distinctions in music making. Merriam, *The Anthropology of Music* 247-248.

34. See, for example, Edwin Erickson, "Tradition and Evolution in Song Style: A Reanalysis of Cantometric Data," *Behavior Science Research* 11 (1976) 227-308; also Steven Feld, "Sound as a Symbolic System: The Kaluli Drum," *Bikmaus* 4 (1983) 78-89; id., "Sound Structure as Social Structure," *Ethnomusicology* 28 (1984) 383-409.

35. Feld, "Sound Structure" 405.

36. John Miller Chernoff, for example, would contend that "music's explicit purpose, in the various ways it might be defined by Africans, is, essentially, socialization." *African Rhythm and African Sensibility* 154.

37. Margaret Mary Kelleher, "Liturgy: An Ecclesial Act of Meaning," *Worship* 59:5 (1985) 482.

38. This is what Nattiez refers to as the poietic dimension, the esthesic dimension, and the trace or neutral level. Nattiez, *Music and Discourse* 11-12.

39. Lomax, "Song Structure and Social Structure" 426.

40. Arthur Vidich, "Participant Observation and the Collection and Interpretation of Data," *American Journal of Sociology* 60 (1955) 354-360.

41. See *Environment and Art in Catholic Worship* (1972) nn. 28 and 41; this is the author's presupposition about the place of the assembly in Roman Catholic worship music as well.

42. Kelleher, "Liturgical Theology: A Task and a Method," *Worship* 62:1 (1988) 6.

43. The Social Science Study Group of the North American Academy of Liturgy (NAAL) [of which Kelleher was a member] provides further explanation of these terms in its 1986 draft of an "Instrument for Describing and Interpreting the Public Meaning of Ritual Events." At the beginning of the instrument the following definitions are given:

Normative meaning [Kelleher's "official meaning"]: that which according to official interpretations and authoritative commentators, ought to be communicated by the rite. Such meanings are easily accessible through study of the official documents and commentaries themselves.

Private meanings: the particular understandings and motivations which individual worshipers bring to the rite, in light of which they make sense of what they experience there. These meanings surface when participants are asked how they understand the rite or why certain things are done or said.

Public meaning: That which is actually communicated by the rite as it is celebrated in this place and by these people. This will approximate the "normative meaning" more or less closely, but it can never fully realize it on any given occasion and may actually depart from it in significant ways. This kind of meaning is much more difficult to identify than the other two, yet the "public meaning" reveals the values of the group.

While the NAAL definitions begin to chart out something of the relationship between public and official meaning, neither it nor Kelleher suggest whether there is any necessary relationship between private, official, and public meaning. Within the frame of symbolic causality, one could surmise that repeated ritualization expressing a particular public meaning would, at least implicitly, cause—and not simply allow—a fusion of the public with personal meaning. Kelleher is more cautious, noting that "The performed [i.e., public] meaning *may* also include new meanings which are being made available for a community's appropriation as well as some which are in the process of being criticized, rejected or transformed." "Liturgical Theology" 6.

44. See, for example, MSCC n. 9 and the various references cited in that text.

45. CSL n. 112.

46. The concept of the integral role of the assembly in public worship was effectively raised by Yves M.J. Congar, "L'Ecclesia ou communauté chrétienne, sujet intégral de l'action liturgique," *La Liturgie après Vatican II*, ed. J.P. Jossua and Y. Congar (Paris: Cerf, 1967) 241-282; more recently, see Catherine Vincie, "The Liturgical Assembly in Magisterial and Theological Literature and in the 1988 Rite of Christian Initiation of Adults," unpublished Ph.D. dissertation (Washington, DC: The Catholic University of America, 1990).

47. The role of accompaniment is one of the variables in the musical symbol which needs to be taken into account when interpreting the musical form symbol vis-à-vis its ecclesial referents.

48. Kelleher, "Liturgy: An Ecclesial Act of Meaning"; also, id., "Liturgical Theology" 5-6.

49. For a further discussion of this concept, see Joyce Ann Zimmerman, "Liturgical Assembly: Who is the Subject of Liturgy?" *Liturgical Ministry* 3 (Spring 1994) 41-51.

50. In a parallel discussion of British and Kentucky ballad singing, in which the listeners must remain silent and physically passive, Lomax characterizes the association of the performer with the audience, in sociological terms, as "one of exclusive authority: a principal model for conduct in Western European culture." Lomax then opines that "dominance-subordination, with a deep sense of moral obligation, is the fundamental form of role-taking in the Protestant West," and notes that "our cooperative enterprises are organized in terms of an assemblage of experts," Lomax, "Song Structure and Social Structure" 440. One could certainly interpret the above described liturgical-musical scenario in similar terms.

51. *The General Instruction of the Roman Missal*, for example, notes the centrality of the eucharistic prayer (n. 54), and the *Appendix to the General Instruction for the Dioceses of the United States* notes the transitional and secondary nature of the preparation of the gifts (n. 50).

52. One striking example is the relative lack of interest on the part of many worshipers in the eucharistic prayer which *The General Instruction of the Roman Missal* calls a "high point" (n. 54). Such disinterest was well documented in a study conducted by The Notre Dame Center for Pastoral Liturgy, the Georgetown Center for Liturgy, Spirituality and the Arts, the Loyola Pastoral Institute, and the Corpus Christi Center entitled *Liturgical Renewal, 1963-1988: A Study of English Speaking Parishes in the United States*. A summary discussion of this study is presented in Lawrence J. Madden, ed., *The Awakening Church: Twenty-Five Years of Liturgical Renewal* (Collegeville: The Liturgical Press, 1992). Such discrepancies have also been documented in my own field work which, for example, has demonstrated that some communities identify the sung Our Father, especially while the people hold hands, as the high point of the rite. See Edward Foley and Mary McGann, "Why Do Congregations Sing?" *Proceedings of the North American Academy of Liturgy* (1990) 87-97.

53. *General Instruction of the Roman Missal* n. 55b.

54. Besides those previously mentioned (i.e., quality of musical performance, frequency, integration with the rite, accompanied or unaccompanied) other variables include acoustics, spatial deployment, familiarity of the music, and the quality of the musical leadership. Some of these are discussed in Foley and McGann, "Why Do Congregations Sing?"

55. The following principles are the basis for this schema and those that follow: (1) the blocks of capital letters indicate both text and music; (2) the relative length of those blocks of letters indicate the relative length of the respective musical sections; (3) a changed text with repeated music is indicated by superscripted numerals, e.g., AAAA^1 indicates the same music as AAAA, with a different text; (4) a change in music and text is indicated by a change in letters, e.g., BBBB indicates different text and music from AAAA, although the phrases are of comparable length; (5) lower case letters indicates harmonization, e.g., aaaa indicates the same text as AAAA, but now sung in a harmonization to the melody of AAAA; and (6) instrumental lines will be indicated by dashes [e.g., - - - - - - - -].

56. Whereas responsory has been employed narrowly to refer to a type of liturgical chant that includes the responsories of the eucharist (e.g., gradual, and offertory) as well as those of the offices (i.e., *responsoria prolixa* and *responsoria brevia*), the term will be employed here in the more generic sense of a responsorial form.

57. Although this form is often called "antiphonal" as well (see, for example, Randel, *The New Harvard Dictionary of Music*, s.v. "antiphonal singing"), this is, strictly speaking, not accurate. The antiphonal form is

an elaboration of the responsory, in which the people are divided into two choirs, and respond alternately to the leader with a refrain or antiphon. For a further explanation of this form, see Robert Taft, "Essay in Methodology," *Worship* 52:4 (1978) 321-324.

58. From *Praise God in Song: Ecumenical Daily Prayer*, compiled and edited by John Allyn Melloh and William G. Storey (Chicago: GIA Publications, 1979).

59. Some of these are sketched out in the various choral and instrumental accompaniment books, e.g., Jacques Berthier, *Music from Taizé*, vol. 1: edition G-2433 (choir, cantor, guitar, accompaniment); edition G2433-A (instrumental parts for various instruments), all published by GIA Publications, Chicago. A further illustration of the improvisatory presumptions of this music can be found in the various recordings of Berthier's music, e.g., *Taizé 'Cantate!* (Chicago: GIA Publications), no. MS-156.

60. Or, in the language of Martin Buber, while solo performance may say "I-it," and the litany, responsory, and alternatim allow the "I-You" to be realized, the ostinato is more a step toward the "I-Thou." See Buber, *I and Thou*.

61. For the music to *Ein feste Burg*, see above, p. 101.

62. Although sometimes the accompaniment variable in the chorale suggests that the organist is the leader, this is not endemic to the form. In their origin, there was no presumption of instrumental accompaniment for Luther's chorales. Such is implicit in name "chorale," which was derived from the Latin term *cantus choralis* and initially referred to a plainchant style of performance, i.e., unison and unaccompanied. See Randel, *The New Harvard Dictionary*, s.v. "chorale."

63. For a further discussion of these characteristics, see above, pp. 100-103.

8
The Evaluation of Roman Catholic Ritual Music: From Displacement to Convergence[1]

Introduction

THE SECOND HALF OF THE TWENTIETH CENTURY HAS WITNESSED DRAMATIC changes in Roman Catholic worship and its music. Such musical-ritual upheaval has been accompanied by innumerable skirmishes around issues of standards, quality, and criteria for evaluating Roman Catholic worship and its song. The contentious Fifth International Congress on Church Music in 1966[2] was an early testimony to the conflicts that were to arise around the issue of musical quality and the standards for judging that quality in the post-conciliar reform. Many hoped that MCW, the 1972 document of the U.S. Bishops' Committee on the Liturgy,[3] and its celebrated musical-liturgical-pastoral judgment would quell some of the dissension around questions of criteria for liturgical music and promote new levels of ritual composition in this country. Although that document has contributed greatly to the current discussion, it has also created some new problems: partly because of the way it was written and partly because of the way it has been interpreted.

As has been previously suggested,[4] one key problem with MCW is that, while it recognizes the consideration of the musical, liturgical and pastoral not to be separate determinations but a single "threefold judgment" (n. 25), the document yet treats these as three separate judgments and does not demonstrate how they can be integrated one with another. One common pastoral response to this inconsistency is the tendency to discount or ignore the musical judgment in the face of pastoral concerns.[5] Thus, whereas MCW certainly breaks new ground and suggests what we will call a "convergence" model for evaluating worship music, it continues to operate according to what might be called "displacement" criteria. By this I mean that instead of making a judgment about worship music in terms of the convergence of a number of factors—such as the liturgical, musical, and pastoral appropriateness of a piece of music—often this single, tripartite "convergence" of judgments is fragmented into three separate decisions which alternately displace each other. Thus, a decision about the musical quality of a work is displaced by a judgment of its pastoral effectiveness or liturgical appropriateness.

Historical Precedents for Displacement and Convergence Models

Ancient Greece

This tendency to displace one set of criteria with another is not new in the history of Christian worship music or, more generally, in the history of western music. For example, the so-called doctrine of ethos found in the writings of certain ancient Greek philosophers,[6] which held that particular musical sounds or individual modes had a specific emotional, moral, or ethical character, allowed and even required the displacement of one mode for another in order to achieve the desired emotional or ethical response in the listener. Plato discouraged the use of all modes except Dorian or Phrygian, which he considered to be temperate and brave.[7] Although others were less rigorous than Plato in their evaluation of the appropriateness or acceptability of various modes,[8] there was yet the tendency under the influence of this general phenomenon called the "doctrine of ethos" to choose one mode over another because of the individual characteristics or qualities of that mode.[9] More than simply displacing one mode with a another, this "doctrine" implied the displacement of all other criteria in evaluating music—for example, the pleasurability of any given mode—for one based on the perceived moral or ethical character of the music. This single criterion does not necessarily converge or integrate with any others, but displaces them.

Emerging Christianity

Although it is difficult even to identify anything such as early Christian "music,"[10] and there is certainly no pervasive phenomenon or theory setting out criteria for worship "music" in the early Christian community, it does seem that at least some segments of the nascent Christian community were thinking about what "musical" elements might be appropriate in their common prayer. Paul in his First Letter to the Corinthians, for example, suggests that although there are different gifts in the community, there is only one Spirit, and every manifestation of that Spirit is for the common good (1 Cor 12:4-7). Thus Paul counsels the Corinthian community to seek only gifts that build up the community (1 Cor 14:15-16). Paul's admonition might be considered an indicator of what has been called here a "convergence" approach. Paul does not rely upon a single, exclusionary theory about "how" the community's common prayer is affected by various "musical" elements as a basis for making recommendations about what should be employed. Rather, Paul seems focused on the goal of *koinonia*, and would appear to allow for virtually any convergence of elements that would enable this goal to be realized in community prayer.

The contrast being drawn here between the Greek doctrine of ethos and Paul's advice about public worship is not to suggest that the Greek philosophers had no goal for their communities as did Paul for his. Plato, Aristotle, and the other Greek philosophers who addressed this issue were also concerned about the common good, and articulated their various theories around the doctrine of ethos in order to realize more fully this common good. The reason why the ancient Greek approach could be characterized as "displacement" and Paul's approach more as "convergence," therefore, is not because one approach was developed in view of a satisfying goal, and the other was not. Rather, the distinction between these two is drawn in view of the fact that certain ancient Greek philosophers wanted to achieve their goal in view of a particular theoretical construct which effectively excluded the employment of other criteria in judging what music would serve the common good. Paul, on the other hand, does not provide any overarching philosophical or theological framework that establishes the criteria for worship "music."

Another way to characterize the differences between a convergence and a displacement approach in view of this history is to suggest that the ordinary point of departure for convergence criteria is human experience (i.e., an anthropological starting point), whereas the criteria for displacement more readily begin with philosophical (particularly ontological) distinctions. Employing the latter model requires one to rely upon certain abstract principles or theories—prescinding from what people may genuinely feel or perceive—which are thought to articulate something of the essentials of music.[11] The former model, however, requires one to begin with the actual experience of the present music-making community and the consequences of that experience. The displacement model, therefore, could be considered a "theory-practice" model which begins with abstraction and moves to practice, whereas a convergence model is prone to begin with experience, allows one to reflect upon that experience, and shapes future practice in terms of this experience-based reflection, i.e., it is a practice-theory-practice model.[12]

The Rise of Displacement

As Christianity developed and increasingly defined itself in terms of contemporary philosophies, the displacement model began its ascendency, especially in what would eventually be identified as "official worship." Some of this tendency was articulated by early Christian writers who, under the influence of Middle and Neo-Platonism, perpetuated the belief that music was an image of a higher order, that it had an objective and definable significance apart from its usage, and that this significance had moral consequences. Thus musical forms, sounds, and even musicians themselves were accepted or rejected, at least in part, because of what was perceived to be their ontological and moral significance.[13] This is part of the reason why early Christian writers rejected all instrumental music. It was not simply the use of the instrument but the instrument itself which was considered immoral and incapable of uniting with the harmony of all creation redeemed by Christ.[14]

One of the most explicit affirmations of the Christian belief that music had an "objective" significance with moral consequences is found in the work of the Roman philosopher Boethius who became the most influential authority on music in the Christian west during the Middle Ages. His *De Institutione Musica* was a compilation of selections from various ancient Greek writers, many of whom held to some form of the doctrine of ethos. Heavily influenced by the writing of Pythagoras (fl. c. 530 BCE) and Plato, Boethius noted in the introduction to the first book of this work that "music is associated not only with speculation but with morality as well."[15] Through the work of Boethius, and to a lesser extent the writings of the monk Cassiodorus (+ 583), the belief that music embodied the essence of virtue or vice was perpetuated in the church. John XXII (+ 1334), for example, quoted Boethius in his *Docta Sanctorum Patrum* and, in the spirit of this Roman philosopher, condemned those musicians who did not promote devotion with their art but instead created "a sensuous atmosphere."[16]

Another contributing factor to the ascendancy of the displacement model for evaluating worship music was the development of what might be called a Christian "theology of beauty" in the late patristic period. From the time of Plato a consistent theme in western thought had been the association of the beautiful with the "divine." Beauty for Plato was one of the timeless essences, one of the universal Ideas.[17] In the *Symposium*, and even clearer in the *Greater Hippias* (whose authenticity is contested), Plato outlined his belief that the soul achieves a vision of the good—which for him was the supreme Idea and the end of the religious quest— through the beautiful.[18] Thus, for Plato, the beautiful was a key antecedent to what we might call the divine.

This theme found an important Christian proponent in Augustine who believed that beauty—especially that of creation—could lead one to the Creator of all beauty.[19] For Augustine all created beauty is derivative of divine beauty,[20] and it is especially through proportion and rhythm that we become aware of the unity which is essential to this beauty.[21] The most celebrated linkage between the divine and the beautiful was articulated by the fifth-century Neo-Platonic writer Pseudo-Dionysius. In his *The Divine Names* Pseudo-Dionysius counts "beautiful" among one of the primary names of God and believes that God, "the One, the Good, the Beautiful—is in its uniqueness the Cause of the multitudes of the good and the beautiful."[22]

"Sacred" Art

The cumulative effect of these two developments within Christianity—that is, the belief that music had an objective significance with moral consequences, and the adoption of the category of beauty for defining the divine—was twofold. First was the growing tendency within the church to consider and, by consequence, legislate various art forms as though they were an objective reality which themselves could be virtuous or immoral. Second, the standards employed for measuring such musical-artistic virtue or immorality—purportedly universal principles derived from tradition and theological reflection—were in fact the acceptable artistic canons and taste that dominated the ecclesiastical life of that time and place, i.e., the operative definition of the beautiful in contemporary worship. Consequently, what on face value could be considered issues of form, style, and taste, Christianity often translated in terms of morality and sacred beauty. Through the employment of a displacement model of evaluating music or art for Christian usage, and the identification of certain musical-artistic forms as moral and ontologically of a higher order—and thus worthy of both honoring and reflecting the divine beauty—there developed what might properly considered "sacred art" and "sacred music" in Christianity.

The emergence of "sacred music" or "sacred art"—as that thought to both contain and reflect basic Christian beliefs and truths, especially in terms of virtue and beauty—is detectable in the instructions and legislation outlining what art forms are and are not acceptable for Christians. Already in the third century, and more frequently in the fourth century, writers like Novatian (+ c. 258) considered dance and musical instruments "pagan" and unacceptable to Christians.[23] Augustine knew the tension between the arts and worship, and the danger of being moved more by the singing than by what is sung.[24] This tension is part of the reason why certain types of music or other art forms eventually were considered more acceptable—and, therefore, exportable—than others. For example, as part of the seventh-century mission to the English Church, the musical usage of Rome was imported if not imposed[25]—a tradition which Bede (+ 735) called "church music,"[26] apparently in distinction from the musical traditions of the English people, which Bede considered "religious" or "devotional" music.[27] At least for one part of the English mission, receiving the Catholic faith was also linked to a request for architects so that a church could be built "in the Roman style."[28] The same phenomena marked the reform of the Gallican Church under Pepin (+ 768), his son Charlemagne (+ 814), and their successors. Here Roman books, Roman usage, and even Roman chant were imposed upon churches in the realm.[29] Although Roman forms actually intermingled with Gallican forms in architecture, music, and rite so that new hybrids of music, architecture, and worship evolved, these were not considered hybrids at the time but "Roman."[30] This was the standard of acceptability, the standard of what was admittable to the sacred, and this standard "displaced" others. Although it is true that the imposition of certain art forms also served a socio-political purpose, part of the motivation for importing these forms was also their perceived innate superiority and sanctity over local art forms.

Pius X

The ascendancy of a displacement model for evaluating ecclesiastical art and worship music—a model which takes as its starting point an ontological perception of music, whose essence is linked to morality, in which beauty (as determined by certain, usually unspoken, cultural canons) is the means for expressing and encountering the sacred—is epitomized in the 1903 instruction *Tra le sollicitudini* (TLS) of Pius X. In providing general principles for evaluating "sacred" music, TLS discusses music in ontological terms, noting that sacred music should posses certain qualities, "precisely sanctity and goodness of form" (n. 2).[31] Furthermore, TLS states that music must "exclude all profanity not only in itself but also in the manner in which it is presented" (n. 2). Although this principle recognizes the possibility of a profane performance, it also admits that music, apart from any usage, has the potential for profanity in and of itself. Finally, TLS requires that sacred music be "true art" (n. 2). Here the elision between beauty, virtue, and the divine has found full expression.

According to TLS, the most perfect form of sacred music—that is, music which is true art, is in and of itself virtuous, and by its very nature leads us to God—is Gregorian chant. TLS teaches not only that Gregorian chant is the "supreme model for sacred music" but is the standard by which all other sacred or liturgical music is judged, noting that "the more closely a composition for church approaches in its movement, inspiration, and savor the Gregorian form, the more sacred and liturgical it is" (n. 3). Not only, therefore, does TLS make abstract ontological judgments about the virtue, beauty, and holiness of worship music, but posits such characteristics of a specific genre of music in its treasury. This is the final consequence of the displacement model for evaluating music, which not only displaces other criteria in judging worship music, but tends to be so exclusionary that it ultimately suggests the displacement of any music that does not "approach its movement, inspiration and savor." Thus, TLS concludes, "the more out of harmony [other music] is with that supreme model, the less worthy it is of the temple" (n. 3).

The Shift to Convergence

A perceptible shift away from displacement criteria in evaluating worship music—already foreshadowed in the 1955 encyclical of Pius XII, *Musicae Sacrae Disciplina* (nn. 34-35)—was made explicit in the Constitution on the Sacred Liturgy (CSL), which did not rely heavily upon ontological or moral criteria for evaluating worship music but emphasized the function of such music. Thus CSL notes that it is in the wedding of music to words that music forms "a necessary or integral part of the solemn liturgy" (n. 112). Even more significant is the statement that "sacred music will be the more holy the more closely it is joined to the liturgical rite, whether by adding delight to prayer, fostering oneness of spirit, or investing the rites with greater solemnity" (n. 112). Although employing the language of holiness reminiscent of Pius X, CSL clearly moved towards a functional definition of sacred music, stressing that its holiness is not only or essentially a matter of ontology or ethics but, instead, is related to music's ability to shape a community's prayer by wedding itself to text and rite.

It is true that previous documents have discussed the function of sacred music, and TLS itself acknowledges that the principal "office" or function of music is "to clothe with befitting melody the liturgical text . . . [and] to add greater efficacy to the text" (n. 1). What is significant about the discussion of music's function in CSL, however, is that, in terms of criteria for evaluating music for worship, the issue of function is not secondary to previous ontological determinations of sacrality or ethics. Rather, the very decision about the sacrality of the music begins with and is contingent upon a functional consideration, i.e., to what extent it engages the community and joins itself to the ritual. At the most fundamental level, the determination of the sacrality of the music is linked to the primary "functional" consideration of the "full, conscious and active participation" of the faithful, which was not only the "aim to be considered before all else" in the "reform and promotion of the liturgy" (n. 14) but also has become a basic norm for shaping the reformed rites as envisioned by CSL.[32] It is in these terms that one can understand CSL's reference to the "ministerial function supplied by sacred music in the service of the Lord" (n. 112).

The priority CSL gives to music's function in worship and the virtual absence of ontological or ethical criteria for the evaluation of worship music demonstrates its affinity with a convergence rather than a displacement model for evaluating worship music. A strong indication of this is CSL's inability to hold up any music, even Gregorian chant, as the "supreme model" against which all other music need be judged. To the contrary, CSL "approves of all forms of genuine art possessing the qualities required and admits them into divine worship" (n. 112). These "qualities," according to CSL, do not appear to be intrinsically related to any form, style, or tonality—such as Gregorian chant—but rather belong to certain functional capacities of the music, e.g.: (1) its ability to wed itself to the text; (2) its ability to joint itself to the rite; (3) its ability to add delight to prayer; (4) its ability to foster oneness of spirit; (5) its ability to invest the rites with solemnity; and especially (6) its ability to foster the full, conscious and active participation of the community.

It was CSL's affinity with a convergence approach to evaluating worship music that prepared the way for the developments in MCW noted at the beginning of this essay, and which prompts us to explore this model even further.

Exploring the Elements of Convergence

The suggestion that the evaluation of contemporary worship music requires a consideration of various converging factors rather than the acceptance of a single philosophical framework which displaces all other criteria, leads us to explore what some of those converging factors might be as well as how they might relate to each other. Before delineating these factors, however, something needs to be said about the goals or purposes that such individual elements—as well as the convergence approach itself—need to serve.

The Purpose of Liturgy

CSL recognizes that worship is for God and for people, i.e., a "great work, wherein God is perfectly glorified and the recipients made holy" (n. 7). This bifurcation in worship's purpose does not suggest any necessary conflict but rather points to an essential complementarity in this bi-directional goal. The glorification of God through Jesus Christ signifies human sanctification. Conversely, human sanctification in Jesus Christ is an authentic act of praise to God. These complimentary purposes must themselves converge rather than displace each other.

Though there are many possible ways in which to assess whether or not this two-part worship goal is being realized, a convergence approach is orientated toward grounding that assessment in human experience. Theologically, this means assessing the quality of praise in terms of the sanctification of the community.[33] Musically-liturgically, CSL has demonstrated this to mean assessing the "holiness" of the music (i.e., its capacity for praise) in terms of its ability to fulfill certain ministerial responsibilities vis-à-vis the community.[34] The most important of these from the viewpoint of CSL is the "full, conscious, and active participation" of the community. It would seem, therefore, that an appropriate approach to assessing our worship or the quality of our worship music, which is for the praise of God and the sanctification of the community, is to assess to what extent it enables the full, conscious, and active participation of the people: an act which authentically symbolizes both praise and sanctification.

Evaluating to what extent a community is fully, consciously, and actively engaged in worship is itself a complex task. Margaret Mary Kelleher provides a useful framework for apprehending some of this complexity in her previously discussed distinction between public meaning, personal meaning, and official meaning.[35]

Appraising an assembly's active participation in view of Kelleher's framework translates into engagement on a private, public, and official level. Roman Catholics believe that worship is an ecclesial act, in which baptized individuals come together, and employing official approved forms and texts, offer praise and are transformed in the process. Thus the criteria for active participation are not only shaped in view of an individual's decision about what they believe participation to be (private meaning), nor simply in terms of canonical or other liturgical requirements for participation (official meaning), but that these two converge in the actual perceived and enacted participation (public meaning) of a community.

There are many musical and extra-musical factors that need to converge in order to facilitate the full, conscious, and active participation of the assembly on a private, official, and public level in our worship. An introduction to some of these follows.

Extra-Musical Elements

It might strike some as odd to suggest that many elements that are part of a convergence model for evaluating worship music are not properly musical. These, nonetheless, have a distinctive effect on the community's engagement in worship music. They include:

The Cultural Context. People of different cultures have different ways of expressing and creating their social identity through their music. Similarly, people of various cultures have different ways of symbolizing praise and sanctification through their worship and their music, a fact well recognized by CSL (nn. 37-40). The specific cultural context of a community needs to be considered as a primary frame when assessing the participation of an assembly in song, and in evaluating the music that is to engage them. Some cultures are oriented to the singing of hymns out of hymnals; others, to improvised call-response forms. Some cultures may tend toward ebullience in their sung worship, whereas others prefer subdued music or even silence. This larger cultural context is a critical framework for understanding the nature of participation and, thus, for evaluating how music enables such participation.

The Temporal Context. Liturgical time and chronological time are two aspects of the temporal context that also have an effect on the participation and the evaluation of our worship music. Christmas comes once a year. It is often this factor, more than other specifically musical factors—such as the quality of a composition or the elegance of the texts—which raises the quality of musical worship on the 25th of December. Furthermore, chronological time has a significant effect on the character of participation in musical worship. In a university community, for example, 9:00 A.M. Sunday worship can be deadly; whereas in a community in which there are many families with young children, 9:00 A.M. is often a very effective time for engaging a community in sung praise.

Pastoral Needs/Expectations. Another factor affecting the quality of participation in worship and its music is the pastoral need or expectation that individuals and a community bring to the liturgy. In a time of profound grief or joyous celebration, for example, there may be more need for auditory engagement. Such engagement, though equally intense, may be expressed in radically diverse ways: from deep, communal silence to unrestrained festive song. Furthermore, these situations will dictate something of the adequacy of the music for engaging the community in sung prayer. For example, some texts or music that would be considered adequate by a community at another time might prove too weak or insubstantial to bear the weight of the current worship moment. Ordinary time can respect ordinary music, whereas moments of extraordinary angst or jubilation may pose different kinds of musical and liturgical demands.

Quality of Liturgical Ministries. MCW recognizes that "no single factor affects the liturgy as much as the attitude, style, and bearing of the [presider]" (n. 21). The quality of the presiding has an effect on the quality of the sung worship. Besides the presider, however, other ministries, including the preaching, hospitality, and reading also can profoundly affect the quality and effectiveness of worship and its music. My own field work, for example, has convincingly demonstrated for me that there can be a perceptible correlation between the quality of the proclaimed word and the level of the assembly's engagement in the responsorial psalm or acclamation that follows. Although the caliber of the text or the musical setting will also influence the community's level of engagement in the music, extra-musical elements such as the quality of the liturgical ministries will be at least as influential in such matters.

Architectural Setting. Many elements in the spatial arrangement of a worship space affect the engagement of the community in worship and its music. The acoustics—which not only determine how the assembly hears others, but if and how its members can hear themselves—are a prime concern. Furthermore, the physical distance between ministers and the assembly affects both the visual and auditory engagement of the community. So does the very configuration of the assembly, and the way its members perceive themselves in relationship to the size and scale of the space. Even though a church may possess a splendid sound-reinforcement system, if a community feels dwarfed by a building, the people's musical-liturgical participation may be proportionately timid.

Musical Elements

Apart from these extra-musical elements, a broad range of properly musical elements needs to be taken into account when employing a convergence approach to evaluating worship music. These include:

Musical Leadership. One of the extra-musical elements affecting the quality of the musical-worship experience is the quality of the ministerial leadership. A similar point needs to be made about the musical leadership. The engagement of the assembly in the worship, for example, often has less to do with any decision about the quality of the composition, or the appropriateness of the text, or the integration of the music with the ritual, as much as the quality of the musical leadership. This quality needs to be measured in distinctly musical terms (e.g., accuracy in pitch and rhythm, quality of tone, consistency in tempo, etc.) as well as in liturgical-ministerial terms (e.g., the hospitality of the music ministers, their prayerfulness, ability to model appropriate praise, etc.).

Musical Tradition. Another often unspoken factor having considerable bearing on the quality of a musical-liturgical event is the musical tradition of a local church, a local community, or even a specific worship gathering. Aside from the larger cultural context, noted above, there are varying musical traditions from community to community, or even within subdivisions of a community. Some communities, for example, have a stronger tradition of sung worship in general, whereas others have a tradition of singing at certain times in the rite, or even for singing certain pieces of music. These specific musical traditions are critical when assessing the quality of the musical liturgy.

Quality of the Musical Composition. The community's assessment of the quality of the musical composition also has a significant impact on the people's engagement in the worship. Their usually implicit evaluation of the singability of a piece of music, its rhythmic interest, the amount of challenge in the length of phrases, the level of difficulty in the intervallic structure or the ambitus of the work, etc. Note that this evaluation is framed not in terms of some conservatory standard or textbook definition, but in terms of the real experience of a local community and its assessment of the quality of a musical composition. No matter what a textbook might say about the excellence of a composition, if a community does not like it, it will be less effective in engaging its members in worship.

Quality of the Text. Closely related to a community's perception of the quality of its music is its perception of the quality of the texts that are set to music. Again, this is often more an implicit than an explicit evaluation, but one which a community often subconsciously makes over and over again. Does the text meet the people's needs in terms of its imagery, poetics, inclusivity, and expression of dogma, and does it stretch them while respecting the amount of change or challenge they can tolerate? It is the balance between these two polarities—a community's comfort with the texts as appropriate expressions of its belief, and the same community's level of tolerance when the norm of that expression is challenged or stretched—which defines the range for assessing the viability of a text for engaging a community in sung worship.

Interplay of Music and the Rite. A final element that needs to be considered when employing a convergence model for evaluating music's ability to engage the assembly is the interplay of the music with the ritual. Does the music effectively express the meaning of the rite and provide appropriate musical expression for and distinction between primary and secondary elements in the worship? It is here—more than with almost any other element which we have considered—that the convergence between private, official, and public meaning can be most challenging. This challenge arises because so many people in the same community can hold very different opinions on the meaning of various segments of a rite (e.g., the eucharistic prayer): opinions which often differ dramatically from the official instructions on the rite.

The Interrelation of Extra-musical and Musical Elements

The delineation of various musical and extra-musical elements that need to be taken into consideration when employing a convergence model for evaluating worship music is only one step in this process. A second, more complex issue is how these elements relate to each other. It should not be presumed that each of these elements is of equal import for engaging a community in sung worship, nor should it be assumed that such factors interact with parity.

The physical sciences might provide an insight as to how these various elements interrelate. For example, from organic chemistry we learn that the chemical structure of certain elements promotes their reactivity and allows them to easily combine (e.g., hydrogen and water into H_2O), whereas other elements only combine under extreme pressure or temperature. For example, methane gas combines with water to become carbon monoxide and hydrogen gas ($CH_4 + H_2O - Co + 3H_2$) only at high temperature (800-1000 degrees Celsius), increased pressure (10-50 atmospheres), and requires a catalyst (like nickel).

Analogously, certain factors in a convergence equation for the engagement of the assembly appear to combine more readily, whereas others require certain pressures or catalysts to occur. For example, I would suggest that effective liturgical leadership somewhat easily combines with the factor we have identified as the interplay of music and the rite in the promotion of the assembly's participation. Or, at times of great pastoral expectation, there may be much more of a need to rely upon certain local musical traditions which readily surface at such moments to support and invite the engagement of the community. On the other hand, a text that is challenging in its poetic expression or theological content may require the catalyst of particularly gifted musical leadership in combination with an articulate liturgical leadership (such as a presider or homilist to break open the text) for the text to be effective. Whereas my own field work and that of some of my students have demonstrated that these elements combine in different ways and under different circumstances, there is not enough data at this time to suggest clear patterns for these combinations. Much more work needs to be done here.

Conclusion

For centuries worshipers have recognized the power of music in worship. So too have worshipers effectively employed this musical power through the centuries to offer praise and inspire the community. Offering a new model for evaluating worship music on the cusp of the twenty-first century is not meant to disparage the manner of evaluating music in the past, nor to suggest that contemporary perspectives on worship music are innately superior to those of another era. Rather, this foray into models and methods for evaluating worship music begins with the premise that things have changed: the form of our worship, the style of our music, the manner of ministering in worship, and even our concept of what it means to be present at worship. This significant and fundamental transformation of our worship challenges us to a new kind of musical-liturgical participation, and new ways of thinking about our musical-liturgical participation.

Ultimately it is not only a convergence of factors or perspectives that I am suggesting here, but a convergence of people. The division of musicians into various camps, each with their own "approach" (read "agenda"), does not enrich either the worship of the church nor the atmosphere for even discussing that worship. Rather, it is divisive and has the potential for turning worship into civil war. In order to change this situation we not only need competent and charitable participants in the dialogue, but an end to the belief that some styles or bodies of music are not only ontologically superior but possess a greater capacity for mediating the holy. This is not to say that people are to give up their preferences or tastes for certain types of music, but rather that these be recognized as just that: preferences, not metaphysical priorities. Maybe in this way musicians and liturgists, assemblies and worship leaders can journey even further into the mystery we call liturgy, for the glory of God and the sanctification of the community.

Notes

1. I am grateful to the many students who have participated in my seminar on "Music and Ritual" at Catholic Theological Union over the past ten years, where some of these ideas were first explored.

2. For a report of that meeting, see *Sacred Music and Liturgy Reform after Vatican II: Fifth International Congress for Church Music (Chicago-Milwaukee, 1966)*, ed. J. Overath (Rome: Consociatio Internationalis Musicae Sacrae, 1969).

3. Much of whose work was anticipated in the 1968 document of the U.S. Bishops' Committee on the Liturgy entitled *The Place of Music in Eucharistic Celebrations*.

4. See my "Music in Catholic Worship: A Critical Reappraisal," *Liturgy 90* (February-March 1991) 8-12.

5. MSCC addresses the apparent tension between the musical, liturgical, and pastoral judgment by stressing that these, in fact, are three facets of a single judgment and cannot be made sequentially or in opposition to each other (n. 82).

6. Warren Anderson argues that this was more a basic phenomenon within many ancient Greek writings about music than it was a unitary theory. See his *Ethos and Education in Greek Music: The Evidence of Poetry and Philosophy* (Cambridge, MA: Harvard University Press, 1966) 177.

7. *Republic* 3:398c-399d.

8. Aristotle (+ 322 BCE), for example, allowed virtually any type of music for relaxation in his *Politics* 8.1339a-1342b.

9. Thus, for example, we hear from Aristotle the story of Philoxenus (c. 436-380 BCE) who attempted to compose his dithyramb "The Mysians" in Dorian mode, but ultimately could not and had to return to Phrygian, which was the appropriate harmonia. *The Oxford Classical Dictionary* (Oxford: Clarendon Press, 1949), s.v. "music, and the philosophers."

10. For a more extended discussion of the difficulties associated with discussing "music" in the emerging Christian community, see my *Foundations of Christian Music: The Music of Pre-Constantinian Christianity* (Bramcote Nottingham: Grove Books, 1992).

11. For example, what is beautiful music, what is the effect of music, what is the relationship between music and morality, etc.

12. For a further discussion of the differences between a "theory-practice" model of knowledge, and a "practice-theory-practice" model, see Don Browning, *A Fundamental Practical Theology*.

13. See, for example, the discussion of Clement of Alexandria in Robert Skeris, *Chroma Theou* 130-140.

14. For a further exploration of this idea, see James McKinnon, "The Meaning of the Patristic Polemic against Musical Instruments," *Current Musicology* 1 (1985) 69-82.

15. Boethius, *Fundamentals of Music* 2.

16. *Docta Sanctorum Patrum* 3.1 as cited in Romita, *Ius Musicae Liturgicae* 48.

17. This is especially in the *Phaedo* 65d, 75d, 78d, 100b, etc.

18. *Symposium* 201c, 204e; *Greater Hippias* 296e-297b, etc.

19. For example, *Enarrationes in Psalmos* 41.7.

20. *De Civitate Dei* 11.23.

21. *De Ordine* 2, 15, 42.

22. *The Divine Names* 4.7, as translated in *Pseudo-Dionysius: The Complete Works*, trans. Colm Luibheid, The Classics of Western Christianity (Mahwah, NJ: Paulist Press, 1987) 77.

23. *De Spectaculis* 3:2-3.

24. *Confessiones* 10:33.

25. Bede, *Historia* 2:20, 4:18.

26. ". . . *sonos cantandi in ecclesia*" (4.2), "*modulandi in ecclesia a more Romanorum*" (4.2), and *carmina ecclesiae*" (4.12).

27. ". . . *carmina religioni et pietati*," 4.24.

28. 5.21.

29. *Admonitio Generalis* 79.

30. This was consonant with a growing trend in the medieval west to idealize the Roman way in all things ecclesiastical, so that to be Christian often meant conforming to Roman usage, including the perceived artistic tastes of the Roman Church. For a further discussion of "Romanitas," especially as it influenced medieval worship, see Angelus Häussling, *Mönchskonvent und Eucharistiefeier*, Liturgiewissenschaftliche Quellen und Forschungen 58 (Münster: Aschendorff, 1973) 90-98.

31. Translation of TLS from R. Kevin Seasoltz, *The New Liturgy*.

32. See, for example, the discussion of this primary norm in Frederick R. McManus, *Liturgical Participation: An Ongoing Assessment*, American Essays in Liturgy (Washington, DC: The Pastoral Press, 1988).

33. CSL itself begins its discourse on the nature of the liturgy with a soteriological exposition in n. 5, and already in n. 2 frames its discussion of the liturgy in terms of human salvation and sanctification (i.e., liturgy = "making the work of our redemption a present actuality").

34. Six of these were enumerated above.

35. See above, p. 152.

INDEX

"A Mighty Fortress"—100-3
Abraham, Gerald—23
Achtemeier, Paul—50, 61, 62
acolyte—77
acoustic environment—56; acoustic space—112-3, 119, 124; also see "auditory environment"
active participation—57, 131, 153, 180, 181, 182
Acts of Paul—76
Adorno, Theodor—33
African-American music—13, 14, 34, 35
Aknin, Joseph—10
Alcini, Ilario—28
Alexander the Great—49, 60
alphabets—39ff
alternatim—161-2
Ambrose of Milan—6, 78, 85, 86
Ameln, Konrad—25, 26, 28, 91, 105
American liturgical music—see "U.S. liturgical music"
amidah—68, 71, 82; also see *"tefillah"*
Amos—43, 45, 59
Analecta Hymnica Medii Aevi—24, 25
Anderson, Herbert—v
Anderson, Warren—188
Andrews, Herbert—24
Anglès, Higini—20, 24
anthropology and music—12, 13, 14, 33, 175
antiphonal—144, 171-2
Apel, Willi—26
Aramaic—51
archisynagogos—68, 71
architectural setting—184
Archives du chant—18
Aristotle—188
Arnold, Denis—16
Asian-American liturgical music—35
assembly in music and worship—65, 68, 77, 123, 131, 137-8, 139, 152-72, 180; also see "active participation" and "congregational song"
Athanasius of Alexandria—78

auditory environment—9, 37-63, 75; also see "acoustic environment"
Augustine of Hippo—10, 21, 30, 78, 80-1, 121, 126, 177, 178
Avenary, Hanoch—5, 20, 30, 83, 84, 86

Bach, Johann Sebastian—4, 8, 27, 89, 131, 134
Bangert, Mark—15, 34, 35
Baptist liturgical music—28
Bardon, Paul—32
barform—92-4, 100-2, 105, 164
Barker, John—105
Barr, Cyrilla—24
Barré, Michael—59
Bauman, William—28
Bayer, Bathya—5
beauty—177, 179
Bede—178
Beethoven, Ludwig van—131
Beilliard, Jean—28
belief—145-172
Bellah, Robert—141
Benham, Hugh—23
Berger, Klaus—20
Berger, Teresa—32
Berthier, Jacques—132, 162, 172
Besseler, Heinrich—23
Bible, music of—5, 37
Billerbeck, Paul—84
Billings, William—18
Binder, Abraham Wolf—19
birkat ha-minim—71, 83
Blacking, John—130, 143
Bland, Kalman—30
Blaukopf, Kurt—33
Blidstein, Gerard—82
Blissenbach, Wolfgang—19
Blume, Friedrich—2, 8, 23, 90, 105
Boethius—10, 30, 176-7, 189
Boman, Thorlief—48, 60
Botte, Bernard—85
Bower, Calvin—30
Boyd, Malcom—24
Bradshaw, Paul—84

191

Brahms, Johannes—131
Brand, Eugene—11, 33
Britton, Allen Perdue—27
Brooten, Bernadette—82
Brown, Dierdre—33
Brown, Howard Mayer—23, 26
Brown, Raymond—58, 73, 84
Browning, Don—30, 188
Buber, Martin—113, 124, 172
Burnim, Mellonee—14, 34
Bush, Douglas—23
Buszin, Walter—16, 31, 32, 104
Buxtehude, Dietrich—27
Byrd, William—27
Byzantine liturgy—22; the music of—6, 22

C(a)ecilian movement—8, 27, 28
Caglio, Ernesto Moneta—28, 85
Caldwell, John—22
Campenhausen, Hans von—84
cantata—8
cantiga—7
cantillation—20
cantio—7, 91, 105
cantique—7
cantometrics—150, 169
cantor—6, 65-87, 137, 144, 163-4, 172
canzona—25
Carissimi, Giacomo—27
carol—7
Carpenter, Edmund—124
Carroll, Joseph Robert—15
Carthage, Third Council of—79
Casey, R. P.—86
Cassiodorus—176
Cassirer, Ernst—146
Catholic Theological Union—v, 188
Cattin, Giulio—6, 22
causality—145, 147, 151
Chadwick, Henry—30
chant—7, 104; also see "Gregorian chant," and "Old Roman chant"
Charlemagne—178
Charles, Sydney—18
Charlesworth, James—21
Charpentier, Marc-Antoine—26
Chernoff, John Miller—130, 132, 143, 169

Chiat, Marilyn—19
choir—78, 137-8, 154, 155, 163-4, 172
chorale—89-106, 164-5, 172
Christ-Janer, Albert—27
Christmas—91, 183
Chupungco, Anscar—34
church law and music—7, 9, 28, 29, 144, 178
church music—15, 178
Clark, Linda—36
clausula—25
Cleall, Charles—30
Clement of Alexandria—30, 77, 81, 126, 189
Clifford, Richard—59
Cobb, Buell E.—27
Cohen, B.—30
collections of liturgical music—4, 18
Collins, Adela Yabro—62
Collins, Mary—32
communion rite—32
comparative musicology—33
composer—90, 104, 134, 152; also see "Milwaukee Symposia for Church Composers"
concealed oralism—44-49; 53, 56, 60; also see "residual orality"
Cone, James—13, 34
confessor—79
Congar, Yves—170
congregational song—7, 23, 24, 25, 91, 94-8, 103-4, 123, 137
Conomos, Dimitri—22
Constantine—80
Constitution on the Sacred Liturgy—107, 120, 121, 123, 131, 145, 166, 170
Cooke, Bernard—87
Cooke, Deryck—168
Coote, R.B.—43, 59
Corbin, Solange—2
Corelli, Arcangelo—27
Cornelius, Steven Harry—35
Cornelius of Rome—77
Counterreformation, music of—7-8; also see "Caecilian movement"
Couperin, François—27
Coutourier, C.—126
Coward, Harold—61, 62
Crawford, Richard—27

Crocker, Richard—7
Crossan, Dominic—62
Croucher, Trevor
Crowe, Frederick—53, 62
culture and liturgical music—12-15, 28, 32, 34, 130-1, 140, 142, 143, 182-3
Cutter, Paul F.—22
Cyprian of Carthage—77
Cyril of Jerusalem—79, 87

Damian, Ronald—27
dance—57, 115, 116, 130, 178
Davidson, James Robert—15
Davies, John Booth—33, 109, 112, 124
Davies, William—83
deacon—77, 79, 86
deaconess—77, 79
DeClerck, Paul—126
Deichgräber, Reinhard—20
Deiss, Lucien—32
Delling, Gerhard—20, 76, 84
Denta, R.C.—60
Desprez, Josquin—18
Deuteronomistic movement—43
dialogue—47, 113, 118, 124, 140
Dick, A.B.—43, 44, 58, 59
Didaskalia—77
Diehl, Katherine Smith—26
discographies—4
Dix, Gregory—63
DjeDje, Jacqueline Cogdell—14, 35
Dodd, C.H.—62
Dölger, Franz Josef—20
Donakowski, Conrad—25
door keeper—77, 79; also see "porter"
Doran, Carol—15, 33
Dorian mode—96, 102, 174, 188
Dreisoerner, Charles—34
drumming—144
Drummond, R. Paul—28
Duchesneau, Claude—10, 29, 32
Duclos, A—29
Dufay, Guillaume—18
Duncan, Stephen Frederick
Dussel, Enrique—150, 168
Dyer, J.—21
ecclesial identity—151-172

Edgar, William—30
Egeria—86
Eisenstein, Judith—30
Eisler, Hanns—33
Elbogen, Ismar—19, 66, 81, 82, 83
Eliade, Mircea—126
Ellinwood, Leonard—26, 28
Ende, Richard von—16
entertainment model—138-40
entrance rite—133, 134
Environment and Art in Catholic Worship—136, 141, 143, 144, 169
Ephrem the Syrian—21
Epiphanius—66
episcopacy—80
Episcopal liturgical music—29, 36
Epperson, Gordon—125, 167, 168
Erickson, Edwin—169
Etherington, Ch. L.—16
ethnoart—149, 168
ethnocentrism—130-1
ethnomusicology—7, 12, 13, 14, 33, 34, 143, 149
ethos, doctrine of—174-7, 188
eucharistic prayer—80, 133, 171, 186; music of—11, 134
Eusebius of Caesarea—78, 85, 87
evaluating worship music—128-42, 153, 173-89
event, the musical-liturgical —3, 132, 143, 151, 154
exorcist—77, 79
Ezechiel—45

faith—see "belief"
Farmer, Henry—30
Faruqi, Lois Ibsen al—31
Fassler, Margot—17, 22
Feld, Steven—151, 169
Fellerer, Karl—2, 8, 16, 24, 27, 34
Ferguson, Everett—21, 86
field observation—13, 14, 36
Fifth International Congress on Church Music—173, 188
Figeras, José Romeu—25
Finey, Theodore—16
Fink, Peter—15, 123
Finnegan, Ruth—57, 59
Fischer, Balthasar—21

Fischer, J.L.—149, 168
folk music/song—90, 91, 92, 105, 130, 143; also see "popular music"
Fontain, Jacques—21
Foote, Henry W.—28
forms, musical—145-172
Fortune, Nigel—8
Frescobaldi, Girolamo—26, 27
Friedrich, Gerhard—62
Froger, P.—30
Frost, Maurice—27
Fuchs, Ernst—53
Funk, Robert—62
Funk, Virgil—v, 28

Gabrieli, Giovanni—18, 26
Gallo, F. A.—23
Gamber, Klaus—30
Garside, Charles—31
Gebauer, Victor—8
Geertz, Clifford—146
Geisslerlieder—7, 105
Gelineau, Joseph—11, 17, 21, 28, 32, 75, 77, 84, 85
Gennadius of Constantinople—81
Gerhardsson, Birger—61
Gérold, Théodore—21
Gerson-Kiwi, Edith—19
Gibbons, Orlando—27
Gibson, Gerard D.—4
Gloria in excelsis—91, 133; also see "Glory to God"
Glory to God—133; also see "*Gloria in excelsis*"
glossolalia—21
Glover, Raymond—29
Gneuss, Helmut—24
Goldberg, Geoffrey—6
Goody, Jack—55, 57, 58, 63
gospel—53
gospel music—34, 35, 132
Gottfried, Gottfried—21
Gottwald, Norman—58
Gounod, Charles—27
grave digger—79
Gray, Michael H.—4
Greek language—51, 75
Gregorian chant—7, 8, 13, 23, 24, 28, 90, 91, 93, 95, 100, 131, 179, 181
Grelot, Pierre—20
Grey, Donald—126
Grimes, Ronald—13, 34
Grindal, Gracia—33
Grontkowski, Christine—60, 61
Grout, Donald—16
Guiraud, Pierre—167
Gushee, Marion—7
Gutmann, Joseph—19, 59

Hahn, Ferdinand—83
Haïk-Vantoura, Suzanne—17
Hameline, Jean-Yves—28
Handel, Georg Frideric—27
Hanin, Aloys—29
Hannick, C.—21
Harnoncourt, Philipp—28
Harvey, Louis-Charles—34
Häussling, Angelus—189
Havelock, Eric—39, 57, 59, 60, 124
Hayburn, Robert—23, 27, 29
Haydn, Franz Joseph—27
hazzan ha-knesset—66, 70, 71, 72, 81
hearing and revelation—38-9, 44-8, 53-5, 59, 75; epistemology of—110-113; organs of—46-8, 109; physiology of—111-2; preeminence of—50, 54, 55, 75, 89; also see "sound"
Hebrew language—40, 41, 48-9, 69, 75
Hebrew thought—48-9, 60
Heinemann, Joseph—5, 19, 82, 83, 84
Hellenization—49-50, 56
Henderson, Frank—32
Hennecke, Edgar—85
hermeneutics—36
Herrmann, Siegfried—57
Heskes, Irene—16
Heyer, Anna—3
Higginbottom, Edward—26
Hiley, David—7, 23
Hippolytus—77, 85
Hispaniae Schola Musica Sacra—18
Hispanic music—14, 34, 35
historical studies of music,—2-9,
Hitchcock, H. Wiley—16, 26, 27
Hoelty-Nickel, Theodore—31

Hoffman, Elizabeth—28
Hoffman, Lawrence—5, 15, 17, 19, 83
Hofmann, F.—15
holiness of music—179, 182, 187
Holleman, A.W.J.—21, 22
Holy, holy—133, 155; also see *"Sanctus"*
holy, music as—126, 179, 180, 182, 187
Homer—49
Hoon, Paul—30
Hoppin, Richard—23, 24
Horbury, W.—83
Hucke, Helmut—22, 28, 31
Huels, John—144
Hughes, Andrew—22
Hughes, Anselm—23
Huguenots, music of the—26
Huijbers, Bernard—11, 28, 124
Hume, Paul—16
Huot-Pleuroux, Paul—16
Hutchings, Arthur—25
Hutmacher, Robert—132
hymn, hymnody—11, 26, 32, 77, 83, 135, 156, 183; African-American—35; inclusive language and—33; indigenous—34; Latin—7, 24; multicultural—35; New Testament—6, 76; vernacular—8, 27, 97, 104, 164; also see *"cantio"* and *"chorale"*
hymnals—9, 14, 29, 183; ethnically identified hymnals—34, 35

ICEL—see, International Committee on English in the Liturgy
Idelsohn, Abraham Z.—2, 4, 66, 69, 82, 83
improvisation—132
inclusive language—11-12, 32, 33, 136-7, 144, 185
India, liturgical music of—14
individualism—141
institution narratives—55
instrument, instrumentalist —6, 8, 134-5, 137, 139, 163-4, 172, 176, 178, 189
International Committee on English in the Liturgy—32, 33
Ionian mode—96, 102

Irwin, Joyce—11, 31
Irwin, Kevin—32, 124, 167
Isaiah—45, 71-2
Israel, ancient—40-40

Jackson, Irene V.—34, 35
Janota, Johannes—25
Jeffery, Peter—7, 17, 19, 21, 22, 23, 81
Jenny, Markus—26, 31
Jeppesen, Knud—24
Jeremiah—43-4, 58-9
Jeremias, Joachim—61, 63
Jerome—79, 87
Jerusalem—6
Jesus, in synagogue—71-2, 74, 84; language of—51-2; prayer of—71
Jewish music, Judaism and music—2, 4, 5-6, 9-10, 13, 30; also see "Bible," "Masoretic accents," "prayer leaders, Jewish," "synagogue,"
John Chrysostom—79, 87
John XXII—10, 177
Johnson, Elizabeth—32
Johnson, Larry—vi
Jonas, Hans—110, 124
Joncas, J. Michael—29, 36
Jones, Cheslyn—84
journals, musical—3, 17
Jousse, Marcel—62
jubilus—80, 81; also see "melisma"
Judah ben Illai—68
Julian, John—8
Justin Martyr—85
Justinian—69

Kelber, Werner—54, 59, 62
Kelleher, Margaret Mary—36, 152, 169, 170, 182
Keller, Evelyn Fox—60, 61
Kemmer, John—33
Kennedy, Michael—168
kerygma—52-3
keyboard music—26
Kimelman, Reuven—83
King, A. Hyatt—17
Kittel, Gerhard—44, 47, 59, 60
Klauser, Theodor—87
Klepper, Robert—29

koinonia—175
Kornmüller, Utto—15
Krahe, Maria-Judith—31
Kresteff, A.D.—30
Kroll, Josef—21
Kümmerle, Salomon—15
Kurzschenkel, Winfried—31
Kyrie—86, 133; also see "Lord have mercy"

LaCroix, Richard—21
laity, role in liturgical music—see "assembly," "congregational song"
Lampe, G.W.H.—81
Landman, Leo—66, 82
Langer, Susanne—111, 115, 124, 147-8, 149, 168
language—147-8; music as—116, 148
Laodicea, Council of—78, 80, 81, 83
Lasso, Orlando di—27
Lattke, Michael—20
lauda—7, 24, 25
law—see "church law"
leadership, musical—137-40, 184-5
Leaver, Robin—8, 25, 26, 27, 34
Lebon, Jean—32
Leclercq, Henri—77, 85, 86
Leeb, Helmut—6, 22, 86
Leege, David—36
Leichentritt, Hugo—24
Leise—7, 25
Léon-Dufour, Xavier—60
Leupold, Ulrich—97, 98, 100, 102, 104
Levine, Joseph—20
Lewis, Anthony—8
Lippardt, Walther—25, 26
Lippman, E.—84
litany—32, 157-8
liturgical judgement, the—132-40
liturgical music—10, 31, 125, 179 et passim
Liturgical Music Today—127, 128, 133, 134, 136, 137, 138, 142
liturgical musicology—34
Loh, I-To—34
Lomax, Alan—150, 151, 152, 168, 169, 170
Lombard, Peter—121-2

Lord have mercy—133; also see "*Kyrie*"
Lovelace, Austin—132
Lowens, Irving—27
Lukken, Gerard—167
Luther, Martin—26, 31, 89-106, 121, 164, 172
Lutheran liturgical music—11, 25, 27, 29, 31, 89-106
Lydian mode—95
Lynch, Mary—vi
lyricism—76, 77, 135-6

ma'amadot—67, 73
Maahs, K.H.—60
MacDonald, George—98, 103
MacDougall, Hamilton—28
Machaut, Guillaume de—18
Madden, Lawrence J.—171
Madsen, Wanda Jean—35
Maimonides—10, 30
Manns, F.—20
manuscripts, musical—3
Manzarrata, Tómas de—29
Marshall, Madeleine Forell—27
Martin, Emil—31
Martin, Ralph P.—20, 84
Masoretic accents—17
Mateos, Juan—86
Mauck, Marchita—vi
Mauk, Frederick—143
Maultsby, Portia—35
McCorckle, Donald—16
McGann, Mary—vi, 11, 36, 124, 144, 171
McIntyre, Joseph—58, 59
McKim, LindaJo—29
McKinnon, James—6, 20, 21, 22, 189
McLuhan, Marshall—124
McManus, Frederick—189
Mearns, James—24
Mehrtens, Frits—16
Meistersinger—93, 100, 105
melisma, melismatic—96, 99, 102; also see "jubilus"
Melloh, John Allyn—172
memorization—57
Merriam, Alan—33, 168

Messenger, Ruth Ellis—26
meter—99, 103
Methodist liturgical music—26, 27, 29, 34, 35, 36
Mexican mission music—35
Meyer, Leonard—168
Meyer-Baer, Kathi—17
Michaelis, Wilhelm—62
Michel, Alain—24
Middle Ages, music of—6-7, 23, 24
Miller, Terry—27
Millgram, Abraham—82, 83
Milwaukee Symposia for Church Composers—v, 29, 32, 34, 127-144
ministers of music—137-8, 1534
Minnesinger—93
mission music—34, 35
Mitchell, Nathan—34
mithpallel—66-7, 73
Mocquereau, André—28
mode—95-6, 174
Molitor, Raphael—24
Monumenta Liturgiae Polychoralis Sanctae Ecclesiae Romanae—18
Monumenta musicae sacrae—4
Monumenta Polyphonae Liturgicae Sanctae Ecclesiae Romanae—18
morality and music—10, 174-7, 179, 180
motet—24, 25
Mowinckel, Sigmund—19
Mozart, Wolfgang Amadeus—2, 27
Mullenberg, James—58
Murphy, Roland—57
Musch, Hans—15
Music in Catholic Worship—v, 29, 108, 127-44, 166, 173, *188*
music ministers—139, 140, 154, 156, 171, 158-65, 184, 187
Musica Divina—18
Musicae sacrae disciplina—29, 179
musical judgment, the—128-32, 140-1, 173-4
Musicam sacram—29
musicology—see "comparative musicology," "ethnomusicology," "liturgical musicology" and "theomusicology"

Mützell, Wilhelm—27
Myers, Helen—143
Nattiez, Jean-Jacques—125, 168, 169
Nettl, Paul—25, 105, 125
neumatic settings—96, 99, 102
Neusner, Jacob—19, 61
New Grove Dictionary of Music and Musicians—27
New Grove Dictionary of Music and Musicians—2 *et passim.*
New Testament, music of—6, 20-21, 70, 74-6
Niceta of Remesiana—10, 30
Nketia, J.H. Kwabena—144
North American Academy of Liturgy—v, 32, 169
notation—3
Notre Dame Study of Catholic Parish Life—14, 36
Novatian—178
Nulman, Macy—19

O'Connell, Robert—30
Odes of Solomon—21
offertory song—133
Old Roman chant—7
Ong, Walter—39, 57, 58, 75, 84, 112, 124
ontology—175-6, 179, 180, 187
oral societies—38ff, 57, 59
oratorio—8
organ—8, 26
Origen—30, 77
orthodoxy—135, 136
Ortique, Joseph—15
Ostdiek, Gilbert—12
ostinato—162-4
Our Father—171
Overath, Johannes—27
Oxyrhynchus—22

Paléographie musicale—18
Palestrina, Giovanni Pierluigi da—7, 18, 24, 131, 132
Palisca, Claude—16
Panikkar, Raimundo—125
paper—61
parables—53-4, 62

Parks, Edna—27
passion music—8
Passionslied—25, 26
pastoral judgment—140-2, 173-4
pastoral performance standard—138-40, 156
Patrick, Millar—26
Paul of Tarsus—71, 72-3, 74, 84, 123, 175
Peirce, Charles—146
Pelikan, Jaroslav—27
Pentecost—91
Pepin—178
performance practice—3, 138-40, 143, 150, 152, 166
periodicals, musical—see "journals"
Perrin, Norman—61
Pharisees—50, 72
Phos hilaron—21
physiology—see "hearing, physiology of"
Picard, François—28
Pidoux, Pierre—26
Pike, Alfred—31
Pirro, André—23
Pius X—10, 13, 28, 29, 107, 126, 179, 180
Pius XII—29, 179
piyyutim—69, 70
Pizzani, Ubaldo—30
plainchant—see chant
Plato—49, 60, 61, 112, 124, 174, 175, 176, 177
Pliny the Elder—61
poetry and liturgical music—12, 135-6, 185
Polyphonia Sacra—18
polyphony—7, 24
Popp, Linda—35
popular music—129-30; popular religious song—7; also see "folk song"
Porte, Jacques—15
porter—79; also see "door keeper"
Postman, Neil—144
Pottie, Charles—32
Poultney—David—15
Power, David—167
practice-theory-practice—176, 188

Pratt, W.S.—26
prayer leaders, Christian—72-4, 77, 84, 183; Jewish—66-70, 72, 82, 83
preaching of disciples—52; of Jesus—51-2
preparation of the gifts—171
presbyter—79, 86
Presbyterian liturgical music—29
Prete, Mary—vi
priesthood, Christian—78; Jewish—67, 82
printing of music—17
prophecy—40, 43-44
Prosper of Aquitaine—126
Protestant Church music—25, 28 31; also see "Baptist," "Episcopal," "Lutheran," "Methodist," "Reformation"
psalmist—77-9, 81, 86, 87, 137, 144; also see "cantor"
psalmody—6, 8, 26, 27, 33, 76-7, 78, 85, 97, 103, 135; also see "psalmist"
Pseudo-Dionysius—177, 189
psychology and music—12, 33, 34, 108
Purcell, Henry—27
purpose of liturgy—181-2
Pythagoras—176

Quasten, Johannes—21, 85, 125
Quinn, Frank—32

Rahner, Karl—122, 126, 146, 165, 167
Rainoldi, Felice—29
Ramshaw-Schmidt, Gail—32
Randel, Don—16, 168
range—94-5, 102
Rankin, Susan—23
Rattenbury, J. Ernest—27
reader—76-9, 86, 184
reading aloud—50; also see "reader," "Torah," "Word of God"
recordings, musical —3, 4
Reese, Gustav—23
referential meaning—144-72
Reformation, music of—7-8, 25, 31
Reiber, Erich—81
Reilly, James—31
religious music—10, 15, 31, 178

Renaissance, music of—6, 23, 24, 131
Répertoire international de litérature musicale (RILM)—17
Répertoire international des sources musicales (RISM)—3
residual orality—40, 42, 50, 58; in Ancient Israel—44-9; in the New Testament—53-5; also see "concealed oralism"
responsorial forms—77, 85, 158-60, 171
revelation and hearing—38-9, 44-8, 53-5, 59, 75, 117-21; and seeing—45-6, 54, 59; also see "sound, preeminence in revelation"
rhyme—100, 103
Rice, William Carroll—16
Richardson, W.—21
Ricoeur, Paul—54, 62, 167
Riedel, Johannes—25, 27, 105
ritual—115-7
ritual music—v, 1, 9, 11, 12, 34, 108, 113-23, 131, 132, 173-89
ritual studies—13, 34, 35
Robertson, Alec—16
Roche, Elizabeth—23
Roche, Jerome—23, 24
Rohring, Klaus—28
Roman Catholic liturgical music—8, 18, 27, 28, 31, 35, 36, 108, 121-3, 127-144, 151-189
Romanitas—189
Rome—6, 178
Romita, Fiorenzo—23, 189
Roper, Cecil—26
rosh ha-knesset—68
Rossler, Martin—16
Routley, Erik—8, 9, 27, 31, 32, 33, 139, 144
Rowley, H.H.—5
Ruf—7

Sa'adya—10
Sabel, Hans—16
sacramental nature of music—109, 121-3
Sacred Harp—27
sacred music—10, 15, 31, 178, 179, 180

Sadducees—50
Sadie, Stanley—27
Saliers, Don—36
Sanchez, Máximo Brioso—20
Sanctus—95; also see "Holy, holy"
Sanders, E.P.—61
Sanders, Jack—6, 69
Santeria—35
Schafer, F. Murray—56
Schalk, Carl—15, 25, 105
Schalz, Nicolas—31
Schell, Johanna—29
Schillebeeckx, Edward—53, 62, 122, 126
Schiller, Benjie-Ellen—6
Schmemann, Alexander—81
Schmidt, Darl—85
Schmidt, Günther—26
Schmitt, Francis—28
Schnackenburg, R.—20
Schneemelcher, Wilhelm—85
Schrage, Wolfgang—72, 84
Schreiber, Baruch David—20
Schreiter, Robert—v
Schubart, Wilhelm—85
Schubert, Franz—27
Schuhmacher, Gerhard—28
Schulz, Hans-Joachim—22
Schütz, Heinrich—18
Schwann catalogues—4, 18
scribes/scribalism—42-3, 58
Searle, Mark—13, 32, 34, 36
Seashore, Carl—12
Seasoltz, R. Kevin—28, 123, 189
Seay, Albert—23
Second Vatican Council—9, 11, 28, 142
seeing—see "revelation and seeing," "vision"
Selfridge-Field, Eleanor—26
semiology/semiotics—15, 36, 125, 146, 167
Semmelroth, Otto—122
Sendrey, Alfred—16, 19
senses, epistemology of—110; also see "hearing, epistemology of," "vision, epistemology of"
sequence—25

Shelemay, Kay Kaufman—33
sheliach tsibbur—68, 71-4, 77, 81, 82, 84
shema—47, 68, 82
Shiloah, Amnon—30
Shinan, Avigdor—20
Shulhan Arukh—69
signification—145-72
Silbiger, Alexander—26
Silva, Owen Francis da—35
Silver, Harry—168
Sirota, Victoria—31
Sithole, Elkin—35
Skelley, Michael—167
Skeris, Robert—21, 30
Sloboda, John—33
Smallmann, Basil—26
Smith, Howard C.—27
Smith, J.A.—6, 20
Smith, William Sheppard—20
Smothers, E.R.—21
social structures—149-51
sociology and music—12, 33, 34, 108
Söhngen, Oskar—16, 28, 31, 126
Solesmes, monks of—18, 28
sonata da chiesa—25
Sonne, I.—30
sound, nature of—9, 108-113; preeminence in revelation—75, 117-21; also see "revelation and hearing"
Sozomen—78
Spalatin, George—97
Spanish missions, music of—14
Sparksman, Brian—86
speaking, organs of—46-8
Spector, Johanna—20
speech, organs of—48
Spencer, Jon Michael—10, 31, 35
spirituals—34, 35
Stäblein, Bruno—21, 24
Stäblein-Harder, Hanna—4
Stefani, Gino—16, 21, 25, 31, 34
Stevenson, Robert—25, 28
Stiller, Günther —8
Storey, William G.—172
Strack, Hermann—84
structures, musical-liturgical —11, 32, 132-5, 145-72; also, see "forms, musical" and "units, liturgical"

Strunk, Oliver—22
Stubbins, G.-W.—15
Stulken, Marilyn—29, 35
Stumpf, Karl—12
Stutton, Brett—36
style, musical—128, 132, 133, 135, 143, 187
subdeacon—77, 79
Swain, Joseph—32
syllabic settings—96, 99, 102
symbol—115-6, 120, 125, 136, 146-8
synagogue—5, 19, 20, 66-8, 71-2, 81, 82, 83; also see "Jesus, in synagogue"
Szövérffy, Josef—7, 22, 24

Taft, Robert—v, 22, 87, 172
Talmud—66; Babylonian—30, 82, 84; Jerusalem—82, 83
tefillah—83; also see *"amidah"*
Telemann, Georg Phillipp—27
Temple—67, 69
Terrien, Samuel—20, 45, 46, 59, 126
Tertullian—76, 85
texts and music—9, 11-12, 96-8, 102-3, 114-5, 120-1, 132, 134, 135-7, 147, 180, 185, 187
Theodore of Mopsuestia—87
theology and music—1, 2, 9-12, 30-1, 89, 107-126
theology of celebration—145-7
theomusicology—10, 31
theorists, medieval—23
theory-practice—176, 188
Thomas Aquinas—145, 167
Thompson, Bard—16, 26
Tillich, Paul—125
time—183
Todd, Janet—27
Torah—67; oral Torah—50; reading the Torah—82
Tra le sollicitudini—10, 13, 123, 126, 179
translation of texts—11
Trent, Council of—7, 24, 166
Tresmontant, Claude—48, 60
Troeger, Thomas—12, 33
trope—25

Turner, C.—30
typikon—78

United States, music of—8, 27-8, 151-72
units, liturgical—133-4
Universa Laus—29, 125

Valentin, E.—15
van der Leeuw, Gerardus—31, 125
Varèse, Edgard—149, 168
Vaux, Roland de—40, 57, 58, 59, 61
Veuthey, Michael—29
Victor of Vita—78
Vidich, Arthur—169
Vincie, Catherine—170
virgins—79
vision, epistemology of—49, 111; pre-eminence of—49, 51, 54, 60
visual arts—149-50
visual representations of God—45-6
Vivaldi, Antonio—27
von Rad, G.—60

Walker, Wyatt T.—35
Walton, Janet—17
Watts, Isaac—26
Weber, Max—33
Weissenbäck, Andreas—15
Weisser, Albert—16
Wellesz, Egon—22, 83
Wengst, Klaus—21
Werblowsky, R. J. Zwi—19
Werner, Eric—16, 19, 30, 83, 86

Wesley, Charles—26, 27, 34
Wesley, John—26, 27
White, James—25
Widoger, Geoffrey—19
widows—77, 79, 86
Wienandt, Elwyn—25, 35
Wilder, Amos—51, 52, 54, 61, 62, 63
Wilhelmi, G.—20
Wilkey, Jay W.—31
Willcock, Christopher—159
Williams, Peter—26
Wilson, Blake—24
Winter, Miriam Therese—31
Wiora, W.—25
Wohlberg, Max—20
Wolff, Hans Walter—60
women, liturgical music and—20, 67; also see "inclusive language"
word of God—43, 45, 47, 52, 55, 59, 60, 75, 89, 120-1; reading the word—68, 71, 76-8, 85, 183
Wren, Brian—12
Wright, Addison—57
writing—39-44, 50, 51, 54, 57, 58

Yeats-Edward, Paul—16
Young, Carlton—29
Yudkin, Jeremy—23

Zeitlin, S.—82
Zimmerman, Joyce Ann—170
Zuckerkandl, Victor—126
Zwingli, Ulrich—31

DATE DUE

S 11-9-99			
D 12-9-99			
ILL 4791227			
WITHDRAWN			